JURISPRUDENCE OR LEGAL SCIENCE?

Modern jurisprudence embodies two distinct traditions of thought about the nature of law. The first adopts a scientific approach which assumes that all legal phenomena possess universal characteristics that may be used in the analysis of any type of legal system. The main task of the legal philosopher is to disclose and understand such characteristics, which are thought to be capable of establishment independently of any moral or political values which the law might promote, and of any other context-dependent features of legal systems. Another form of jurisprudential reflection views the law as a complex form of moral arrangement which can only be analysed from within a system of reflective moral and political practices. Rather than conducting a search for neutral standpoints or criteria, this second form of theorising suggests that we uncover the nature and purpose of the law by reflecting on the dynamic properties of legal practice. Can legal philosophy aspire to scientific values of reasoning and truth? Is the idea of neutral standpoints an illusion? Should legal theorising be limited to the analysis of particular practices? Are the scientific and juristic approaches in the end as rigidly distinct from one another as some have claimed?

In a series of important new essays the authors of *Jurisprudence or Legal Science?* attempt to answer these and other questions about the nature of jurisprudential thinking, whilst emphasising the connection of such 'methodological' concerns to the substantive legal issues which have traditionally defined the core of jurisprudential speculation.

Jurisprudence or Legal Science?

A Debate about the Nature of Legal Theory

Edited by
Sean Coyle and George Pavlakos

·HART·
PUBLISHING

OXFORD AND PORTLAND, OREGON
2005

Published in North America (US and Canada) by
Hart Publishing
c/o International Specialized Book Services
5804 NE Hassalo Street
Portland, Oregon
97213-3644
USA

Hart Publishing is a specialist legal publisher based in Oxford, England.
To order further copies of this book or to request a list of other publications please write to:

Hart Publishing, Salter's Boatyard, Folly Bridge,
Abingdon Rd, Oxford, OX1 4LB
Telephone: +44 (0)1865 245533 Fax: +44 (0)1865 794882
email: mail@hartpub.co.uk
WEBSITE: http//:www.hartpub.co.uk

British Library Cataloguing in Publication Data
Data Available
ISBN 1-84113-504-6 (hardback)

Typeset by Datamatics Technologies Ltd, India
Printed and bound in Great Britain by
MPG Books Ltd, Bodmin, Cornwall

Contents

Preface

This volume springs from a workshop with the same title which was held on 25–26 October 2002 at Queen's University, Belfast under the auspices of the Forum for Law and Philosophy. That meeting constituted the first in a series of 'Workshops in Analytical Jurisprudence' that shall regularly invite state of the art papers to address topical issues in legal philosophy. In choosing this subject to launch the series, we thought it appropriate to explore the question of the nature of legal philosophy in general, by examining the relationship between metaphysical issues (is law a set of rules? is law distinguishable from morality? etc) and the philosophical assumptions and motivations which underpin and drive them. In doing so we hope to have shed some light on the state of legal theory as it stands today, and to have offered some insight into the reasons why modern legal theory takes the distinctive form it does.

The essays which comprise the present volume are original contributions presented to the workshop, with the exception of Robert Alexy's seminal paper, 'The Nature of Legal Philosophy'. This paper appeared originally in (2004) 17 *Ratio Juris* 156–67, and we should like to thank Robert Alexy and Blackwell Publishing Ltd, who kindly granted permission to reprint. Both the workshop and, subsequently, the book would not have been possible if it were not for the generous financial support of the Mind Association, the Research and Regional Services Office at Queen's University Belfast, the Queen's Law School, Hart Publishing and the European Forum of Philosophy at LSE. To these organisations we owe our profound thanks.

Both the workshop and the subsequent composition of this book have been intellectually most stimulating and rewarding. All of the workshop participants have contributed to the editing and shaping of this volume, and all came up with insightful comments and suggestions which proved invaluable for improving the final result. We thank them all for their commitment and enthusiasm. Finally, we would like to offer our warmest thanks to Richard Hart for his encouragement, patience and support.

SC and GP
London and Belfast
May 2004

List of Contributors

Robert Alexy is Professor for Public Law and Legal Theory at the Christian-Albrechts University of Kiel.

Sean Coyle is a Reader in Jurisprudence at University College London.

Jonathan Gorman is Professor of Moral Philosophy at Queen's University Belfast and Head of the School of Philosophical Studies.

Carsten Heidemann holds a PhD in legal philosophy from the University of Kiel and practices as a barrister in Kiel.

Philip Leith is Professor of Law at Queen's University Belfast.

John Morison is Professor of Jurisprudence at Queen's University Belfast and Head of the School of Law.

George Pavlakos is City Solicitors Educational Trust Lecturer in Jurisprudence in the School of Law at Queen's University Belfast.

Veronica Rodriguez-Blanco is Lecturer in Jurisprudence at the University of Birmingham.

Introduction

GEORGE PAVLAKOS AND SEAN COYLE

What is the nature of legal theory? What are its main aims, and how is legal theory related to legal practice? We might, for example, regard the legal theorist's task as consisting in the analysis of legal practice. Theory would then be related to practice in much the same way as science relates to everyday life: as a series of interconnected observations, reports and theories which aim to reveal the structure of that experience, to make sense of a complex phenomenon by subjecting it to the principles and assumptions which make the phenomenon possible. Since law is a social institution, legal theory in this sense aims to describe the conditions which make that social institution possible and intelligible. Legal theory, in this sense, is quite separate from legal practice, and aims at a body of knowledge quite different to the knowledge sought by the ordinary lawyer. For whilst the ordinary practitioner's interest lies generally in the detailed resolution of particular doctrinal debates, the legal theorist's concern is with the analysis of the general framework of concepts, ideas and assumptions within which those debates take place.

We can refer to this conception of legal theory as 'legal science'. The underpinning thought of legal science is that, by clarifying the framework of thought within which the ordinary lawyer moves, the specifically *legal* problems and debates with which the lawyer wrestles are elucidated and revealed. It is this desire for clarity which entails that legal theory (that is, in the form of 'legal science') must be sharply distinguished from the particular terms of the legal problems which stand in need of the theorist's illumination.

Legal theory might, however, be understood in a rather different way. For rather than aiming at detachment and scientific neutrality, the legal theorist might be seen as engaging directly with the legal and doctrinal issues which make up the business of the ordinary legal scholar. Legal theory in this sense is not concerned with the attempt to produce conceptual clarifications and analyses which are needed *prior* to participation in those debates, but with the wider legal, moral and political significance of those debates themselves. The aim of legal theory is then to understand the place of important legal ideas within the moral and political life of the state and society, both as a reflection of the values which guide and drive that society, and as an explanation of how that form of political life evolved and developed. We might refer to this understanding of the theorist's task as 'jurisprudence'. The main issue between jurisprudence and legal science can thus be understood as the question of whether legal theory represents a *prudentia* which engages in practical accounts of law, or a *scientia* that studies objective facts about it.

In recent years, legal theorists have turned their attention towards the nature of legal theory with a renewed interest. The overwhelming tendency has been for accounts of the nature of legal theory to be expressed in the shape of methodological observations concerning the *form* of theoretical inquiries into law. Methodological questions of this kind exert their own fascination, but they are rather far removed from the kind of question which has traditionally motivated and occupied the legal philosopher. It is for this reason that this collection of essays seeks to connect the question of the nature of legal theory with the substantive questions of legal theory: what is law? How is law related to moral value, and what is the connection, if any, between the truth of legal propositions and the truth of moral statements? Can one view the law in a value-neutral way? How can law's existence as a social phenomenon be reconciled with its normativity and claim to authority?

These and other questions are taken up in the essays below, and examined in the light of particular conceptions of the nature or function of legal theory. The remainder of this introduction will attempt to give an indicative, thematic exploration of the insights contained in those essays and to situate them in a wider intellectual context.

LEGAL SCIENCE, ANALYSIS AND OBJECTIVITY

The idea that the law is open to scientific and analytical study is not new: the leading writers on common law during the eighteenth and nineteenth centuries frequently expressed the desire to present the law as a 'science of principles' rather than a collection of procedures and remedies. Rather than merely describing and arranging, the jurist's task was presented as that of explaining the law systematically and coherently, as an expression of more abstract principles which might claim to reflect necessary truths about the world or human nature.[1] This move towards 'scientific' explanation therefore entailed a shift away from a conception of law as based on social custom and practice, towards a conception of law as deriving from rational principles which transcend those practices. These intellectual conditions fostered a form of juristic scholarship which centred upon the rational exposition of principle rather than the examination of social practices.

Latter-day proponents of legal science share the view of their intellectual ancestors that juristic scholarship must in some way transcend legal practice in order to reveal the nature of that practice. In particular, proponents

[1] See S Coyle, 'Two Concepts of Legal Analysis', this volume.

of legal science believe that theoretical inquiry into law must enjoy a level of detachment from the specifically legal problems addressed by the practitioner, if it is to make sense of and clarify those problems. This scientific detachment is often expressed in terms of neutrality and objectivity, and one of the aims of legal theory is seen as consisting in establishing the possibility of 'value-free' accounts of law. In one sense, all of the contributions described below constitute differing attempts to understand the conditions under which a general science of law is available, and to ponder the ramifications of 'objective' or 'value-free' explanations.

For much of the twentieth century, analytical legal theory has assumed that objectivity can be maintained only in combination with a value-free account of law's normativity. Many theorists have tried to capture legal rules and concepts through analytic definitions and exhaustive sets of semantic criteria. Moreover, the most significant challenge to this picture within the analytic tradition, that of HLA Hart, seemingly replaces it with a similarly 'objectivist' method of analysis which conceives of legal rules and concepts on the basis of value-free social facts.[2] In recent years, our understanding of the relations between normativity and objectivity has undergone a significant change: a line of thought, originating with Dworkin, has repeatedly and forcefully urged that, despite the unavailability of value-free explications of law's normativity, value-laden explications need not be less objective than value-free ones. Two developments are crucial in this context. The first refers to the increasingly plausible idea that values can be conceived as mind-independent, objective entities. The second consists in the thought that evaluative language directly refers to such mind-independent entities. From these thoughts emerges a different conception of analysis of evaluative terms as requiring explanation in terms of their mind-independent 'counterparts'.[3]

In the light of these developments, the question of the nature of legal theory arises in a new and pressing shape: is legal theory to be regarded as a *scientia* that studies norms as essentially mind-independent social facts? Or is it instead to be treated as a *prudentia* that deals with norms and reasons for action as intellectual products, which can be regimented and understood in various, possibly conflicting, ways?

Whether or not social norms turn out to be 'objective' in this sense, most of the authors in this volume hold the view that it is possible to inquire into the nature of law in a general way, at least to the extent that it is possible to stand at some critical distance from legal practice and reflect upon its most general characteristics.[4] This would be true, they believe, even if such reflection should eventually lead to the conclusion that there is very little to

[2] But see Coyle (above n 1).

[3] See G Pavlakos, 'Normative Knowledge and the Nature of Law' (this volume).

[4] The principal opponents of such a view are Coyle (above n 1) and P Leith and J Morison, 'Can Jurisprudence Without Empiricism Ever be a Science?' (this volume).

say about the practice of law once we step outside it. For even in this case (as George Pavlakos argues),[5] theoretical inquiry will have clarified the focus or the point of the practice, a clarification that is absolutely essential for determining what counts as part of the practice. An 'interpretive' stance on law — one that argues against the meaningfulness of any general philosophical inquiry about the law — is therefore, on this view, itself a 'general' theory in this sense even if it otherwise shuns the characteristic beliefs of legal science.[6] It is, therefore, the generality sought by such theories (the attempt, that is, to provide an account of law which does not depend on variable 'local' arrangements) which marks out legal science as a distinct form of theoretical inquiry, rather than strict adherence to the possibility of *value-free* explanations of law.

The generalist ambition of these theories is revealed by their search for an adequate account of very general, or 'basic' or 'foundational' properties of law. Central to an understanding of law, on this view, are the action-guiding character of law and its institutional nature. To say that law is action-guiding is to state that law is one of the parameters that determine our action. To the extent that we value action it is important to be able to identify the law. It is for this reason that, in the eyes of the proponent of legal science, legal theory must be kept distinct from legal practice. Law's normativity supplies its action-guiding and reason-giving properties, but it also renders pressing the question of how legal norms are distinguishable from the norms of other normative orders which claim for themselves the authority to regulate action: morality, ethics, instrumental rationality, custom and so on. The role of legal science is then that of clarifying the parameters of legal reasoning, and of studying and identifying the differences between legal norms and norms of other kinds.

To say that law is institutional is to state that law is embedded in an authoritative apparatus which both creates norms through pre-specified procedures that require the cooperation of specially designated officials, and enforces the law by applying sanctions to those who fail to comply with its requirements. The institutional aspect of law raises a plethora of questions,

[5] G Pavlakos (above n 3).

[6] See the essays by Pavlakos and Rodriguez-Blanco, this volume. In a recent essay, Ronald Dworkin argues as follows: 'I argued that a general theory about how valid law is to be identified . . . is not a neutral description of legal practice, but an interpretation of it that aims not just to describe but to justify it — to show why the practice is valuable and how it should be conducted so as to protect and enhance that value . . . But [Hart], on the contrary, simply describes these activities in a general and philosophical way, and describes them from the outside, not as an active participant in the legal wars but as a disengaged scholar of those wars.' (See Dworkin, 'Hart's Postscript and the Character of Political Philosophy' (2004) 24 *OJLS* 1–37, p 2.) Later in the same essay, however, he asks: 'What does the claim that "the law" requires something really mean? What in the world makes that claim true when it is true, and false when it is false? . . . We want, moreover, to answer these questions not just for a particular legal system, like English law, but for law in general, whether in Alabama or Afghanistan, or anywhere else.' (at 19)

prominent amongst which is the issue of the legitimacy of the legal order: in so far as law is action-guiding, what justifies the regulation of action through an authoritative system of sanctions? Depending on the answer to that question, different legal theories will bestow different weight on the importance of the institutional conditions of legal validity and their impact on the nature of legal phenomena.

Some of these themes are taken up by George Pavlakos and Carsten Heidemann. Heidemann directs his attention to the institutional nature of law, addressing in particular the nature of law's claim to authority and the correctness of its normative standards. Heidemann discusses the view that, in so far as law makes a claim to correctness, it makes a moral claim, and there is therefore a connection between law and morality. On this view, moral values exist as facts and thus objective entities, and legal officials refer to these, making it seem reasonable that legal reasoning has the character of a 'science' about those facts. In fact, he claims, this appearance is misleading: it is not the factuality but the mind-dependence (or mind-independence) of those norms which is at issue. The attempt by legal officials to discover the content of legal norms (to find out, that is, what obligations exist under the law) is both part of an institutionalised, social practice and manifestly 'real'. Thus the distinction between 'science' and 'prudence', he says, 'concerns less the character of the object of legal cognition than it does the *methods* by which normative or non-normative facts are ascertained'. Heidemann wants to understand the conditions which must hold before legal reasoning can exhibit the conditions of *either* science *or* prudence.

For Heidemann, then, the possibility of 'scientific' investigation into law depends upon the cognitive status of legal norms. Yet, as the term is used throughout this introduction, Heidemann's discussion — in so far as it attempts to clarify a general analytical framework for law — is one which already moves within the characteristic assumptions and beliefs of 'legal science'. It is a strength of Heidemann's analysis that it reveals, in part, the relationship between these beliefs about the character of legal theory and the issues of objectivity and mind-independence on which it may rely.

In his chapter, George Pavlakos takes up the theme of legal validity in a more general way. Theoretical inquiries aim to increase our knowledge of the law, he argues, and hence we might distinguish between kinds of theory on the basis of the kind of insight they provide into the law. On this account, legal science *clarifies* our knowledge of the law, understood as the truth-conditions of legal propositions, but does not *add* to legal knowledge; whereas jurisprudence, conceived as a form of practical knowledge, generates new knowledge of the law. The bulk of the essay is then given over to a painstaking analysis of the conditions which make possible the generation of legal knowledge, and normative knowledge more generally. Because jurisprudence is a form of practical inquiry, there is an inevitable engagement between the activity of jurisprudential theorising and the objects of that theorising: given that law is (on this view) action-guiding and normative, no 'Archimedean' standpoint is available from which to contemplate legal norms as fully-fledged mind-independent objects open to neutral description. Any theoretical insights supplied by jurisprudential investigation will therefore be interpretive and, ultimately, themselves action-guiding. Legal science, on the other hand, views legal norms as mind-independent entities which form part of the furniture of the external world: they are objects open to scientific description, analysis and study. The neutrality of legal science — and the engagement of jurisprudence — are subjected to close scrutiny. Yet, as Pavlakos argues, an investigation into the metaphysical presuppositions and conditions for scientific neutrality and normative engagement *itself* rests upon the possibility of detached, critical distance of such inquiries from the particularities of legal practice. What results is a detailed analysis of the exact conditions under which theories of both kinds supply knowledge of the law.

In his essay 'The Nature of Legal Philosophy', Robert Alexy also argues for the possibility of a general philosophical inquiry into law's nature, albeit one that stands in a dialectical relation with the features of concrete legal phenomena. According to Alexy, the nature of legal philosophy is intertwined with the nature of its subject matter, the law, there being no privileged viewpoint between the two for the inquiry to start. On the face of it, it is not possible to determine the nature of legal philosophy unless we relate it to the nature of law; but in order to know anything about the law we need to engage in the kind of inquiry that legal philosophy practices. Far from presenting a case of circularity, Alexy informs us, the relation between law and legal philosophy is that of the hermeneutic circle. It consists of successive pendular movements between the pre-understandings of the philosopher and the subject matter, the law. Along these lines, the nature of legal theory is revealed next to the nature of law in a piecemeal way, each successive instance of 'revelation' serving as the foundation for the next movement. Furthermore, the entire hermeneutic process of cognition moves from the abstract to the concrete.

At the highest level of abstraction, Alexy believes, legal philosophy sets out to demarcate the conceptual boundaries of law. It engages in the analysis of central legal concepts (norm, obligation, right, validity) and generates necessary truths that hold in all possible contexts (*a priori*). Examples of such analysis are the explications of the concept 'norm' as *meaning content* (Kelsen) or as *natural cause* (Olivecrona). Such differences in view are not free of important consequences: while the former would allow norms to feature as elements of an inferential system, the latter would restrict their role into that of elements within a causal network. What is more, Alexy suggests that this type of analysis, when applied to the concept 'law' itself, reveals two necessary characteristics thereof: its coercive character and its deontological structure.

Following on from the abstract level of conceptual analysis, legal philosophy switches into a concrete engagement with legal phenomena as they occur in the context of actual legal systems, past and present. On this occasion, philosophical inquiry amounts to propositions about law's nature whose truth depends on specific evidence within specific contexts (*a posteriori*). The purpose here is to assess the conceptual framework that resulted from the abstract conceptual analysis against the background of actual instantiations of the legal phenomena. Given the two necessary characteristics of law, its coercive character and deontological structure, concrete philosophical analysis needs to address a factual and a normative aspect. The coercive element of law turns legal philosophy into an inquiry into the factual dimension of law. As such it is interested in the institutional and authoritative aspects of the legal system and comprises what is often labelled legal positivism. In contrast, the deontological element of law turns legal philosophy into a species of normative philosophy, or the philosophy that asks the question about what ought to be done. To that extent, legal philosophy becomes a special case of practical reasoning alongside morality and ethics.

The three levels of analysis, the conceptual, the factual and the normative, are not disconnected from one another. To think the opposite, Alexy argues, is to abide by a 'restrictive maxim' that would isolate legal philosophy from either of general philosophical and practical reasoning. In contrast, a complete understanding of legal phenomena requires a 'comprehensive ideal' of legal philosophy, one in which the nature of legal philosophy arises as that of a general systematic inquiry directed specifically at its subject matter, the law.

A rather different view of 'scientific neutrality' is offered by Jonathan Gorman.[7] For while Gorman's interests transcend the question of the relationship of theory to practice, he views 'Reason' as an eternal and external standard by which law and legal reasoning are measured. Like the classical common lawyers, Gorman aims to understand what makes the law *rational*; but like Heidemann, he also wishes to explore the conditions in virtue of which theoretical inquiries into law are intelligible. He begins by asking the traditional jurisprudential questions of what is law, whether that question is completely distinguishable from the question of what law ought to be, what is justice, etc, but then he states that answers to these questions depend upon a conception of truth and knowledge, or understanding. The questions we need to ask about the nature of this knowledge and understanding (that is, the ordinary lawyer's knowledge and understanding) are, in turn, conceptually prior to not only the doctrinal disputes with which the lawyer deals, but even the interpretation of the questions of legal theory themselves. These are distinctly philosophical questions because we need

[7] J Gorman, 'The Truth of Legal Analysis', this volume.

not only an answer to them but also a justification, or reason, for their being the right answer, and these reasons lie outside the law as such.

By using Hohfeld's analysis of rights to explore the nature of legal analysis, Gorman explores the issue of what an analysis of jural relations, or legal reasoning, really is. Are the insights supplied by theoretical perspectives on law 'objectively' true, or only on the basis of subjective beliefs and contingent practices? Hohfeld's analytical scheme, it turns out, is offered both as an *analysis* (of conditions which hold locally) and as a standard of *criticism* (which transcends those local conditions). As such, that analysis — and perhaps all jurisprudential analysis — can appear, at once, as a project of rational reconstruction *and* as a project of conceptual clarification. While the former project is stipulative, and thus 'detached' from the practice it wishes to understand, the latter is essentially descriptive of that practice. We should nevertheless be wary, urges Gorman, of the idea that the facts of legal understanding are separate from theories about them: the stipulative and descriptive aspects of legal analysis are better seen as two differing models of legal reasoning — models which structure our understanding of what legal understanding is. The choice between these models is not arbitrary, however, but judged on basis of reason (just as, if anything warrants truth of Hohfeld's stipulative recommendations, it is reason). Hence legal theorists must 'draw on and develop' our understanding of what reason requires in law.

The rationalism of this suggestion contrasts not only with the empiricism of Leith and Morison, and the 'jurisprudential' stance of Coyle — both of which, in their different ways, emphasise the socially and historically variable contexts in which legal practices are played out — but also with the views of Veronica Rodriguez-Blanco. For like Pavlakos, Rodriguez-Blanco seeks to reveal the metaphysical commitments of conceptual analysis, not its relationship to reason. She begins by contrasting methodological disputes with substantive questions of what law is. The former roughly pose the question of whether legal theory should address internal ('participant') or external perspectives, and whether it aims to give a descriptive or an evaluative account of law. She states that the majority of consciously methodological studies adopt the methodology of the social sciences, and these pairings are a consequence of that adoption. Yet despite overwhelming theoretical interest in the internal/external and descriptive/evaluative distinctions, she argues, these are marginal to substantive theoretical understandings of law: natural law theories have been structured along both external-descriptive lines and internal-evaluative ones, so while such methodological pairings may decisively shape particular theoretical stances, they make little difference to substantive account of law. Consequently, Rodriguez-Blanco wants to abandon that methodological debate in favour of a different question: one which pertains to the metaphysical presuppositions of legal theory. In particular, she addresses the question of whether an 'abstinent' or a 'descriptive' perspective is preferable.

The former view consists (roughly) in the claim that legal reasoning has no particular metaphysical consequences or commitments; the latter argues that we must use conceptual analysis in order to uncover the metaphysical commitments of legal discourse. This dichotomy, Rodriguez-Blanco argues, lies alongside the internal/external dichotomy but is more revealing of the intellectual commitments and alleged 'objectivist' claims of the various theoretical standpoints to which it is applied. Her aim, accordingly, is to re-conceive that methodological debate along lines which reveal the connection of metaphysical presuppositions with substantive theoretical views about the law and legal reasoning. In fact, she concludes, conceptual analysis depends upon metaphysical and moral convictions and is not metaphysically or morally 'neutral'.[8] Hence, she argues, legal theory should be grounded in, but not confined to, conceptual analysis as traditionally conceived.

JURISPRUDENCE VS LEGAL SCIENCE

The term 'legal science' has been used to describe a view of legal theory as separable from the facts of legal practice. Legal science aims to give a 'neutral' account of legal practice by engaging in conceptual analysis of the 'foundations' of that practice. This mode of analysis is viewed as taking place prior to engagement in the substantive disputes with which the lawyer grapples, and aims to clarify the terms of those disputes by clarifying their structure and assumptions. One task of legal science therefore consists in asking whether the facts of legal practice are, in the end, 'objective' or 'subjective'. It is for this reason that the distinguishing characteristics of legal science are best understood as lying in their generalising ambitions and their separation from ordinary legal practice. The above accounts of legal theorising fall within the category of 'legal science' because they claim to supply analytical perspectives on law which (as Gorman observes) go beyond, or exist apart from, the particular features of the socially extended practices they purport to depict. The stark differences between the various conceptions of legal theory therein are nevertheless underpinned by a strikingly similar conception of the *kind* of theoretical insight legal theory exists to supply: a conception far removed indeed from the views of the common lawyers who first wondered about the possibility of a 'science of laws'.

The two essays which begin and end this collection — that of Sean Coyle, and that of Philip Leith and John Morison — take a different view. Yet despite profound similarities in the motivations of these essays, and in their views of the shortcomings of 'legal science', equally profound are

[8] But see both Leith and Morison (above n 4) and Coyle (above n 1), who argue that conceptual analysis is of limited interest in the context of legal theory precisely in virtue of its 'neutrality'.

the striking differences between them in terms of general orientation and their conception of the nature and tasks of legal theory. For while Coyle seeks to reject legal science in favour of an older tradition of 'jurisprudence', Leith and Morison argue for the establishment of legal theory as a 'genuine' science of law. This is not, however, science in the sense used elsewhere in this volume, but rather a version of the methodology of the social sciences, firmly rooted in empirical investigation rather than conceptual analysis.

Leith and Morison reject the claims of analytical jurisprudence in favour of empiricism. Only then, they claim, can legal theory be transformed into a science. Leith and Morison blame 'formalism' for many of the short-comings of modern legal theory, which they see as indulging in pointless semantic exercises which remain essentially divorced from, and of no interest to, an understanding of legal practice. Legal theory should instead, they claim, attempt to locate law within wider social practices, and understand the contribution of law to such practices (such as governance). This form of theoretical investigation, however, has become so far removed from the mainstream of modern legal theory that it 'is not visible at all'.

Coyle shares with Leith and Morison the view that legal theory has become increasingly remote from legal practice, but disagrees about both the cause and the remedy for this detachment. Leith and Morison place the blame squarely on Hart, and see the only way of bringing legal theory back on track as limiting jurisprudence to the examination of law in action. Hart, they point out, while claiming to be engaging in sociology, is in fact doing no such thing. Hart's central theoretical insights, on this view, purport to reveal analytical insights into the nature of law, but are in reality far removed from any real insight into the nature of legal practice as it is actually carried on.[9] Jurisprudence, they argue, should consist in empirical study and theoretical critique of results of that empiricism. In doing so, it should emulate the forms and methods of science, and provide a genuine insight into the living law: an insight which does not confine itself to irrelevant musings on the nature of rules and abstract speculations about conceptual connections between law and morality.

Having revealed what they regard as the flaws of modern legal theory, Leith and Morison go on to give examples of their own style of jurisprudence: they argue, for example, that investigations of barristers present a challenge to received jurisprudential conceptions of 'rules' and the sense in which law is made up of 'rules'. Legal reasoning, they argue, has much more to do with the variable temperaments of judges as to how a case is presented and reasoned. The traditional idea of traditional 'lawyers' law' is

[9] This theme is taken up by Veronica Rodriguez-Blanco in her essay on legal metaphysics, in which she suggests a quite different view of Hart's claim to be writing an essay in 'descriptive sociology', and of the value of that approach.

quite far removed from this: barristers may not be specialists in this kind of law, but locate their expertise within a wider conception of 'legal knowledge' which includes much more practical and mundane things such as judge's characteristic likes and dislikes, the needs of clients and solicitors, etc. In this sense, Leith and Morison argue,

> [p]ersuasion is at the heart of the legal process and the barrister's job is to ensure that solicitors and clients, witnesses and opponents as well as judges and juries are persuaded to see the world in the way that the barrister urges. Rules are not platonic/atomic structures with a core and a penumbra: they exist to be used in a rhetorical context where particular views can be urged and specific solutions to real problems achieved.

Our legal theory must reflect and respond to such realities.

Coyle disagrees with Leith and Morison both about the reason for legal theory's separation from legal practice, and about the significance of that separation. The project of 'neutral' conceptual analysis of law, he argues, will come to be seen as a possibility only where the pressing political questions which traditionally drive jurisprudential inquiry recede into the background of popular thinking. Where individual liberties are under threat, for example, or where there is widespread disagreement over the form or limits of governmental power, the task of legal theorists will be seen as that of putting forward and defending particular political conceptions of the law's point or purpose. Doctrinal exposition will then seem to be intimately connected to wider political debates, and of considerable importance in the shaping and outcome of those debates. Where individuals' anxieties centre instead upon relatively minor questions, such as rates of taxation, or upon questions of political policy which are not directly threatening to one's way of life, attempts to reveal the political foundations of law will seem much less pressing and worthwhile, and theoretical inquiry will instead take the form of the minute analysis of extant institutions, and the drawing of 'general' conclusions about the 'nature' of law as a social practice.

Rather than restricting the role of legal theorising to empirical investigation, Coyle believes that legal theory should be directed at understanding legal practice as a series of variable and contingent arrangements which have formed against the background of various political and historically extended practices. The role of law, he argues, is inevitably shaped by the form of political life in which it participates: law is at once something created by that life, and something that plays a central role in structuring that life. Accordingly, theoretical insights into law are most illuminating when directed at an understanding of law's place within a system of wider political practices, rather than an investigation into 'conceptual foundations' or semantic properties of legal propositions which are believed to transcend those practices.

JURISPRUDENCE OR LEGAL SCIENCE?

Most of the authors in this volume write from within the tradition of 'legal science'.[10] As a reading of the various chapters makes clear, however, they often differ about the precise characteristics and assumptions of legal science, and hence employ that term in a series of distinct yet closely related ways: these, roughly speaking, centre upon varying conceptions of the meaning and role played by the ideas of theoretical neutrality and objectivity. It is in the light of this that, we believe, the term 'legal science' is best used in connection with theories which purport to understand the nature of law in general terms, or which concede the possibility of generality in theoretical accounts of the nature of law. Jurisprudence, as here conceived, denies that possibility. Theoretical understandings of law, on the latter view, are understandings of the place of law in a system of contingent social and political practices, and of the way in which law develops within those practices as a distinctive source of value and insight *into* those practices. Inquiries into 'the nature of law' are, accordingly, viewed at best as unhistoric attempts to understand the current form of our distinctive, legal practices.

Can the aims of jurisprudence and legal science be reconciled? In one obvious sense they cannot, since jurisprudence emphasises the unavailability of scientifically neutral or objective standpoints in terms of which legal science must be cashed out. It is therefore sometimes said that theoretical standpoints of the kind here labelled 'jurisprudence' entail a commitment to moral and cultural relativism: if the moral, political and rational standards through which we understand our legal and political life are themselves mere realisations of historical possibilities, then what basis exists for rational or comparative criticism? Is it true that there are no general or eternal standards — such as reason — by which we can view and judge our particular form of life? It is in fact doubtful that a rejection of the underpinning assumptions of legal science leads to an all-out commitment to relativism. Relativism trades on the assumption that standards (moral, political or otherwise) which have emerged and operate within one form of life are not capable of forming a basis for meaningful comparisons with standards governing some other, alternative form of life: that we cannot *rationally* prefer one set of such standards to any other, or that we can only express such preferences in an ultimately question-begging way. Jurisprudence is committed to no such assumption, but only to the view that there are no genuinely informative *general* conclusions to be reached about the nature of law irrespective of time or place. Thus, for example, a proponent of jurisprudence may assert that the Roman law concept of *ius*, though it forms the intellectual basis for modern Western systems of law, is inapplicable

[10] As Dworkin rightly observes, 'this is Archimedeanism's golden age.' See Dworkin (above n 6), 2.

to the legal society of ancient Greece, which focused not upon conceptions of right, but upon civility and excellence. This assertion is nevertheless compatible with the (questionable) assertion that a legal order conceived on the basis of rights is *superior* to one rooted in conceptions of excellence and civic virtue.

While jurisprudence seeks to explain fundamental features of legal practice against the background of particular political practices and arrangements, it does not thereby confine theoretical speculation to contingent contexts of historical explanation. That being the case, it might be argued that legal science plays a role in exploring the conditions under which the comparisons permitted by jurisprudence, between different systems of values (such as rights, virtues and excellences), might be probed. The question of objectivity and neutrality might then be seen as a question of whether objective or meaningful comparisons between distinct forms of legal and political practice are available, and if so, what makes them available. Perhaps, as Jonathan Gorman argues, the standard of comparison turns out to be reason itself; perhaps it turns out to be something else. To the philosopher (but not, one might expect, the legal practitioner) these are issues worth exploring. Hence, legal science's critical distance from legal practice might turn out to be essential, plausible and — contrary to the view of Coyle and Leith and Morison — no obstacle to an informative view of law notwithstanding its distance from the cares and concerns of the lawyer and doctrinal scholar.

Viewed in this way, jurisprudence and legal science provide two distinctive, but equally valid ways of looking theoretically at law. Jurisprudence explains and judges law and legal reasoning from the perspective of values which have emerged as part of those practices. It seeks to comprehend the significance of those values through sustained engagement with the practices and currents of thought through which they emerged and developed. Legal science, on the other hand, seeks an understanding of the significance of law *a priori*, through the analysis of legal concepts according to standards which are viewed as independent of those concepts, and which stand outside the social and historical contexts in which those concepts figure. Which of these modes of thinking about the law is most fruitful, the reader may judge by closer engagement with the various arguments and essays in this volume.

1

Two Concepts of Legal Analysis

SEAN COYLE[1]

IN HIS DISCUSSION of 'civil laws' in *Leviathan*, Hobbes offers the following account of the main purpose of his argument. The term 'civil laws', he says, refers to those instruments of a civil polity which men are bound to observe, not because they are members of this or that *particular* society, but in virtue of their membership of *a* society. Hence, the aim of the analysis is 'not to shew what is Law here and there; but what is Law; as *Plato*, *Aristotle*, *Cicero* and divers others have done, without taking upon them the profession of the study of the Law.'[2] The kind of investigation being proposed here is suggestive of the way in which a scientist might investigate natural phenomena: theoretical inquiry into law is seen as the analysis of a particular form of social order, the elements of which can be mapped, described, classified and dissected according to recognised standards and criteria. Because the understanding sought is of law as a social phenomenon (it is implied), the conclusions offered by the analysis transcend the moral and institutional peculiarities associated with particular legal orders, and constitute a form of scientific knowledge which exceeds the cultural limits of any given polity.

Posterity has largely accepted Hobbes's judgement of the status of such claims. In modern jurisprudential thought, it is not uncommon to find associated with them the additional virtues of *neutrality* and *generality*. In his 'Postscript' to *The Concept of Law*, Hart observes that the legal theory put forward in that work '. . . is morally neutral and has no justificationary aims: it does not seek to justify or commend on moral or other grounds the forms and structures which appear in my general account of law.'[3] The account is general 'in the sense that it is not tied to any particular legal system or legal culture, but seeks to give an explanatory and clarifying account

[1] I am enormously grateful to those present at the Workshop in Analytical Jurisprudence at Queen's University for their observations and criticisms of an earlier version of this essay, and to Stephen Guest and Holly Cullen for reading earlier drafts. I am especially indebted to Brian Bix, whose helpful suggestions have improved the essay in numerous ways.

[2] T Hobbes, *Leviathan* (Cambridge, Cambridge University Press, 1991) II.26, 183.

[3] HLA Hart, *The Concept of Law,* 2nd edn (Oxford, Clarendon Press, 1994), 240.

of law as a complex social and political institution . . .'.[4] This underpinning similarity in approaches as otherwise diverse as those of Hobbes and Hart suggests a prevailing concern with something other than mere objectivity; it seems to indicate, rather, a deeper set of assumptions regarding the nature of explanation, and of the purpose of legal philosophy itself. For the political theorists of the seventeenth and eighteenth centuries, an account of law was an account of the moral basis of law, and the attempt to understand the importance and distinctiveness of legal rules within more inclusive conceptions of social order. Such explanations were not offered as *neutral* understandings, but they very often did purport to identify necessary truths concerning the moral significance of legal rules; truths which were reckoned to be independent of the form and substance of particular institutional arrangements.

Much of modern legal theory, by contrast, consists in the attempt to offer clarifications of the conceptions and criteria we use in ordinary legal reasoning. The modern legal theorist seldom regards his principal task as the application to law of a specific moral theory; rather, he sees himself as offering an *analysis* of the principles and ideas which lie behind ordinary legal practice. Such analyses are 'neutral' on this view, because they are concerned with the elucidation of the conceptual foundations of our practices rather than with questions about the extent to which those practices serve our fundamental interests, welfare or wider social goals. Questions of the latter sort inevitably presuppose some conception of what our deeper interests are, and of the way in which they might or should be secured through collective action.[5] One theorist might think that legal rules can only bring about an increase in overall welfare by adopting a stringently utilitarian standpoint; another might feel that our interests are best served by maximising autonomy rather than utility, and hence that the law must resemble a Kantian framework of compossible rights and freedoms. The project of conceptual clarification is often thought of as dealing with matters which are *prior* to such questions in the sense of being 'foundational' to them: conceptual analysis is regarded as investigating the internal coherence of moral and legal theories rather than evaluating those theories on moral or political grounds.

The aim of analytical jurisprudence is to *describe* the legal order in philosophical terms rather than to *evaluate* it. We think of the classical political theorists as attempting to identify the necessary form of social relations, and insisting that law define and uphold the structure of those relations. For the modern theorist, the plausibility of a theory of law depends not on its moral desirability, but upon its ability to offer a penetrating insight into the

[4] *Ibid*, 239. For an excellent discussion of these claims, see S Perry, 'Hart's Methodological Positivism' (1998) 4 *Legal Theory* 427–67.
[5] See J Finnis, *Natural Law and Natural Rights* (Oxford, Clarendon Press, 1980).

form and structure of our legal practices. In either case, the virtue of a theory rested in the degree of analytical insight it provides, whether of juridical relationships or societal relationships more generally. Differing conceptions of what counts as 'genuine' or 'useful' insight into law thus reflect basic disagreement over the nature of law itself. This evident truth has in turn encouraged the belief that the central task of legal theory is to uncover the true nature of law.

It is tempting to characterise modern jurisprudential debate on this subject as an argument between those who attempt to exhibit the content of legal rules as a reflection of specific moral values, and those who seek to analyse the *form* of those rules as elements of a social practice. We tend to associate the former of these approaches with natural law (or idealism); the latter with legal positivism. Yet, in so far as those who espouse idealism or natural law theory are the intellectual heirs of the seventeenth-century natural rights theorists,[6] we can see *both* positivists *and* naturalists as participating in a broadly similar conception of legal *theory*: one which seeks to propound the fundamental features of law in general, an account which (as Hobbes remarked) neither requires, nor is available to, those who study the rules, principles and doctrines of law *here* and *there*. When understood in this way, the debate between idealists and positivists turns on the question of whether genuinely neutral understandings of law are possible. That the understanding sought is *general* is, very often, taken for granted.

THE CLAIMS OF 'LEGAL SCIENCE'

Is this form of juristic scholarship possible? Both idealists and positivists, it has been suggested, conceive of legal theory as being essentially separate from legal practice.[7] Lawyers, on this view, apparently employ relatively settled criteria for recognising what counts as sound doctrinal legal scholarship; but the task of the legal philosopher is to explore deep philosophical problems concerning the basis and significance of the ordinary lawyer's

[6] Modern writers on natural law are the heirs of the natural rights tradition to the extent that they conceive of the legal order as a systematic body of rights. We might employ the term 'Idealism' to refer to this conception, and regard natural law theory and idealism as distinct yet somewhat overlapping ideas. I am not interested in natural law theories which primarily concern the conceptual relationship between law and morality (and which can claim a dubious historical ancestor in the Thomist tradition).

[7] Dworkin — who certainly counts as an idealist for these purposes — might be regarded as something of an exception. Yet, to put matters in a language which Dworkin would recognise, whilst his 'conception' of legal theory is one within which jurisprudence is 'the general part of adjudication, silent prologue to any decision at law', his 'concept' of legal theory fits very much within the generalising spirit with which I am concerned. Such generalist ambitions are evident in passages such as this one: '. . . the most abstract and fundamental point of legal practice is to guide and constrain the power of government . . . The law of a community on this account is the scheme of rights and responsibilities that meet this complex standard.' See R Dworkin, *Law's Empire* (London, Fontana, 1986), 90 and 93 respectively.

assumptions. By isolating and articulating the philosophical principles which underpin the ordinary lawyer's concepts and criteria, the legal philosopher attempts to reconstruct the legal order in terms of the moral and philosophical theory presupposed in the application of its rules, principles and doctrines. Such questions do not arise in legal practice: the ordinary lawyer confronts the legal order as a body of highly technical rules, definitions and distinctions which require specialised techniques of interpretation and application. By applying these techniques, the lawyer can ply his trade without raising any of the deeper questions uncovered by the legal philosopher.

We can refer to this conception of philosophical analysis as 'legal science', given the suggestive parallels with the scientist's investigation of natural processes: the processes occur independently of the scientific analysis, but seem to require scientific explanation in any case. Likewise, a philosophical understanding of the nature of law is not required by those who engage with legal rules on a daily basis; yet the obvious bearing of law on our moral lives makes a philosophical account of the lawyer's assumptions pressing.[8] This distinction between legal practice and the theory of law is perhaps most starkly articulated in the philosophy of Jeremy Bentham. In a long footnote to his discussion of common law, Bentham states that '[a] rule of Law must be predicated of some certain assemblage of words — It can never be predicated of a bare assemblage of naked ideas.'[9] The reason for this, he says, is that only a verbally formulated rule has the requisite certainty associated with binding legal standards. The suggestion is that only posited rules, and not ideas formed from them, could claim to be an authoritative statement of the law. In due course, Bentham recast this distinction as a distinction between 'authoritative' and 'unauthoritative' propositions of law: the former consist in the express declaration of a legislator; the latter express 'either (first) the will of certain judges acting as such, or else, secondly, inferences drawn from what is supposed to have been such will, or thirdly, what is supposed to have been the will of a legislator.'[10]

Bentham apparently experienced considerable difficulty in articulating exactly what he meant by this distinction, yet it is clear that much of its significance, for him, lay in the distinction between stipulated rules, on the one hand, and reports or explanations of those rules, on the other. Stipulated rules consist of certain words, usually arranged into sentences, clauses and sub-clauses; but whether we are dealing with entire paragraphs or distinct sub-clauses, we can be sure that whichever words we single out as constituting a discrete command are still propositions of law. Not so with purported

[8] Dworkin, for example, sees the central task of legal philosophy as the production of a morally satisfactory justification of law's apparent power to interfere in the moral lives and choices of ordinary citizens: see *Law's Empire* (above n 7), ch 6.

[9] J Bentham, 'A Comment on the Commentaries' in *A Comment on the Commentaries and a Fragment on Government* (London, Athlone, 1977), II.10, 259n.

[10] *Ibid*, II.10, 260.

explanations or attempted interpretations of written rules: here, the form of words depends upon the commentator's subjective *idea* of the rule, and no part of his explanation or gloss can claim to represent an authoritative statement of law. At best, we have 'the shadow of the shadow of a shade' which is nevertheless 'worshipped as the substance'.[11] The tendency to conflate these two distinct kinds of proposition, Bentham argued, leads us to adopt a distorted picture of law: one which views the legal order as a systematic and internally coherent body of rules and principles underpinned by more general values, and which disguises the true form of law as a series of particular commands. The distinction between authoritative and unauthoritative propositions thus reflects a more general division between the projects of expository and censorial jurisprudence. For the attempt to supply a content for law beyond that stated by authoritative words will become the construction of justifications for applying a rule in a particular way according to 'underpinning' moral values. Hence, in the case of unauthoritative propositions, Bentham thought,

> . . . it would have been better, had [they] never been characterised by the name of Law: had [they] never been characterised by any other name than that of Jurisprudence . . .[12]

We might accept Bentham's distinction between 'law' and 'jurisprudence' as aptly describing a widespread belief among practising lawyers that black-letter rules are conceptually distinct from the justifying arguments which support them. Many of the intuitive judgements we make about the authority of textbooks, statutes and judicial decisions as sources of law come from this belief. We rightly distinguish between, on the one hand, the statutory provisions and judicial pronouncements which make up the law, and, on the other, the textbook commentary which reports and arranges the rules in a pedagogically functional manner. We tend to think of textbooks as *describing* a particular area of the law, but not as an authoritative *source* of law: any authority possessed by the textbook is entirely derivative from the rules it purports to describe. At the same time, we seldom conceive of court judgments as embodying a sharply delineated and definitive statement of the law. The sifting of the *ratio decidendi* from the *obiter* remarks is seen as relying on complex and elusive considerations which demand great skill on the part of the jurist. It is thus tempting to suppose that we can distinguish between clear cases, which involve the straightforward application of settled rules, and hard cases, where there is no very clear legal rule which can be told apart from various conflicting justifying arguments. If we are to take beliefs such as these seriously, it seems that we are obliged to accept something like Bentham's distinction between authoritative and unauthoritative

[11] J Bentham, *Of Laws in General* (London, Athlone, 1970) XV, 188.
[12] *Comment* (above n 9), II.10, 261.

propositions of law: the term 'law' (we could argue) should be reserved for settled rules, whereas 'jurisprudence' refers to doctrinal legal reasoning *about* the content of legal rules.

Bentham's view sustains the picture of the ordinary lawyer as confronting a system of technical and highly articulated rules the application of which, at least in straightforward cases, remains independent of wider questions of social policy and moral desirability. At the very least, we might concede, it enables us to locate with greater precision the points at which considerations of social policy intrude upon otherwise neutral legal arguments. On this view, the legal philosopher is engaged in the same sort of activity as the juristic commentator: both offer particular visions of the black-letter rules, the former at a considerable degree of abstraction, the latter at the level of concrete legal institutions. Yet the difficulty Bentham experienced in the formulation of his distinction should alert us to the immense difficulties which face the attempt to offer rigid categorical divisions of this kind in the context of the common law. For it is far from clear that complex areas of the legal order, such as contract law or the law of real property, can be represented as an exhaustive list of precise black-letter rules. As one distinguished legal historian put it, '[in] the common law system no very clear distinction exists between saying that a particular solution to a problem is in accordance with the law, and saying that it is the rational, or fair, or just solution.'[13]

Bentham viewed doctrinal reasoning and philosophical evaluation of legal rules as being closely related. For the construction of justifying arguments is, he thought, the task of the censor rather than the expositor, who should limit himself to straightforward reports of the black-letter rules. But if, as Simpson suggests, the black-letter rules are ultimately inseparable from the wider doctrinal questions, it follows that the tasks of the doctrinal writer and the legal philosopher are not radically far apart. Bentham's use of the word 'jurisprudence' to describe both activities is suggestive: the modern legal writer regards the word as possessing two distinct, and apparently unconnected, senses. The first sense is that given by practising lawyers who understand the word to refer to a body of judicial opinion, and hence as a set of principles concerning (for example) the conditions under which a purchaser for value might undermine the conditions of a trust of land, or the meaning of 'merchantable quality' under s 14(2) of the Sale of Goods Act (1979). The second sense is that employed by legal theorists to refer to the activity of legal philosophy, considered as asking *general* questions independently of particular legal institutions and arrangements. The analytical ambitions of 'legal science', then, might profitably be regarded as an attempt to keep these two senses of 'jurisprudence' apart.

[13] AWB Simpson, 'The Common Law and Legal Theory' in *Oxford Essays in Jurisprudence*, 2nd Series (Oxford, Clarendon Press, 1973), 77–99.

Yet the very motivations for drawing such a distinction are, as we have seen, undermined by the terms in which the argument itself is framed. For it is both possible and desirable to reject Bentham's very strict dichotomy of 'law' and 'jurisprudence' whilst affirming his perception of an intimate connection between doctrinal argument and legal theory. The ordinary lawyer usually regards a body of judicial opinion as exhibiting order and coherence at the level of principle. A series of judicial decisions can generally be represented in different ways according to the underpinning principles assumed to be at work in the decisions, an insight reflected in the language in which talk of judicial opinion is framed: the search for the *ratio decidendi* is the search for *reasons* rather than articulated *rules*. The exposition of legal doctrine thus depends upon the ability to depict the law as pursuing coherent projects at all. Were this impossible, the law's claim to protect settled expectations, and to offer a rational basis on which such expectations can be weighed against one another where they conflict, would give way to a series of ever-changing moral and political judgements about how best to define and reconcile conflicting interests in the light of wider social goals. Jurisprudential inquiry might therefore be seen not as an investigation into the 'nature' of law in general, but as an exploration of currents of thought which have shaped our assumptions about the legal order, and of the reasons for perceiving them as central or important. The legal order is both complex and normative: the character of the understanding sought, in relation to it, bears not upon the 'foundations' of its rules, principles and doctrines, but upon their wider *significance* to our form of life.

This conception of the tasks of legal theory can be found at work in the writings of HLA Hart. Hart opens his book, *The Concept of Law*, by briefly mentioning some of the most influential conceptions of law advanced by legal philosophers: for example, that 'real' law consists exclusively in judicial pronouncements, or that the law is best represented as a system of interlocking rights, and so forth. These examples are raised only to be dismissed; they are, Hart claims, exaggerations of 'partial truths' about law.[14] Yet the relationship of this statement to the main body of Hart's book is often imperfectly understood. The central thesis of that book is that law fundamentally consists in *rules* (or, more precisely, the practices which comprise them), and that the concept of law is best illuminated through an analysis of law as 'an affair of rules'. Exactly what form of jurisprudential inquiry, then, is being proposed here? Temptingly obvious is the following explanation: the earlier theories foundered (Hart is saying) because they highlighted only inessential, contingent features of law, whereas the notion of a rule captures what is necessary and fundamental about law. The earlier theories represent *partial* truths because (for example) law certainly *involves* determinations of right as an important feature of legal reasoning;

[14] Hart (above n 3), 2.

judicial practice represents the cutting-edge of law, and hence entices us to draw revealing distinctions between 'dead' rules and 'living' rulings; and so on. But closer examination reveals the notion of a rule as the basic one which underlies each of these 'insights' into the nature of law: rights are theoretically interesting only because they are conferred by rules; judicial decisions are worthy of scrutiny only in relation to the claim that judges do, or do not, decide cases according to fixed rules. All of these phenomena are, on this view, elements of a wider rule-following practice, and an understanding of the form of that practice provides a quite general understanding of law, untied to local variations in institutional arrangements.

We should reject such an explanation. Its plausibility lies in our readiness to assume that the presence of 'partial' truths suggests the existence of a deeper or more comprehensive truth awaiting the lucky ones who are able to penetrate the conceptual fog. Rules, we are led to believe, are 'central' in a way that other concepts, such as rights, are not. Yet such a claim is very far from Hart's apparent intention in discussing the earlier examples. His discussion of them is intended as indicative rather than suasive: we are to reject the earlier theories not because they are *false*, but because the search for necessary or foundational truth in the context of law is itself misconceived. In claiming that an analysis of law in terms of rules is preferable to rival explanations, in terms of its analytical power, Hart is not purporting to establish a metaphysically significant truth about law, but rather the claim that an understanding of law as a system of rules affords the best explanation of the current form of our legal practices. An analysis in terms of rules represents but one way in which those practices can be understood: law is not *inevitably* conceivable as a system of rules, but only takes that form as a result of various historical forces acting upon juristic thought. The task of the theorist is therefore not that of supplying insights into the 'necessary foundations' of the legal order, but to display the assumptions which give shape to legal practice as a distinctive historical product.

It is possible to regiment legal practice according to various conceptions and ideas: law can take on (for example) the appearance of an integrated system of rights, a collection of remedies, judicial outcomes or a corpus of rules and principles. The task of the legal philosopher is not the discovery of which of these possible understandings is the 'true' one, but consists rather in exhibiting those understandings as received explanations which vie and compete in the light of current problems and preoccupations. On this view, these alternative regimentations are 'partial' because they exaggerate the centrality to law of patterns of thinking which ebb and flow in the tide of history: patterns of thought which reflect shifting conceptions of the nature of social life and the relationship of law to political values. Major shifts in our thinking about law tend to reflect broader social or political change (one might bring to mind the 'revolutionary' legal theories of Hobbes or Marx); but in general change is gradual, and expressive of ideas recognised as having influenced our practices and assumptions only in retrospect. Instances of conceptual upheaval, in which a received way of looking at law is comprehensively undermined by an emergent insight, will therefore be rare. Instead, we may expect there to be, at any time, numerous overlapping conceptions of the legal order, each emphasising aspects of the legal order deemed by their champions to be crucial, or central.

A perspective which emphasises rules might therefore be in tension with established understandings of the legal order as possessing rational coherence at the level of principle. For it is far from clear that a body of posited rules should inevitably form an internally consistent system. In a situation of prolonged social instability, for instance, law may well be looked upon primarily as a body of authoritative commands: it might be felt that legal rules should possess the virtues of firmness and clarity; correspondingly little attention being devoted to the question whether, taken together, those commands conform to particular standards of reason or can be subsumed under more general principles. The values and motivations of the legislator might owe as much, if not more, to political expedience and instrumentalism as to rational coherence. Yet we may be loath to give up the notion of the legal order as a rationally coherent system, even in the face of an array of posited provisions. Rather than seek to reconcile these positions, the legal theorist might be conceived as examining the influence of these ideas and their interrelationship. Let me continue to use the word 'jurisprudence' to refer to this conception, in order to distinguish it from the claims of 'legal science'.

'JURISPRUDENCE'

The legal theorist, on this view, offers an account of the legal order based not upon the preliminary analysis of concepts, but on suggestive understandings of the normative significance of legal rules and doctrines. Particularly instructive in this regard is the suggestion by AWB Simpson that forms of legal writing are often indicative of more general views about the nature of law.[15] The idea of law as *capable* of being presented as a rational system is (he suggests) not inevitable, but rather a contingent product of the textbook tradition which had its beginnings in the early seventeenth century. It is, however, in the eighteenth century that one can most clearly trace the intellectual commitments of modern jurisprudential debates about the nature of law. The following remarks represent a brief gesture in the direction of such an account.

[15] AWB Simpson, 'The Rise and Fall of the Legal Treatise: Legal Principles and the Forms of Legal Literature' (1981) XLVII *University of Chicago Law Review*, 632.

Let us go back to Hart's claim that the modern legal order is best understood as a system of rules. The idea that law is properly analysed in terms of rules is not new: Pufendorf, writing in 1672, had observed: 'That reason should be able to discover any morality in the actions of a man without reference to a law is as impossible as for a man born blind to choose between colours.'[16] His point was, of course, that any understanding of human behaviour which attempts to rise beyond the level of mere observation necessitates resort to generality and classification, indicative of a moral theory understood in terms of moral *rules*. But a perspective which gives priority to rules as the bedrock of a moral theory is itself an historical product. The seventeenth-century natural lawyers focused on *rights* first and foremost: no theoretical attention was centred on rules as the distinctive means by which a society might give effect to abstract entitlements, and regulate competing rights. Only with the removal of the theological underpinnings of the natural rights theories in the early eighteenth century, and the rise of the idea of legislative will, did rules become worthy of sustained theoretical attention as the vehicles by which rights are adjudicated and conferred.

A very different picture of the legal order was present in the traditional common law scholarship of the fifteenth and sixteenth centuries. The legal writings of this period were organised around the assumptions and preoccupations of legal *practice*, and hence emphasised procedure and remedies. The focus on matters of immediate practical significance meant that there was no pressing reason to regard the law as an ordered, rational system; and, by and large, it did not occur to legal commentators to do so.[17] The majority of the legal writings of the time consisted in the form of abridgments and glossaries; and where a systematic presentation of the rules did seem desirable, the notion of systematicity was largely confined to presentation under headings arranged in *alphabetical* order.

The form of legal scholarship practised by the traditional common lawyers did not encourage the construction of bolder classificatory schemes. Where philosophical speculation on law seemed appropriate, the lawyer moved within a conception of law as an embodiment of a society's shared conceptions of the good. Legal rules and doctrines were seen not as serving underpinning rational principles, but as evolving over time: the rules represented developing responses to recurrent problems which were subjected, in

[16] S Pufendorf, *De Iure Naturae* (translated as: *The Law of Nature and of Nations*) (London, 1749), I.2.6.

[17] The systematic treatment given to tenures in Littleton's *Tenores Novelli* [c 1481] seems to form a notable exception. Thus despite the efforts of Coke and Matthew Hale, Stair's lament in the *Insitutions* that '. . . there are not wanting of late of the learnedest lawyers, who have thought it both feasible and fit, that the law should be formed into a rational discipline, and have much regretted that it hath not been effected, yea scarce attempted by any' was not entirely rhetorical: see *Institutions* (1681), 1.1.17.

Coke's memorable words, to 'the fire of experience'.[18] The standards of reason involved in the articulation and application of common law rules were immanent rather than transcendent. The rules were seen as emerging not from more general principles, but from long usage and experience: the common law was looked upon as a repository of accumulated wisdom and immemorial custom. So long as the rules were perceived as evolved responses to the problems of collective living, rather than as rational dictates, there was no obvious reason for regarding the corpus of rules as forming a comprehensive or systematic response to human social life.

From the beginning of the seventeenth century, in the writings of Grotius, Locke, Rousseau, Kant and others, the emphasis shifted from the idea of law as a collection of *remedies* to the idea of law as a system of interlocking *rights*. This intellectual shift required the development of a systematic jurisprudence: law came to be seen as a system of horizontal and vertical patterns of entitlement. The idea that every individual was possessed of rights and duties, towards both other individuals and the state, gave rise to the notion of formal equality, itself entailing the assumption of universal postulates beyond the rules which outlined a particular individual's *actual* entitlements. Law came to be depicted as a rational order governed by transcendent standards of reason, of which the positive rules are merely instances. It is this vision of the legal order that is at work in Blackstone's *Commentaries*, a work often regarded as a typical example of early eighteenth-century natural law scholarship. This assessment of Blackstone's work, however, ignores the sense in which the assumptions of the position are already deeply positivist. Once law is seen as governed by rational principles regarded as transcendent rather than immanent, the 'rules' come to be regarded as related to those principles *deductively*, rather than as coming into focus only gradually and incompletely. Since the general principles can be interpreted in different ways according to the moral values and purposes they are held to serve, the idea of *canonical* rules becomes important. For legal rules, we are tempted to think, are set apart from open-ended moral debate precisely in that they are ascertainable and final: law, therefore, comes to be conceived in terms of the immensely plausible idea of a body of authoritative standards, in which questions of legal validity are untied to subjective moral belief.

[18] Sir E Coke, *Institutes* I [1628], s 138. See also G Postema, *Bentham and the Common Law Tradition* (Oxford, Clarendon, 1986), ch 1 and 2. Coke's words might in fact be regarded as marking a watershed in common law theory: for on the one hand, the emphasis on common law being rooted in custom provided the basis for later convention-based analyses which explored the dynamics of legal judgment from within a bottom-up model of legal authority; whilst on the other hand, the notion of an immanent morality paved the way for understandings of the common law as a communal moral exercise which went beyond the bottom-up model and advocated forms of idealism. (Dworkin's writings provide an excellent example of the way in which an account of the latter kind might be developed.)

The tension between these inherited traditions (the perspective which emphasises articulated rules, and the notion of law as a body of rational principles) has shaped our received views and attitudes toward legal writing. Blackstone's *Commentaries* are part of a tradition which views the treatise writer as systematically expounding the law: his propositions are understood as *describing* the legal order, conceived as a body of general principles, definitions and doctrines. But once the positivistic assumptions of the position are recognised, it becomes necessary to distinguish (as Bentham did) between propositions *about* law and propositions *of* law. The question of the basis of the treatise writer's propositions therefore becomes pressing: no longer can they be said to derive their authority from their conformity to standards of reason or justice; rather, they can claim to possess authority only in so far as they are an accurate statement of judicial decisions or legislative provisions. But if this is so, why not jettison altogether the idea of transcendent principles, and realise instead that legal rules have their origin in court rulings and Acts of Parliament? The *source* of legal rules becomes important: the focus of legal thinking shifts from the content to the *form* of legal rules.

The role of textbooks, on this view, is reduced to the reporting, clarifying and ordering of the mass of rules which emanate from these sources. The textbook writer's propositions are no longer regarded as possessing any *intrinsic* authority. Bentham, in particular, viewed textbooks with distaste: he saw their peculiar mix of exposition and justification as apt to mislead the unwary reader into believing that the law consists of principle rather than command. Latter-day positivists have abandoned Bentham's hostility to principle, but have in the main retained this account of authority. Rational or systematic reconstruction of the legal order according to systematic conceptions (such as rights) is seen as inevitably 'partial'. At the same time, however, we continue to regard the common law as a distinctive body of principles and ideas, essentially different in character from statute law.

Much of modern legal theory is concerned with reconciling these conflicting ideas. The assumption of systematicity and coherence comes to be seen as more a matter of squaring overlapping *policies*, than of expounding an underlying moral vision. The law is regarded as pursuing various, often interrelated, projects (such as compensation, deterrence and protection of the environment); the job of the commentator is, then, to present the law in such a manner as to give expression to the policy served by the rules in such a way that the law's other projects are not undermined. Hard cases arise, on this view, where policies conflict, or where it is impossible to articulate, on the basis of a general policy, a sufficiently specific principle governing particular circumstances. In such cases, it is consistency of approach and purpose, rather than the articulation of an underlying moral vision, which is seen as supplying the grounds for decision. It is from such ideas that the distinctive concerns of modern legal philosophy flow: where legal reasoning is viewed as expounding an underpinning moral theory, problems associated with judicial discretion do not arise; but where the courts are seen as giving effect to underlying *policies*, we must begin to face difficult questions about the appropriateness of judges deciding upon the meaning, scope and relative merits of related policies.

Hart's claim that law should be understood in terms of rules is (I contend) best interpreted as offering a sustained reflection on modern society's weddedness to rules as the means by which our lives are structured. As such, it is a suggestive account of the way in which legal practices are related to wider political values, such as freedom and public moral reasoning. For the classical political theorists, rules stood in opposition to freedom: the laws of a state were perceived as fetters upon the active pursuit of moral or political ends not in accordance with the terms of legal rules. Political debates about the law thus tended to centre upon questions of authority and legitimacy which would have seemed of central importance and relevance to educated individuals living through those times. Questions about political liberty will exert a general fascination only in conditions in which individual freedom is threatened by social order in a real way. In such conditions, there can be no obvious dividing line between academic speculation and political life: the treatise writer's attempts to comprehend and to justify the conceptual structures of the legal order, and its relationship to individual liberty, will seem both relevant and profound. In circumstances of protracted social stability, by contrast, the concerns of the academic writer will seem to most individuals as possessing only a tenuous connection with the substance of everyday life.

Unlike the pamphlet writers of the late seventeenth and early eighteenth centuries, a modern legal writer can no longer realistically hope to exert any direct influence over political life or popular opinion through his writings. Where authoritarian rules are not seen as intruding upon the pedestrian concerns of each individual citizen, we no longer perceive as being important what a conception of legal practice says about the form of law in its relationship to wider social practices. Academic life is seen as increasingly isolated and separate from the fabric of social life: the gulf between 'theory' and 'practice' will seem very wide. It is therefore no coincidence that the modern legal theorist associates his activities most closely with the claims of 'legal science'.

The claims of legal science can thus be seen as *themselves* reflecting the assumptions of modern legal and political culture. For a strong faith in rules and formality will in turn give rise to the impression of the theorist as standing essentially outside the law-making process. Yet the very different conception of the theorist's activities sketched above, which I have termed 'jurisprudence', is not of merely historical interest. Rather, it seeks to reveal the origins and significance of rival accounts of law which continue to influence the way we think about the legal order. By uncovering the normative significance of legal conceptions and ideas, the theorist is able to reveal much that is important in apparently dogmatic and irrelevant debates (such as debates about the nature of rights, or debates about the nature of legal reasoning). The appearance of sterility and irrelevance, felt by many who confront these debates for the first time, arises in large part from the characterisation of legal theorists as neutral technicians seeking to reveal necessary truths or 'conceptual foundations' as a prelude to scientific description of the legal order. What is most perplexing about such descriptions is their claim to be logically prior to the myriad doctrinal disputes and questions posed by the ordinary lawyer as part of legal practice. Rather than attempting to delineate a conceptual framework in which such questions can be posed, the theorist should (I have argued) seek to reveal their wider philosophical significance.

THE RETURN OF LEGAL SCIENCE

It is, I have contended, in the spirit of the latter enterprise, rather than the former, that Hart's claim that law is a system of rules should be understood.[19] In saying that law consists in the union of primary and secondary rules, Hart was not proposing the construction of a particular conceptual framework for the analysis of legal systems. His aim was rather to offer an account of the relationship of law to social practices more generally. Suppose someone were to advance the following suggestion: a very reasonable interpretation of Hart's overall purpose is that he seeks to understand law by reference to the attitudes of its participants. Since he is not interested in the features of any *particular* legal system or legal culture, it would seem that the analysis must proceed by delineating the purely formal features of the practices wherein the participants' attitudes are manifested. This approach then retains the notion that legal theory should explore the significance of rule-following practices in law within the context of wider social and political practices, but suggests that a reliable understanding of those practices can only be arrived at by an analysis of the general conditions under which the practices are possible. These conditions, according to Hart, turn out to be a reflective attitude to a practice of recognition.

It is true that such an account strongly resonates with the claims of legal science: by attempting to isolate quite general features of legal practice, Hart might be said to be offering a conceptual framework which might then be applied to particular legal systems in much the same way that the proponent of legal science claims to offer an account of law essentially untied

[19] For an analysis of Hart's work as falling within the tradition of 'legal science', see W Twining, 'Academic Law and Legal Philosophy: The Significance of Herbert Hart' (1979) 95 *LQR* 557.

to the specific institutional arrangements and moral values adopted by particular societies. The appearance of neutrality is, however, illusory. For in supposing that it is possible to offer a complete characterisation of a practice of recognition without involvement in the moral values internal to that practice, the legal scientist relies on a conception of analysis in which the project of *describing* a normative practice is rigidly distinguished from that of *evaluating* the practice. Is a rigid distinction between these two projects possible?

We have good grounds for rejecting such a possibility. As Hart was well aware, in a practice of any complexity, the attempt to reduce the attitudes held by participants towards the practice to a definitive, finite proposition may well lie beyond our powers of expression. Take a very simple example: suppose I regularly help out at a shelter for homeless persons, motivated by strong feelings concerning the plight of the homeless. Suppose further that, over time, my help is not only appreciated by the other volunteers, but that they come to rely upon my turning up as part of the smooth running of the operation. Now, we can aptly distinguish this practice from a mere *habit*, in that it is something that I feel I ought to go on doing (or at least, I might feel that I should not suddenly cease to turn up out of mere whim). It might nevertheless be possible for me to provide some indications of circumstances in which I would regard myself as released from the obligation: if I break my leg, I may feel unable to offer my assistance until the injury heals; I may have a pressing commitment on a particular occasion which I feel outweighs my regular engagement at the shelter; my car might not start; I may feel unwell, or I may eventually revise my views on homelessness as an individual rather than a social problem (and so on). Yet it would be impossible for me to provide a quite general statement of the conditions under which I could regard myself as legitimately released from my regular practice: though I have, in Hart's term, a 'critical reflective attitude' to my practice, I may be quite unable to reduce that attitude to a particular form of words, in the guise of a canonical proposition or *rule*. Even in this extremely simple example, my views on the extent of my obligation may rely on very fine judgements in particular circumstances which defy any attempt to freeze them into final canonical form.

If, in cases such as this simple one, it is impossible for one individual to provide an exhaustive and final description of his own rule-following behaviour, so much less will it be possible to provide a complete description of a general social practice. Each participant in a social practice, Hart said, 'not only [follows the rule] in a certain way himself but "has views" about the propriety of all [following the rule] in that way.'[20] In a great many cases, of course, these 'views' will overlap; for without substantial agreement in individual judgements no coherent practice could emerge at all. But given

[20] Hart (above n 3), 51.

that individual participants are likely to disagree about the appropriate motivations for continuing with the practice in certain situations, and may differ over the wisdom of conforming to the practice at all in others, we should not pin our hopes on the availability of perspectives which are capable of furnishing 'descriptions' in the legal scientist's sense: each 'description' will rely on particular judgements about how (and if) the practice should continue in given situations, and hence upon evaluative assumptions relating to the purpose and moral value of that practice.

Suppose the proponent of legal science attempts to defend analytical neutrality in the following way. The values according to which the participants regard the practice (he might argue), though of course possessing moral significance, are nevertheless capable of being *described*. Since participants in the practice will generally disagree about the way in which the practice should continue, it is the task of the legal theorist to propose, on *analytical* grounds, the moral theory which makes best sense of the practice as a whole: for example, the participants' assumptions might be most insightfully characterised by a series of Kantian principles concerning the relationship between rights and individual autonomy; alternatively, they may represent utilitarian beliefs about the way such choices should be structured in the light of broader social values. It is (the theorist might continue) no part of the task of legal science to *criticise* these values, except on grounds of internal consistency, but simply to reveal their presence as the conditions which make discourse about the practice coherent.[21]

If such inquiries are supposed to form the core of the legal theorist's activities, then it appears that somewhere along the line a point has got lost. For such inquiries have little to do with the central questions which preoccupied the classical political theorists and legal writers of the past: the notion that theoretical inquiry is confined to attempts to rationalise complex social practices according to fixed values (values which are then said to comprise the 'foundations' of those practices) would strike those writers as a crude and curiously perverse way in which to gain insight into the nature of the practices studied. 'Neutrality', here, is bought at the expense of a deep cultural understanding of the practices under investigation: in attempting to provide a unifying explanation based on fixed values, the legal scientist would be forced to embrace abstraction and generality;[22]

[21] See eg, DN MacCormick, '*The Concept of Law* and The Concept of Law' reprinted in R George (ed), *The Autonomy of Law* (Oxford, Oxford University Press, 1996), 163–93 at 177: understanding of law at the level of particular institutions is, he says, 'as much a matter of making the phenomena intelligible by matching them to a model, as it is anything like the neutral observation of an always-already present feature of the "real world" of the law . . . it is intrinsic in the work of legal doctrine and legal theory to engage in such rational reconstruction and model-building.'

[22] See NE Simmonds, *The Decline of Juridical Reason* (Manchester, Manchester University Press, 1984), ch 1. I deliberately exclude from the scope of these remarks those theories which seek to advance particular moral theories (such as liberalism) on grounds of their *moral* superiority, or desirability.

rather than seeking to understand the significance of opposing explanations, he must treat rival conceptions as 'misguided'.

It is, in any event, unclear whether such accounts can truly claim to be neutral in the appropriate sense (we might refer to this sense as 'methodological neutrality'). Methodological neutrality presupposes the possibility of adjudication between various rival moral theories on grounds of their analytical power in explaining the form of our social practices. Evaluative considerations cannot, of course, be entirely excluded from such assessments, since the theorist's motivations for rejecting a candidate explanation might relate to the drawing out of absurd consequences which most could agree on as being undesirable or implausible. But (many theorists feel) such considerations are both minimal and relatively uncontroversial. This explanation should not satisfy us: for it treats the analysis of judgements as an investigation of brute facts capable of being described and catalogued in the way of scientific phenomena. As we have already noted, however, this is at best a highly misleading picture of the nature of such judgements. Individual moral judgements are rarely detachable from the wider moral context within which the individual describes his views about a practice. This does not mean merely that an individual's judgements tend to be specific determinations of more general outlooks (for so much is obvious); it implies that the articulation of reasons for action in specific contexts are part of an individual's self-understanding of the broader significance of the practice. Because the individual's reasons for action are not determined in any *logical* way by his broader moral outlook, the attempt to ground specific judgements in wider principles will seldom be genuinely independent of the terms in which those principles are described.

In the majority of individual moral judgements, no very clear line can be drawn between the *formulation* and the *application* of general moral principles. Description and evaluation in such cases come to much the same thing: there comes a point at which an individual's self-description of his practice shades into normative ideas of what is the *right* way of continuing. In the case of wider social practices, too, theoretical understandings of the grounds of a practice are not rigidly distinguishable from moral explanations of how the practice *ought* to be conceived, or understood.[23] Such understandings can still be offered as *descriptions* of social practices (except on highly restrictive understandings of 'description'), as long as we are prepared to abandon the pseudo-scientific concern with 'neutrality'. Hart's somewhat puzzling use of the term 'descriptive sociology' to characterise his theory can be understood along these lines. The theory offers a descriptive account of legal practices in a way that chimes with positivist understandings of analysis: the examination of legal concepts such as rights, and rules, takes place within an analysis of their contribution to social life and social

[23] For a qualified denial of this, see L Moore, 'Description and Analysis in *The Concept of Law*' (2002) 8 *Legal Theory* 91.

practices; yet the perspectives thus offered on various legal conceptions (unique as they may be to the philosopher rather than the practitioner) are hardly independent of the theories about politics, justice and morality generated by the doctrinal disputes in which they figure. The theory of law does not offer analytical clarifications of legal concepts *prior* to engagement in such controversies; it rather examines the way that political and moral values are reflected and played out in the context of their use.

CONCLUDING REMARKS

The theory of law is, or ought to be, a contribution to legal practice rather than an attempt to expose its 'necessary form'. The understandings sought by the proponents of 'jurisprudence' and 'legal science' are in many respects the same: both seek to reveal the tacit commitments of legal practice as expressions of broader moral and political theories. Yet it is through an appreciation of the substance of legal practice, and not the attempt to uncover its supposed formal underpinnings, that the richest understandings are to be found. By endeavouring to supply scientific knowledge of the *form* of legal practice, the theorist provides only the most abstract view of our social life: in seeking to transcend the limits of particular cultural and institutional arrangements, the theorist offers a form of knowledge of the law too remote to be of interest to the ordinary lawyer or commentator. Only by seeking to locate legal principles and conceptions within wider currents of moral and political thought, can a deeper insight into our legal practices be found.

2

The Truth of Legal Analysis

JONATHAN GORMAN

WHAT IS LAW? How can we tell whether an answer to that question is the correct one? Indeed, what does the question mean? Is it a different question from the question of what law ought to be, so that morally-independent legal analysis is possible, as John Austin insisted? Or must we understand law to have some essential relationship to — for example — justice, so that legal analysis is really moral analysis, and the truth of legal analysis amounts to the truth of moral analysis? But then, what is justice? How can we tell whether an answer to that question is the correct one, either? What does 'correctness' amount to? The problems which relate to the nature of the truth of answers to such questions about law arise before we need concern ourselves with the interpretation of the questions themselves. The problem of the correctness of legal analysis does not require a prior solution to the familiar issues regarding legal positivism. Our problem here concerns truth and understanding in these contexts. Truth is not a mere academic concern. The truth of a proposition gives it *authority*, and the search for authority is a perennial concern of both philosophers of law and of lawyers.[1]

We shall begin with the question 'what is justice?' We shall leave open the issue of how far this may or may not contrast with the question 'what is law?' If we wish to know — rather than merely to have an opinion about (even a currently widely shared and legally authorised opinion about) — what justice is, we require not only an understanding of and an answer to the question 'what is justice?' but, more importantly for us here, the *justification* for its being the correct answer. For this, it is more plausible to turn to Plato's *Republic* than to ask a lawyer. That this is more plausible shows that, despite recognising that law and justice ought to have some important connections with each other, a distinction in principle between law and morality is widely accepted. That the order of presentation of the argument of this paper uses this fact does not, however, necessitate a commitment

[1] The arguments presented here are, in part, a unification of a number which appear *passim* in my *Rights and Reason* (Chesham, Acumen Press/Montreal, McGill-Queen's University Press, 2003).

here to legal positivism. That a lawyer might, in the end, be the right kind of person to ask can be left open here. Again, that the order of presentation of the argument of this paper begins with Plato rather than some other moral philosopher does not necessitate a commitment to Plato's position.

In *The Republic* we find an answer to the question 'what is justice?',[2] the reasoning why we should believe the answer, and an explanation of what its truth amounts to. The dialogue or conversational form of *The Republic* is crucial to the position which Plato is presenting. The protagonist, Socrates, does not answer our question 'what is justice?' directly. He asks this question of the other people with whom he is conversing, but he does not deny their answers. Rather, he assumes that they are right, and then draws conclusions from their answers, conclusions which are presented as being correctly and logically drawn according to mutually shared standards of reasoning. At many points in the conversation Socrates invites his antagonists to recognise that the conclusions logically drawn from their answers are unacceptable, and they typically agree. Given that they share the reasoning and share dislike of the conclusion, the upshot is their recognition that they have not expressed themselves sufficiently accurately in the first place. A shared intellectual search results, governed by the shared and exact standards of logical reasoning, into what it is that, 'deep down', they recognise justice really to be. It is the logical reasoning involved in Socrates' and the others' contributions to the dialogue which constrains the outcome and is essential to yielding a knowledge of what justice really is.

The plausibility of Plato's position derives from the plausibility of the view that you cannot be just unless you *know* what it is to be just, and Plato's rationalist theory of knowledge is essential to this. Reasoning provides *knowledge* of the ethical: the idea of justice which is in question is not merely something in our several heads, but something which we all — not just the parties to the Socratic conversation — *share*, something *presupposed* in the ongoing dialogue as there to be discovered, something *about which* we have knowledge and so something *independent* of each of us rather than dependent on personal desire or choice, and so something both *unchangeable* and *universal* and therefore *authoritative* for each of us. Moral truth is grasped by the exercise of reason, and can be grasped in no other way. Reason provides the ultimate justification. The truth of our moral understanding, for Plato, consists in correspondence to a rationally apprehended abstract reality, his world of 'Forms'. This reality is itself rational, so that the authoritative truth about justice is warranted by reason.

This approach contrasts in many fundamental ways with that of Thomas Hobbes in his *Leviathan*, where, in chapter 13, he said: 'The desires, and

[2] It would take too much space here to summarise what Plato's answer actually is; in any event, it would be irrelevant to do so.

other passions of man, are in themselves no sin. No more are the actions, that proceed from those passions, till they know a law that forbids them: which till laws be made they cannot know: nor can any law be made, till they have agreed upon the person that shall make it'.[3] Law should then be understood as made by the 'person agreed upon', that is, the sovereign. Here the answer to the question 'what is justice?' is effectively the same as the answer to the question 'what is law?'. The sovereign, in making law, thereby determines all 'sin', or right and wrong. All justice, all morality is then grounded in law. Law cannot then be judged by morality, as if there were standards for this which were independent of the sovereign. In Hobbes's system it is the rational self-interest of the people which ultimately rationally justifies the state and its law, and so also the standards of justice.

Among many differences between this approach and Plato's, note in particular that reason for Hobbes seems at first sight comparatively weak and indeterminate, since 'rational self-interest' means that reason is merely instrumental in achieving what we desire. Moreover, Hobbes stresses that different people have different views about what does or does not conform to the requirements of reason.[4] Yet, despite these familiar points, Hobbes shares with Plato a perception of geometry as the paradigm case of the independent eternal authority of reason, as 'the only science that it hath pleased God hitherto to bestow on mankind'.[5] Essential to Hobbes's theory of the state is, as it is for Plato, this understanding of reason as setting all of humanity a *common standard*, as something we all share and therefore as something *independent* of our choice. At the foundation of Hobbes's philosophical approach we find the idea of reason as setting a mutually shared standard, an external and unchanging standard expressing demands for consistency independent of we many error-prone individuals.

What is authoritative, both in Hobbes's state of nature and out of it, is reason, which operates as an *external* impediment against the freedom to think (and so, in so far as we are rational, act) as we wish. Consider individual judgement about what reason requires. Hobbes understands this to be prone to error, but the possibility of error arises only because there is some external standard against which it might be measured or criticised. If reason were purely an 'internal' as opposed to an 'external' standard, with no attempt to refer to something external to individual choice, then exercising our individual judgement about what reason, so understood, 'requires' would be very like trying to operate with a private language, as Wittgenstein understood that.[6] Such a standard would not constrain us at

[3] T Hobbes, *Leviathan*, ed J Plamenatz (London, Collins, 1962), 144.
[4] 'Diverse men differ not only in their judgement on the sense of what is pleasant and unpleasant to the taste, smell, hearing, touch and sight, but also of what is conformable or disagreeable to reason in the actions of common life', *ibid*, 167.
[5] Plato, *The Republic*, para 527b–c; Hobbes (above n 3), 77.
[6] L Wittgenstein, *Philosophical Investigations* (Oxford, Basil Blackwell, 1968).

all. Hobbes's argument, by contrast with this, effectively understands reason as some external standard about what reason 'really' requires. He certainly presumes this external standard to exist in the state of nature, for it is this which enables us rationally to contract our way out of the state of nature. On the other hand, he certainly presumes some internal standard also to exist, for this is what drives his argument characterising the state of nature to the conclusion that our lives in it would be nasty, brutish and short.[7] There are, then, two standards of reasoning in Hobbes, with the final justificatory work being done by the external standard. Essential to at least our moral understanding for Plato,[8] and to both our moral and our legal understanding for Hobbes, is the understanding of reason as setting an unchanging and external shared standard. This standard is thus independent of human choice and so seems to reflect some abstract reality beyond us and beyond the experiences which our mere senses deliver to us.

John Locke adopts the same kind of view in his second *Treatise on Government*, with God-given reason telling us that we must respect each other's rights to life, health, liberty and property.[9] Reason sets an external standard for Plato, Hobbes and Locke, and the truth warranted or constrained by it involves some curiously abstract reality external to human beings. This 'reality' Plato understood as a heavenly world of 'Forms' which he sought to interpret, although Hobbes and Locke made little comparable attempt to make sense of their God-given reason. Whatever the mysterious metaphysical detail, the morality and law which are grounded in such reason are supposed to share the authority of reason's independence from human choice. That independence is heavenly or God-like for Plato, Hobbes and Locke. The authority of God — if reason can get us that far — certainly seems a plausible enough justification for morality and law. Yet is not all this merely a rationalist error? Are we not using God to justify reason, and yet reason to justify God? Can reason yield authoritative knowledge about morality and law? Did Locke, when writing his treatises on government, forget his own empiricism expressed in his *Essay Concerning Human Understanding*, which was published in the same year (1690)?

If we follow the much more clear-minded David Hume, we may as empiricists believe that reason cannot yield truth of any kind, but can only help us to operate with the truths which experience gives us: in other words, reason can warrant the *validity* of our arguments, but the *truth* of our conclusions depends entirely on the truth of our premisses, and for empiricists

[7] Hobbes (above n 3), 143.

[8] If we conceptually contrast law with morality, Plato's *Republic* speaks of morality but not of law. We find the legal theory and detail elsewhere, in *The Statesman* and *The Laws* respectively. However, it is very doubtful if Plato should be seen as a proto-legal positivist. For Plato, and like Hobbes, law and morality share the status of being public standards of right and wrong.

[9] J Locke, *Two Treatises on Government* (London, Dent, 1924), 119.

it is experience alone which determines what we know such truths to be. Yet generations of empiricists have not been able to show how to guarantee the truth of what we believe on a sentence-by-sentence basis. Quine's approach illustrates the pragmatic and holistic form which much empiricism has taken in the last half-century. On this view our system of beliefs is justified as a whole, and not independently. Individual sentences which express what we claim to know are not individually warranted: 'Any statement can be held true come what may, if we make drastic enough adjustments elsewhere in the system'.[10]

For example, 'experience' may suggest that an explorer is observing a black swan, and must then revise a prior belief that all swans are white; and yet the prior belief may be preserved by sorting 'experienced' reality in a different way: since all swans are white, this black thing cannot be a swan, but must be some other kind of bird. The description 'black swan' is not warranted by experience but rather by pragmatic decision in the light of prior theory. What is 'known' here — black swan or not? — is then a matter of *decision*: there is a choice about how to make our observation descriptions consistent with our overall theory. So there is human choice after all, but we nevertheless cannot believe what we like. The available alternatives are *constrained*: it is consistency — that is, *reason* — which is the ultimate authority for what we may justifiably claim to know, even for the empiricist. Empiricism does not provide a way out of the difficulties suggested by the supposed metaphysical independence of reason, and we need that independence to give authority to the moral and legal values constructed upon reason.

It is indeed odd to think, for example, of human rights as being — like the standards of reason — Platonic-style metaphysical entities which exist independently of us as rules in the natural order of things rather than as part of a rule-governed social practice. Surely we do not have to think of human rights and rational standards as really existing things, and adding 'abstract' to our description of them makes the matter less perspicuous rather than more. Yet how else should we understand the independent authority of moral and legal values, and what else could it mean for statements about those values to be true? Should we hold human rights and reason to be just a matter of unconstrained social choice? But then how could statements about human rights be true? Could 'truth' be available in a holistic system where the choice of what to believe might be entirely unconstrained? Alluding to Wittgenstein's point mentioned earlier, a language which is 'private' to a community is no better founded than a language which is 'private' to an individual, if in neither case is there any constraint on what is said in it. Authority is entirely lacking.

[10] WVO Quine, 'Two dogmas of empiricism', in *From A Logical Point of View*, 2nd edn (New York, Harper & Row, 1961), 20–46 at 43.

The way in which concepts of justice and reason may be understood as independently authoritative can be helpfully expressed in terms of the question whether such understanding is 'subjective' or 'objective'. Understanding may be held to be *subjective* in so far as its function is held to consist in the removal of ignorance, doubt or puzzlement on the part of those who have it.[11] Understanding may be held to be *objective* in so far as its function is held to be the achievement of a correct or truthful view of the way things really are or the way they actually work. It may be noted, assuming for the moment that these explanations of 'subjective' and 'objective' are correct, that the kind of understanding which successfully removes puzzlement may or may not give a true account of the way things really are, while our best explanations of the way the world works may be impossible for most people to understand — indeed, we may imagine that the truth about things is such that no human being can grasp it.

The contrast between 'subjective' and 'objective', as explained so far, typically expresses a *realist* position: the view that there is a reality or truth independent of what we believe it to be. On such an approach, that we actually use the concept of — for example — 'human rights' in a certain way (a way involving reference to 'meanings' or to a particular range of criteria for determining what human rights we 'really' have), is no guarantee that we are doing so *correctly*, that is, objectively rather than subjectively. On such a realist approach, it is not our actual social practices which ground the correctness of our understanding of rights but rather an external and mysterious metaphysical something which has no necessary connection with those social practices. And yet if we too readily reject such Platonic mystery, and insist with Wittgenstein on limiting our understanding to our actual use of words, then we risk a subjective relativism which may be quite inappropriate to a proper understanding and which would not reflect the everyday sense that human rights and other moral and legal values have some kind of independence or objectivity which gives them the authority which we commonly believe they have. Subjective explanations are there to fob off the curiosity of children, but 'proper' explanations must be objective and mirror the independent external world.

It is an important issue whether there are such things as human rights or natural justice. Some theorists affirm such things, however mysterious their status. Some theorists deny that there are, and believe that such values are a subjective creation on the part of human beings. But both the assertion and the denial of the existence of human rights are ambiguous. To assert that human rights 'exist' is an assertion that can be interpreted both realistically

[11] I have expressed this elsewhere, in particular in 'Kellner on language and historical representation', (1991) 30 *History and Theory* 356–68, and 'From history to justice' in A Jokic (ed), *Essays in Honor of Burleigh Wilkins: From History to Justice* (New York, Peter Lang, 2001), 19–69.

and anti-realistically. To take an example from contemporary physics, do extra dimensions exist? Stephen Hawking expresses in a popular way an anti-realist approach for physics, referring to what he calls a 'positivist' approach. 'Which is reality, brane or bubble? They are both mathematical models that describe the observations. One is free to use whichever model is most convenient.'[12] We may suppose such things to exist, but such a supposition is no more than a claim that our best theory purports to refer to them, and *we* choose which is 'best'. The philosophical question is whether any sense is to be made of their 'really' being there *independently* of what the theory says: summarily, the philosophical realist says yes, the anti-realist, no.

We may wish to deny that human rights or other moral values exist, if existence is given some Platonic realist interpretation. But it may be that human rights exist in an anti-realist interpretation of existence. Similarly, if we deny that human rights exist, we may be denying a realistic interpretation of the existence of human rights and affirming an anti-realistic interpretation, or we may be denying their existence under any interpretation. In the light of this choice of denials, we may recall HLA Hart's remark:

> Perhaps few would now deny, as some have, that there are moral rights; for the point of that denial was usually to object to some philosophical claim as to the 'ontological status' of rights, and this objection is now expressed not as a denial that there are any moral rights but as a denial of some assumed logical similarity between sentences used to assert the existence of rights and other kinds of sentences.[13]

The 'other kinds of sentences' here are those declarative sentences which, for Hart, might be more plausibly interpreted in a realistic way than are sentences referring to rights. Hart might be thinking of physics here, for example. Yet once we adopt an anti-realist interpretation of physics, we can no longer see a clear contrast between the ontological status of rights and that of the referents of physical theories: perhaps they all 'exist' in *our* world.

Rather than an external and mysterious metaphysical something, an anti-realist understanding of rights and other values may then be grounded in our actual social practices. The contrast between 'subjective' and 'objective' therefore need not be taken to presuppose Platonic metaphysical realism in this context.[14] It is a central philosophical problem whether there is such a thing as the way things actually are independently of human understanding,

[12] S Hawking, *The Universe in a Nutshell* (London, Bantam, 2001), 54 and 198.
[13] HLA Hart, 'Are there any natural rights?' in A Quinton (ed), *Political Philosophy* (Oxford, Oxford University Press, 1967), 53–66 at 54.
[14] Some areas of discourse may be more appropriate to being interpreted realistically, and others anti-realistically.

and it is a familiar anti-realist response that the ultimate test of the merit of explanation or understanding may only be in terms of the removal of subjective doubt or puzzlement. The contrast between 'subjective' and 'objective' has to be explained differently if an anti-realist approach is adopted: typically, 'subjectivity' may be taken to suggest that the relativistic and incommensurable positions of many different communities, or even the psychology of many particular individuals, can be the only standard for judging our rights or duties. In such a case, a range of alternatives exist and we have no way of deciding justifiably between them. There is, we might say, no 'truth' of the matter.

By contrast, 'objectivity' may be held to depend on some kind of worldwide inter-community commonality of standard or acceptance which is neutral with respect to different communities or individuals, and which makes sense of the possibility of translation between different communities of belief and also makes sense of the possibility of external judgement of the approaches of particular communities or individuals. Given this, it is apparent that the word 'independence', as used on many occasions so far, is ambiguous between realist and anti-realist uses. Distinguish 'independence' as referring to an external abstract reality like Plato's 'Forms' from 'independence' as meaning unrevisable by human beings, that is, not open to human choice. We do not need to suppose that standards of reason and morality 'exist' independently of us. We only need the idea that these 'objective' standards, as anti-realistically understood, are such as to constrain our choices about what to hold true.

Such imagined 'objectivity' should ideally constrain our choices to the point of psychological certainty. It does in fact do so, in many practical cases. Thus to revise my present belief that I am now sitting at a desk would require, to be consistent, that I revise so many other beliefs (many shared with you) as to make an alternative belief unacceptable. There are, in fact, no consistently available rivals for my belief that I am now sitting at a desk. What consistency requires here is, from my point of view, unrevisable by me. From my point of view, the standards of reason are thereby external and authoritative just because they are not for me a matter of choice. Yet, as a matter of fact, for many beliefs, including many moral and legal beliefs, there are contingent differences between what different groups of people can consistently choose to accept. Are all moral beliefs uncertain in this way? Must we suppose some metaphysical externality which selects between consistent positions, in order to avoid such relativism?

One way to avoid this is to follow Kant. If we do so, we need no longer understand reason, human rights or other moral ideals as existing in some way independently of human beings, but can nevertheless keep an understanding of them as universal and prior to human choice. Following Kant, we should see human nature, the natural world and the world of morality as all structured in terms of reason. Kant explains that reason is authoritative for us and can motivate us because it structures us as human beings and is also an essential part of our own structuring of the experienced world. Yet reason, and the morality which it underpins, while losing its metaphysical independence, does not lose its eternal character. There is for Kant a fundamental and eternal consistency both of human nature and of experienced reality.

It is that consistency of reality which makes possible modern science. The world, as Hume noted, is a regular place. The success of science both supports and is warranted by Kant's rational foundation of human understanding. The character of human understanding is an essential feature of what it is to be human, and reason is thus able to express our human nature and thereby what is valuable about us as human beings. We may then understand human rights and similar values as expressing and protecting our eternal dignity and autonomy as rational human beings. Our fundamental moral and legal values, on this approach, are not metaphysically *independent* of us but they are *universal* and, if Kant is right, are not subject to human choice. This universality is not a mere contingency of widespread acceptance but reflects the necessity of that which lies at the essence of what it is to be a human being in the world. Alternatives to these objective moral standards are not consistently available. There is a determinate reality here, and it is human nature itself.

Kant's arguments concerning the rational structures of the human mind were particularly based on his analysis of the structures of human language.[15] The way we use language expresses our understanding of the world and of our moral status and duties within it, and so expresses the rational structures of our minds. Current analysis of language continues the Kantian approach beyond the determination of his general structures to involve a fine-grained analysis of particular concepts. Questions about the status of the analysis of legal concepts arise against the philosophical background which has now been outlined, and we shall next examine the status of Hohfeld's conceptual analysis of rights. Hohfeld famously — famously for legal theorists, at least — disambiguates the notions of right and duty into claim-right, privilege, power, immunity, no-claim-right, duty, disability and liability.

Jural Opposites	right [claim-right]	privilege	power	immunity
	no-right [no-claim-right]	duty	disability	liability
Jural Correlatives	right [claim-right]	privilege	power	immunity
	duty	no-right [no-claim-right]	liability	disability

[15] The deduction of the categories: see I Kant, *The Critique of Pure Reason* (London, Macmillan, 1968), 120ff.

In what way is Hohfeld's scheme of 'exact' concepts an 'analysis' of fundamental jural relations? We can use his system to solve legal questions, as Hohfeld's editor and Yale colleague WW Cook observed. For example, where a person has property rights of a certain kind, we can *deduce* that someone else has the appropriate correlative duties. More generally, with complex situations, we can deduce a series of relationships involving claim-rights, privileges, powers and immunities, and their opposites and correlatives. Hohfeld quotes the work *Public Service Companies* by a Professor Wyman, as follows:

> The duty placed upon every one exercising a public calling is primarily *a duty* to serve every man who is a member of the public . . . It is somewhat difficult to place this exceptional duty in our legal system . . . The truth of the matter is that the obligation resting upon one who has undertaken the performance of public duty is *sui generis* . . .

and Hohfeld comments on this, 'It is submitted that the learned writer's difficulties arise primarily from a failure to see that the innkeeper, the common carrier and others similarly "holding out" are under present *liabilities* rather than present *duties*'.[16]

As Cook says, these kinds of solutions to legal questions are 'correct' solutions:[17] the *truth* of the matter lies not with Wyman but with Hohfeld. But what makes them correct? Given the truth of presupposed assertions about a person's legal rights, further legal and indeed social truths can then be deduced. These conclusions, it bears stressing, are understood as *true*, as *correct* answers. In terms of Hohfeld's analysis, their truth requires the soundness of the legal reasoning involved, presupposing his clarification of the meanings of the terms used in that reasoning. This is imagined to be a 'scientific' approach, describing a relevant part of reality just as does a scientific theory. Hohfeld's work reflected the philosophical attitude which was to become apparent later in logical positivism: the idea that by scientific standards of meaning the truth is revealed. The book's 'introduction' by Cook says of it that 'its chief value lies in the fact that by its aid the correct solution of legal problems becomes not only easier but more certain. In this respect it does not differ from any other branch of pure science'.[18] But truth requires more than localised consistency of reasoning, and what does the 'truth' of the sentences involved in Hohfeld's reasoning amount to?

Their truth does not and plausibly cannot consist in some sentence-by-sentence correspondence to some metaphysically independent legal or moral 'reality' which stands outside jural systems or actual moral practices.

[16] WN Hohfeld, *Fundamental Legal Conceptions as Applied in Judicial Reasoning* (New Haven, Yale University Press, 1919), 57.
[17] WW Cook, 'Introduction', in Hohfeld (above n 16), 3.
[18] *Ibid.*

We have seen, following Kant, that moral values need not have an independent metaphysical existence, but may be structured in virtue of an essential link to rational human nature and our moral institutions. Now it may be that sentences about, for example, *human* rights are made true by derivation from universal features of human nature, as Kant claims, but it is plain that Hohfeld's analysis of rights is specific to a particular language and a particular jurisdiction and particular time. Nothing in what he says suggests that general features of human nature are involved here, and the attempt to generalise what he says to other times, cultures or jurisdictions would be plainly incorrect. This point, at least, might be thought to enable us to distinguish the question 'what is law?' from the question 'what is justice?'

It is then neither an independent metaphysical existence nor a temporally and culturally universal language or practice which might make Hohfeld's assertions about rights true. Yet neither is it plain that they are true merely in so far as we, in our local situation, *believe* them to be true, for surely not anything we believe will be true. What would then make Professor Wyman wrong and Hohfeld right? We might wish to follow LW Sumner here, and hold that laws and rights exist in so far as they are valid within a legal system, and 'the existence of the system as a whole is a matter of its being sustained by conventional social practices of compliance with and acceptance of its rules on the part of those to whom the rules apply'.[19] In so far as we understand a legal system in terms of Hohfeldian-type concepts with their deductive links, then our legal rights form a system which identifies the jurisdiction in question. Hohfeld's analysis, if true, is then true of that social system.

Well, is it true of that system? Hohfeld says of his analysis: 'Eight conceptions of the law have been analyzed and compared in some details, the purpose having been to exhibit not only their intrinsic meaning and scope, but also their relations to one another and the methods by which they are applied, in judicial reasoning, to the solution of concrete problems of litigation.'[20] Thus his understanding of the meanings of the terms analysed is that they have an 'intrinsic' meaning, and are also those which are actually used in real judicial situations which deal with real legal problems. There is a wealth of references to actual legal usage offered by Hohfeld in support of his analysis, and yet there are also a 'considerable number of judicial opinions' which 'afford ample evidence of the inveterate and unfortunate tendency to confuse . . .'.[21] Hohfeld, while certainly finding much in the law reports in the way of judicial support for his analysis, is *selecting* those which support his position: he is *judging* the judges, as in the following quotation:

[19] LW Sumner, *The Moral Foundation of Rights* (Oxford, Clarendon Press, 1987), 113.
[20] Hohfeld (above n 16), 63.
[21] *Ibid*, 27.

> . . . Lord Westbury, in *Bell v. Kennedy* (1868), L.R. 1 H.L. (Sc.) 307: 'Domicile, therefore, is an idea of the law. It is the *relation* which the *law creates* between an individual and a particular locality or country.' [Compare the confusion in the discussion of the same subject by Farwell, J., in *In re Johnson* [1903] 1 Ch., 821, 824–825.] Contrast the far more accurate language of Chief Justice Shaw, in *Abington v. Bridgewater* . . .[22]

Hohfeld's analysis is not a simple description of legal usage, then. Indeed, he offers a way of speaking which is clearly not familiar to all legal colleagues of his time: 'Those Yale men say rights-powers-privileges-and-immunities as a single word, the way the rest of us say son-of-a-bitch'.[23] But, if the analysis is a false *description* of the ways in which legal people think and judge, then what makes it correct? We have here a semi-formal linguistic system with a range of concepts used in sentences which have certain logical relationships with each other. What is the status of this linguistic entity? Does it describe how language is used? Partly it purports to do so, and is selectively supported on that basis; on the other hand, it also sets a *standard* for how language ought to be used in a legal context. It was precisely a range of difficulties of this kind which affected the approach of the 'logical positivists' — not to be confused with legal positivists — who saw science as the only way of achieving knowledge. We need next to examine these difficulties. Cook's description of Hohfeld's analysis as not differing from any other branch of pure science reminds us of how close Hohfeld was to the developing analytical philosophy of his time.

Logical positivism was an extension of Hume's empiricism: everything we know must be derived from our experiences. Our best scientific theories are justifiable only by reference to our sensations, and are acceptable only in so far as they continue to apply successfully to the world. Logical positivists held in addition that science alone provides proper knowledge, and many believed that science was the only proper way of saying anything at all. They therefore attempted to show that only scientific sentences are meaningful, because only scientific sentences are verifiable. The point of this was to find a criterion which would distinguish proper science from metaphysical, moral and other speculation by showing everything but scientific sentences to be meaningless as true descriptions of the world.

The philosophy of science created within the logical positivist tradition yielded in due course what is still known to many as the 'standard' account. The conclusions are briefly these: a scientific theory consists of a series of sentences which have the logical form of a universal conditional, that is, 'whenever A then B'. Definitions are excluded, and these conditionals are derived from experienced evidence. Given them, we can predict a future B

[22] *Ibid*, 35, n 24.
[23] AL Corbin, 'Foreword' in Hohfeld (above n 16), x.

given a present A, or we can explain a past B by reference to an earlier A, and so forth.

This briefly illustrates the kind of thing a model of science can be. Given such a model of science, and adding to it the further positivist assumption that science is the only way of achieving knowledge, we may then wish, if so philosophically inclined, to conclude two things: first, that the model of science represents or correctly *describes* in summary form actual scientific thought and/or practice; second, that the model of science sets a *standard* for correct thought and/or practice, such that the appropriate reality will be truly described if that model is followed. Hohfeld was not the first to model his approach to law on science, and indeed there is more to being 'scientific' in the legal context than being logically exact in Hohfeld's way, for such exactness permits accurate *prediction* in both law and science.

That judicial decisions should be predictable is an important practical concern, and we may recall Oliver Wendell Holmes's remark that 'the prophecies of what the courts will do in fact, and nothing more pretentious, are what I mean by the law'.[24] Clarity is one of the conditions for predictability, and clarity is widely recognised as a value which the courts and the legal profession should foster. Yet peace-making is valuable too, and the fudges of diplomatically achieved agreements — which have their place in legal practice — are not necessarily well-served by insisting on clarity and predictability.

The application of the standard analysis of science to other disciplines is intended as straightforward. It follows from the positivist assumption that anything that purports to provide knowledge yet which does not match the standard analysis simply fails to provide knowledge at all. Moreover, if we believe the position of the earlier logical positivists, as mentioned earlier, that their analysis is a criterion of meaning as well as a criterion of science, then anything which fails to meet the standard is meaningless as well as empty of knowledge. The result is brutal: swathes of disciplines collapse on the basis of this criterion, even science itself. Subsequent work took two approaches, which presupposed one or other of two views about the status of the model of science, one seeing it as *prescriptive* and the other as *descriptive*. These two approaches were founded on different conceptions of the nature of philosophical analysis, approaches which we see run together in Hohfeld's own presentation. The philosophical issues concerning the status of Hohfeld's analysis are a very close analogue of these issues in the philosophy of science.

The word 'analytical', in the context of contemporary analytical philosophy, is ambiguous in a number of ways. It can mean merely that the

[24] See OW Holmes, 'The Path of the Law' in *The Collected Works of Justice Holmes*, Vol 3, a reference I owe to Roger Cotterrell, *The Politics of Jurisprudence* (London, Butterworths, 1989), 191.

philosophy in question is 'analytical' just in so far as it insists on clarity of meaning, with no more being implied. It typically means more: that the 'analytical' philosophy in question insists on clarity of meaning and also embodies a certain theory of 'clarity' of meaning. There are two approaches here: first, that the embodied theory of 'clarity' of meaning is one that holds that expressions in a natural language are essentially vague and must be translated into the more exact terms of a formal or symbolic — preferably classical — logical system; second, that the embodied theory of 'clarity' of meaning is one that takes natural language, with all its subtleties and distinctions, as inherently exact, so that concentration on ordinary usage will resolve philosophical difficulties and even, following the later Wittgenstein, dissolve them. The logical positivists hold the first of these, and express or model in these terms what is for them our necessarily scientific rationality.

Applying this first approach to legal theory, we should 'rationally reconstruct' what lawyers and judges do. We should note the purpose(s) of law, and show how these rationally ought to be attempted in the light of the scientific model which sets the standard. This approach takes the model of science as prescriptive for lawyers and judges, and the analytical philosopher of law, on this approach, is concerned with what legal reasoning ought to look like. The approach is conceptually stipulative, and Hohfeld's analysis is often taken as stipulative in this sense.

On the second analytical approach to philosophy of science or of law, which derives its conception of analysis — although very rarely with any explicitness — from the later work of Wittgenstein, it is assumed that ordinary language has the fullest possible range of exact literal and rhetorical resources, and that concentration on ordinary usage will resolve philosophical difficulties. Analytical philosophy of law is then conceived as exact ordinary language analysis of what is meant by certain distinctively legal modes of expression, method, evidence, and so forth. On this view we need to grasp what legal reasoning is rather than what it ought to be. We need to grasp 'what actually counts' as legal reasoning, and it is lawyers and judges themselves who may well be held to be the proper and best assessors of this. On this approach analytical philosophy of law is supposed to provide a theoretical or summary description of what lawyers and judges do, and can be falsified by the linguistic 'facts', facts which embody, for example, what is 'correctly' — typically by judicial standards — called a 'right' or a 'duty'. Recall that some courts are more authoritative than others, and that if meanings and correct reasoning are to be stipulated into correctness then the House of Lords or the US Supreme Court exemplify the kind of people to do it, not Hohfeld or the logical positivists. Hohfeld's own deference to legal authority here is as apparent in his work as is its *a priori* stipulative nature, and this demonstrates his confusion between the two analytical approaches.

The difference between the two analytical approaches to philosophy of law can be summarised in terms of two differing standards of 'correctness' here. There is no doubt that the standards set by science as understood within logical positivism would contradict some lawyers' views about what counts as good legal reasoning. On the first analytical approach, so much the worse for legal reasoning, since the standard of correctness is set by the scientific model. On the second analytical approach, so much the worse for the scientific model, since the standard of correctness is set by the best understanding of lawyers. Jurisprudents and philosophers of law have not always been clear about which side of this debate about the nature of philosophical analysis they were actually on.

While a rump of old logical positivism remains, the understanding of philosophy of science was revolutionised by the publication in 1962 of Kuhn's *The Structure of Scientific Revolutions*.[25] Kuhn, primarily an historian rather than a philosopher of science of the standard kind, noted that historical research revealed that science in the past had not operated in ways which accorded with the requirements of the standard model. Kuhn suggested that scientists normally operated against the vague background of an accepted general understanding of the world or 'paradigm' which they sought to articulate with explicit clarity. The history of science disclosed many scientific paradigms. Paradigms did not persist but went through a period of rise and fall and replacement. When a paradigm collapsed it did so not for the reasons suggested by logical positivists, but for a variety of pragmatic — such as social or psychological — reasons. The history of science disclosed a pattern of revolutionary changes between periods of normal science.

We have noted two analytical approaches, one where the standard of correctness is set by a philosopher's stipulative model, and a second where the standard of correctness is set, for law, by lawyers' and judges' own best understanding, or, for science, by what scientists actually do. The first such approach gained its persuasive power in respect of scientific positivism because the philosophers were stipulating using a model of science which was believed to be correct. They were initially taken to be speaking for science itself in trying to impose on others, such as legal theorists, their model of science as the sole standard for knowledge. The positions of those others were rhetorically weak, given the generally undoubted successes of natural science.

But for those who accepted Kuhn's position — and even for those who did not — this approach could no longer be accepted. The positivist philosophers of science were seen as speaking for themselves, not for science, since science — conceived as the real judgements of real scientists in

[25] TS Kuhn, *The Structure of Scientific Revolutions* (Chicago, The University of Chicago Press, 1962).

the real world as disclosed by the history of science — did not fit their model any more than the other disciplines did. Science could not be seen as an authoritative accumulation of 'facts'. Positivist philosophers of science were therefore forced to face a dilemma paralleling that which the practitioners of other disciplines had hitherto faced: given a conflict between real science and their own rational model, which should be taken as pre-eminent? Even the most obstinate positivists could no longer rely on science itself for support, and as empiricists they were in no position to rely on pure reason alone.

Yet, while moving away from imposing on legal understanding the deflated positivist model of science, it is too quick to turn to the 'facts' of legal discourse or practice in the same way that Kuhn turned to the 'facts' of the history of science. This is because Kuhn's arguments were powerfully relativistic. There are no scientific 'facts' on his approach, for what we count as true and what we do not is always relative to some background paradigm, and paradigms change. Moreover, the grounds for their change are not grounds which necessarily disclose some movement in the direction of 'truth', but are typically sociological in nature.

Relativism, a very old philosophical problem, is also a very new one in the postmodern world, and it is continually fuelled by disagreements among the plurality of historical approaches which the ongoing history of historiography discloses. Whatever the importance of history either to philosophy of science or to philosophy of law, no philosopher could for long think that understanding science or law involved a simple appeal to the historical or social 'facts' of actual practice. Even Kuhn's position, it was eventually seen, did not and could not involve an appeal to 'facts' from the history of science, but involved the development of a model for understanding the history of science itself. Thus it is too simple to draw a contrast between philosophy of law as prescriptive for and as descriptive of legal understanding, as if the 'facts' of legal practice and terminology were independent of the theories about it. The contrast should be seen as being between different *models* of legal reasoning: perhaps one based on successful natural science, however that is understood, and the other — 'best legal judgements', perhaps — expressing the legal profession's own best model, its interpretation of its own practice over time. But there is no reason to think that there are merely two choices here, or only one model within the legal profession.[26] Models or interpretations, however, are unavoidable.

The upshot of Kuhn's approach is that it is a pragmatic question which model is the most appropriate to legal reasoning, and moreover that it should not be assumed that only one model should be used. There may well be a multiplicity of legal approaches, or paradigms. Once we are aware of

[26] S Lee, in *Judging Judges*, 2nd edn (London, Faber & Faber, 1989), suggests that each judge has his own legal philosophy and there is no one right answer.

the existence of different paradigms, frameworks, models, or interpretations, then we immediately and once again face the question of *choice*, with the further implications of relativism which lie behind that. While the possibility of choice between models does not imply that one model is no better than another, we at this point have still to develop more determinate rational bases for preferring one to another; moreover, there may well be a moral, or political or other kind of evaluative choice in choosing one over another. Hohfeld cannot merely *stipulate* his way out of difficulties here.

Hohfeld's theory, then, is an attempt to summarise some features of an existing social — in particular linguistic — practice, conjoined with a recommendation that certain further refinements be universally adopted by his profession. There is not here either a description of metaphysically independent rights, or a simple description of rights-talk. While there are descriptive elements in his theory which we may take to be 'true', theoretically these amount to little more than a reminder of how certain past judges or jurists had reasoned. Some of this reasoning was 'good' reasoning and some 'bad', by Hohfeld's lights, with his assessment being made not on the authority of the court in question but *by an appeal to clarity and consistency*. The stipulative recommendations of Hohfeld's table are similarly justified by him by an appeal to clarity and consistency, by the need, as he put it, to 'think straight' in relation to all legal problems.[27] Here the 'truth' of Hohfeld's analysis reflects and is constrained by what he takes to be the eternal and universal standards of reason, rather than the particular features of a local social practice. It is an objective standard of reason which, if anything does, warrants the truth of Hohfeld's claims.

Legal analysts cannot be mere summary describers of local legal practices. They have to commit themselves to the value of reason. Legal analysis then has the authority of reason, whatever that requires and as far as it can be pushed. It is the task of legal analysts to draw on and develop our understanding of what reason requires in the law.

[27] Hohfeld (above n 16), 25.

3

The Nature of Legal Philosophy

ROBERT ALEXY

PHILOSOPHY IS GENERAL *and systematic reflection about what there is, what ought to be done or is good, and how knowledge about both is possible. Legal philosophy raises these questions with respect to the law. In so doing, legal philosophy is engaged in reasoning about the nature of law. The arguments addressed to the question of the nature of law revolve around three problems. The first problem addresses the question: In what kinds of entities does the law consist, and how are these entities connected such that they form the overarching entity we call 'law'? The answer is that law consists of norms as meaning contents which form a normative system. The second problem addresses the question of how norms as meaning contents are connected with the real world. This connection can be grasped by means of the concepts of authoritative issuance and social efficacy. The latter includes the concept of coercion or force. The third problem addresses the correctness or legitimacy of law, and, by this, the relationship between law and morality. To ask about the nature of law is to ask about necessary relations between the concepts of normative meaning, authoritative issuance as well as social efficacy, and correctness of content.*

The question of the nature of legal philosophy connects two problems. The first concerns the general nature of philosophy, the second, the special character of that part of philosophy we call 'legal philosophy'.

THE NATURE OF PHILOSOPHY

There are so many schools, methods, styles, subjects, and ideals of philosophy that it is difficult to explain its nature. A general explanation of the nature of philosophy would presuppose that all, or at least most, of the very different conceptions of philosophy which have appeared in the history of the field have something in common that can be conceived of as the focal meaning or the concept of philosophy.

Perhaps the most general feature of the concept of philosophy seems to be reflexivity. Philosophy is reflective because it is reasoning about reasoning.

Philosophy is reasoning about reasoning, for its subject, the human practice of conceiving, on the one hand, of the world, oneself, and other minds, and, on the other, of human action, is essentially determined by reasons.

Having a conception of the world, oneself, and other minds is to have a conception about what there is. Action, on the other hand, presupposes a conception about what ought to be done or is good. Reasoning about the general question of what there is defines metaphysics *qua* ontology; reasoning about the question of what ought to be done or is good defines ethics. Human practice is not only based — for the most part implicitly — on answers to both questions, it also includes — again, for the most part implicitly — numerous answers to a third question: the question of how to justify our beliefs on what there is and on what ought to be done or is good. This question defines epistemology. Philosophy attempts to make explicit the ontological, ethical, and epistemological assumptions implicit in human practice.

Explicit reflexivity is necessary but not sufficient to explain the nature of philosophy. A teacher who abhors students' chewing gum during his lecture may become reflective by asking himself what the reasons for his attitude are, but this is not enough for him to become a philosopher. Reflexivity must be associated with two other properties if it is to be seen as capturing something genuinely philosophical in nature. The reflection must be reflection about general or fundamental questions, and this reflection must be of a systematic kind. The shortest, most abstract, but nevertheless truly comprehensive definition of philosophy might therefore run as follows: philosophy is general and systematic reflection about what there is, what ought to be done or is good, and how knowledge about both is possible.

This explanation by no means claims to exhaust its subject. Its brevity excludes this, and it may be that even a far more elaborated explanation will never be able to exhaust the nature of philosophy, for behind or between all the concepts one can use to explain its nature there may lie something which cannot be grasped conceptually, despite the fact that philosophy is a conceptual activity. Our explanation, therefore, can only attempt to provide a starting point for an answer to the question about the nature of legal philosophy. One may assume that this question has — as with legal philosophy itself — a certain autonomy, so that we need, indeed, an understanding of the general nature of philosophy only as a first step and not as a final and complete basis on which our understanding of the nature of legal philosophy rests, like a house on its foundations.

My definition of philosophy as general and systematic reflection about what there is, what ought to be done or is good, and how knowledge about both is possible, leads, notwithstanding its extremely abstract and highly tentative character, to three corollaries important for our purposes. First, reflection necessarily has a critical dimension. To reflect on what there is, what ought to be done and is good, and what we can know, is to ask for and to argue about what objectively exists, what is true or right, and what is justified. If one defines normativity as the ability to distinguish what is correct from what is incorrect, these questions are normative questions. Philosophy as a necessarily reflective enterprise therefore necessarily has a normative dimension. The general and systematic character of philosophical reflection leads, second, to an analytic, and third, to a synthetic or holistic dimension of philosophy. The analytic dimension is defined by the attempt to identify and to make explicit the fundamental structures of the natural and social world in which we live, and the fundamental concepts and principles by means of which we can grasp both worlds. Without this analytic bite, philosophy could be neither general nor systematic in a substantial sense.

In legal philosophy, the analytic dimension concerns concepts like those of norm, 'ought', person, action, sanction, and institution. The synthetic dimension is defined by the attempt to unite all of this into a coherent whole. A deeply founded and coherent picture of what there is, what ought to be done and is good, and what we can know, is the regulative idea of philosophy or, in simpler terms, its ultimate aim. This implies that philosophy is necessarily holistic. Our definition of philosophy should therefore be complemented by the following, which is implied by the definition: philosophy is normative (or critical), analytic, and holistic (or synthetic). The three concepts of the definition — reflective, general, and systematic — and the three concepts of the corollary — normative, analytic, and holistic — are descriptions of the same things from different perspectives.

PRE-UNDERSTANDING AND ARGUMENTS

Legal philosophy, as philosophy, is reflection of a general and systematic kind, and it has, exactly like philosophy in general, a normative, an analytic, and a holistic dimension. Its *differentia specifica* consists in its subject: the law. Legal philosophy is not generally directed to the questions of what there is, what ought to be done or is good, and what can be known, but to these questions with respect to the law. Raising these questions with respect to the law is to ask for the nature of law. This seems to lead naturally to the definition of legal philosophy as reasoning about the nature of law.

This, however, seems to cause a problem. It is a circularity problem, which rests on the fact that, on the one hand, legal philosophy cannot be defined without using the concept of law, whereas, on the other, it has the task *qua* reasoning about the nature of law of explaining what law is. How can legal philosophy begin to explore what law is, when it is impossible to say what legal philosophy is without knowing what law is? This circularity, however, is not vicious but virtuous in character. It is nothing other than a version of the hermeneutic circle, and it is to be resolved like all variants of this circle: by starting with the pre-understanding suggested by the established practice and elaborating it through critical and systematic reflection.

The pre-understanding of law is not only the pre-understanding of an entity which is highly complex in itself. To this first complexity is added — as a second complexity — that the pre-understanding as such is capable of extreme variations. The scale extends from Holmes's 'bad man',[1] which defines a rather detached external point of view, to Dworkin's judge Hercules, which represents a rather idealistic internal one.[2] Legal philosophy as an enterprise, which, at the same time, is systematic as well as critical, cannot start from just one pre-understanding. It has to consider all of them and, what is more, has to analyse the relation of all of them to all features of law.

The requirement to consider all pre-understandings which are to be found in law and legal philosophy on the one side, and all features of law on the other side, suggests the idea of something like a catalogue of all approaches and all features. But how does one compose such a list? Simply to pick up and collect each approach and each feature which appears in history or today before our eyes would, as Kant says, 'not be a *rational system* but merely an aggregate haphazardly collected'.[3] One needs no argument in order to say that this would be incompatible with the systematic and critical character of philosophy. Philosophical reflection demands a system. It is, however, much easier to say that a mere aggregate, or, as Kant sometimes puts it, a 'rhapsody'[4] is not enough, than to say how an adequate conceptual system or framework can be constructed. The best answer seems to be: not by an abstract theory of legal philosophy, but by systematic analysis of the arguments put forward in the discussion about the nature of law. No other procedure seems to fit better the general character of legal philosophy *qua* reasoning about the nature of law.

THREE PROBLEMS

The arguments about the nature of law revolve around three problems. The first problem addresses the question: In what kind of entities does the law consist, and how are these entities connected such that they form the overarching entity we call 'law'? This problem concerns the concept of a norm

[1] OW Holmes, 'The Path of the Law' 10 (1897) *Harvard Law Review* 457–78 at 459.
[2] R Dworkin, *Taking Rights Seriously* (London, Duckworth, 1977), 105.
[3] I Kant, 'The Metaphysics of Morals' in *Practical Philosophy (The Cambridge Edition of the Works of Immanuel Kant)* (Cambridge, Cambridge University Press, 1996), 493. See also, I Kant, 'Die Metaphysik der Sitten' in *Kant's Gesammelte Schriften* Vol VI, Royal Prussian Academy of Sciences (Berlin, Georg Reimer, 1907), 203–493 at 357: 'kein *Vernunftsystem*, sondern bloß (ein) aufgerafftes Aggregat sein würde'.
[4] Kant, *Critique of Pure Reason* (Indianapolis and Cambridge, Hackett, 1996), 755.

and a normative system. The second and the third problems are addressed to the validity of law. The second concerns its real or factual dimension. This is the area of legal positivism. Two centres are to be distinguished here. The first is determined by the concept of authoritative issuance, the second by that of social efficacy. The third problem of the nature of legal philosophy concerns the correctness or legitimacy of law. Here, the main question is the relationship between law and morality. To take up this question is to take up the ideal or critical dimension of law. It is this triad of problems that, taken together, defines the nucleus of the problem of the nature of law.

This tripartition claims to be complete, neutral, and systematic. It is complete when it can absorb all arguments that can be put forward for and against a thesis about the nature of law. The only proof possible for this consists in corroborating our triadic model with respect to as many critical instances as possible. The model is neutral when it adds no preferences to the weights of the arguments it absorbs. The proof is the same as in the case of completeness. It is, finally, systematic when it leads to a coherent picture of the nature of law. In this case, the proof cannot consist of anything else than an elaboration of a coherent account.

The last point can be generalised. Only by elaborating the best theory connecting answers to all three questions about the nature of law can the nature of legal philosophy become as clear as possible. It is, however, not only not the case that one can develop such a perfect theory here, but also the case that one may well be sceptical about whether such an ideal of perfection can ever be achieved. Fortunately, it is not necessary to know all, in order to know enough. In order to obtain as much as is necessary for our purposes it suffices to use the triadic model as a framework for the discussion of paradigmatic problems.

FOUR THESES

The consideration of paradigmatic problems vis-à-vis our triadic model shall confirm four theses. This confirmation, again, implies a corroboration of the model. The first thesis says that legal philosophy is not confined to certain special problems connected with law; all problems of philosophy may arise in legal philosophy. In this respect legal philosophy substantially includes the problems of philosophy in general. One can call this the 'general nature thesis'. The second thesis maintains that there are specific problems of legal philosophy. They are due to the specific character of law, which results from the fact that law is necessarily authoritative or institutional as well as critical or ideal. This is the 'specific character thesis'. The third thesis says that there is a special relation between legal philosophy and other provinces of practical philosophy, especially those of moral and political philosophy. One can call this the 'special relation thesis'. A fourth thesis overarches the first three theses. That is, it does not simply join them as a fourth thesis, but expresses an idea behind them. It is the idea that legal philosophy can be successful only if it comes up to the level not only of one or two of these theses but to that of all three. This is the 'comprehensive ideal' of legal philosophy.

While the triadic model of the problems of legal philosophy claims to be neutral, the four theses do not. They involve decisions with respect to the solution of these problems. This becomes clear when one contrasts the comprehensive ideal with something like a 'restrictive maxim'. A radical version of such a restrictive maxim maintains, first, that legal philosophy should never get involved in any genuinely philosophical problem, second, that legal philosophy should concentrate its efforts on the institutional or authoritative character of law, and, third, that legal philosophy should delegate critical normative questions to moral and political philosophy, which for their part should be kept, so to speak, beyond reach. The restrictive maxim mirrors a picture of legal philosophy, that is fundamentally different from the picture of the field corresponding to the comprehensive ideal. Legal philosophy turns into a juridical theory of law, which is separated from general philosophy as well as from moral and political philosophy.

The choice between the comprehensive ideal and the restrictive maxim is a fundamental choice. The character of legal philosophy is determined by it much more radically than by the choice between legal positivism and non-positivism. The choice between positivism and non-positivism is a choice inside the realm of legal philosophy. The choice between the comprehensive ideal and the restrictive maxim amounts to a choice between philosophy and non-philosophy. This is the background against which our paradigmatic problems have to be considered.

ENTITIES AND CONCEPTS

The answers given by Kelsen and Olivecrona in the 1930s to the classical question of what entities the law consists in present our first example. Kelsen defines 'law as norm',[5] and norms as 'meaning',[6] and the 'unique sense' of this meaning as 'ought', and 'ought' as a 'category'.[7] This is the language in which abstract entities are described. Kelsen insists that norms — and thus, law — can be reduced neither to physical events nor to psychical processes. They belong not to natural reality but to an 'ideal reality'.[8] Such an ideal reality, which exists in addition to the physical and

[5] H Kelsen, *Introduction to the Problems of Legal Theory* (Oxford, Clarendon Press, 1992), 13.
[6] *Ibid*, 11, 14.
[7] *Ibid*, 24.
[8] *Ibid*, 15.

the psychical world, would be a 'third realm' in the sense of Frege.[9] The opposite position is to be found in Karl Olivecrona, who, with an eye to Kelsen, maintains that '[t]he rules of law are a natural cause — among others — of the actions of the judges in cases of litigation as well as of the behaviour in general of people in relation to each other'.[10] This question — as an ontological question — is not only a question of general philosophical interest, it is also a question which must be answered in order to determine the nature of law, and it is, therefore, a genuine question of legal philosophy.

An adherent of the restrictive maxim might object that the question of the ontological status of norms is, for lawyers, as unimportant as the question of the real or only imagined existence of a mountain in Africa, identified and surveyed by two geographers, is for these two geographers.[11] The reply to this objection is that the realism problem has a different significance for geographers than the meaning problem has for lawyers. The answer to the question whether norms are meaning contents or natural causes determines the answer to a further question, namely, whether norms can be conceived as elements of an inferential system and, thereby, as starting points of arguments, or whether they are only elements in a causal network. In the first case, legal reasoning oriented towards correctness is possible, in the second, it would be an illusion. This shows how the self-understanding of legal reasoning and, by means of it, the self-understanding of law depends on ontological presuppositions. There are, naturally, several ways for reconstructing these presuppositions. But the mere fact that there exists the necessity of reconstructing them is enough to confirm the thesis that legal philosophy cannot do without arguments that are genuinely philosophical in character.

In any case, the concept of a norm or the 'ought' is a candidate for the most abstract concept of legal philosophy. If one goes one step down from this level of abstraction, the inferential impact of the fundamental concepts of law becomes far more obvious. The distinction between rules and principles is a highly abstract question of the general theory of norms. It has, at the same time, far-reaching consequences for the theory of legal reasoning. If law contains both, then legal reasoning inevitably combines subsumption with balancing.[12] Legal reasoning is thereby essentially determined by structures that are structures of general practical reasoning. This is an important

[9] G Frege, 'The Thought: A Logical Inquiry' in PF Strawson (ed), *Philosophical Logic* (Oxford, Oxford University Press, 1967), 17–38 at 29.
[10] K Olivecrona, *Law as Fact* (Copenhagen, Einar Munksgaard, and London, Humphrey Milford, 1939), 16.
[11] R Carnap, *Scheinprobleme in der Philosophie* (Berlin-Schlachtensee, Weltkreis-Verlag, 1928) 35–6.
[12] R Alexy, 'On Balancing and Subsumption. A Structural Comparison' (2003) 16 *Ratio Juris* 433–49 at 433ff.

reason for not conceiving of legal reasoning as a province in its own right, separate and distinct from other provinces of reason.

All this shows that fundamental philosophical questions must be answered in order to grasp the nature of law. Reflection about the nature of law cannot succeed when separated from general philosophy.

NECESSARY PROPERTIES

Asking for the nature of something is more than asking for interesting and important properties. Questions about the nature of law are questions about its necessary properties. The concept of necessity leads one to the heart of philosophy. The same is true with its relatives, the concepts of analyticity and the *a priori*. Without these concepts it is impossible to understand the meaning of questions of the type 'What is the nature of φ?'. Without understanding the structure of questions of this kind, one cannot understand the main question of legal philosophy: 'What is the nature of law?'; and to fail to understand this question is to fail to know what legal philosophy is.

The possibility of defining the concept of nature as it appears in sentences of the form 'What is the nature of φ?', namely, by means of the concept of necessity, allows for the substitution of the question 'What is the nature of law?' by the question 'What are the necessary properties of law?'. This question leads, by means of the concept of necessity (and its relatives, analyticity and the *a priori*), to the specific character of law. The question of what is necessary turns, when connected with the question of what is specific, into the question of what is essential. This is the area of the specific character thesis.

Two properties are essential for law: coercion or force on the one hand, and correctness or rightness on the other. The first concerns a central element of the social efficacy of law, the second expresses its ideal or critical dimension. It is the central question of legal philosophy to ask how these two concepts are related to the concept of law and, through it, to each other. All — or at least nearly all — questions of legal philosophy depend on the answer to this question.

It is highly contested whether coercion and correctness are necessarily connected with law. This dispute is attended by a meta-dispute about the question of what kind of argument can be given for and against the necessity of such connections. It is impossible to elaborate this here.[13] I will, therefore, confine myself to some features which seem to be instructive for our question concerning the nature of legal philosophy.

[13] R Alexy, 'The Nature of Arguments about the Nature of Law' in LH Meyer, SL Paulson, TWM Pogge (eds), *Rights, Culture, and the Law: Themes from the Legal and Political Philosophy of Joseph Raz* (Oxford, Oxford University Press, 2003), 3–16.

Coercion is the easier case. It seems to be quite natural to argue that a system of rules or norms which in no case authorises the use of coercion or sanction — not even in case of self-defence — is not a legal system, and this is the case owing to conceptual reasons based on the use of language. Who would apply the expression 'law' to such a system of rules? Conceptual reasons of this kind, however, have little power of their own. Concepts based on the actual use of language are in need of modification once they prove not to be, as Kant says — mentioning, *inter alia*, the concepts of gold, water, and law — 'adequate to the object'.[14] Including coercion in the concept of law is adequate to its object, the law, because it mirrors a practical necessity necessarily connected with law. Coercion is necessary if law is to be a social practice that fulfils its basic formal functions as defined by the values of legal certainty and efficiency as well as possible. This practical necessity, which seems to correspond to a certain degree to Hart's 'natural necessity',[15] is mirrored in a conceptual necessity implicit in the use of language. This shows that language, which we use to refer to social facts, is inspired by the hermeneutic principle that each human practice is to be conceived of as an attempt to carry out its functions as well as possible. Unravelling this connection between conceptual and practical necessity makes clear in what sense coercion belongs as a necessary property to the nature of law.

The second central property of law is its claim to correctness. This claim stands in genuine opposition to coercion or force, and it is an essential mark of law that it comprises such a difference. The necessity of coercion, it has been shown, is based on a practical necessity defined by a means-end relation. In this respect, it has a teleological character. The necessity of the claim to correctness is a necessity resulting from the structure of legal acts and legal reasoning. It has a deontological character. To make explicit this deontological structure implicit in law is one of the most important tasks of legal philosophy.

All methods of making the implicit explicit can be applied here. One of them is the construction of performative contradictions.[16] An example of this is a fictitious first article of a constitution which reads as follows: 'X is a sovereign, federal, and unjust republic'. It is difficult to deny that this article is somehow absurd. The idea underlying the method of performative contradiction is to explain this absurdity as resulting from a contradiction between what is implicitly claimed in acting to frame a constitution — namely, that it is just — and what is explicitly declared — namely, that it is unjust. If this explanation is sound, and if the claim to justice, which is a

[14] I Kant (above n 4), 680. See also Kant, 'Kritik der reinen Vernunft' in *Kant's Gesammelte Schriften* Vol III, Royal Prussian Academy of Sciences (Berlin, Georg Reimer, 1904), 1–552 at 478: 'dem Gegenstande adäquat'.
[15] HLA Hart, *The Concept of Law*, 2nd edn (Oxford, Clarendon Press, 1994), 199.
[16] R Alexy, *The Argument from Injustice: A Reply to Legal Positivsim* (Oxford, Clarendon Press, 2002), 35–9.

special case of the broader claim to correctness,[17] is necessarily raised, then a necessary connection between law and justice is made explicit.

It is not difficult to recognise how this argument might be challenged. One simply has to deny that law necessarily raises a claim to correctness. Once this claim disappears, any contradiction between the explicit and the implicit vanishes. The declaration of injustice contained in our first article may then be interpreted as an expression of a claim to power.

This is not the place to discuss the question of whether it is possible for a system of norms to substitute the claim to correctness by a claim to power and nevertheless remain a legal system.[18] This is a question of legal philosophy, not a question about its nature. Here it suffices to say that the discussion about necessary deontological structures implicit in the law belongs to the very nature of legal philosophy.

LAW AND MORALITY

If the thesis that law necessarily raises a claim to correctness should prove to be wrong, it would be difficult to contest the positivist's thesis of the separability of law and morality. The opposite, however, is the case if the thesis about the claim to correctness is true. The thesis would then provide a solid basis for the argument that morality is necessarily included into the law.

The inclusion of morality in the law helps to solve problems, but it also creates problems that one might well be able to circumvent if one followed the positivist's separation thesis. The problems, which the inclusion of morality can help to solve, are, first, the problem of basic evaluations underlying and justifying the law, second, the problem of realising the claim to correctness in the creation and the application of law, and third, the problem of the limits of law.

One aspect of the problem of basic evaluations has already appeared when the relation between law and coercion has been classified as a practical necessity. The concept of a practical necessity is ambiguous. A weak interpretation only refers to a means-end relation, where one treats the choice of the ends merely as a matter of fact or only as hypothetical. This is the import of Hart's concept of 'natural necessity' if one understands the ends only as 'some very obvious generalizations ... concerning human nature and the world in which men live'.[19] The picture begins to change, however, if the general ends of law like legal certainty and the protection of

[17] Justice is a special case of correctness, if justice can be defined as correctness of distribution and compensation; see R Alexy, 'Giustizia come correttezza' (1998) 9 *Ragion pratica* 103–13, 105.

[18] R Alexy, 'Law and Correctness' in MDA Freeman (ed), *Legal Theory at the End of the Millennium* (Oxford, Oxford University Press, 1998), 205–21 at 213–14.

[19] HLA Hart (above n 15), 192–93.

basic rights are considered as requirements of practical reason, and it changes completely if these requirements are considered as necessary elements of the law. Such a strong interpretation of the concept of practical necessity would provide an evaluative or normative basis of the law.

The second problem, which the inclusion of morality promises to solve, is the realisation of the claim to correctness within the institutional framework of the law. An example is legal reasoning in hard cases. Once morality is conceived of as included by the law, moral reasons can and must participate in the justification of legal decisions when authoritative reasons run out. The theory of legal reasoning attempts to grasp this by conceiving of legal reasoning as a special case of general practical reasoning.

The third problem, which seems best solved by means of the inclusion of morality into the law, is that of the limits of law. If extreme injustice is not to be considered as law — at least from the point of view of a participant in the legal system — how should this be justified without recourse to moral reasons?[20]

All of this, however, represents only the one side. The other side is, as already mentioned, that the inclusion of morality in the law creates serious problems. One of the main reasons for the authoritative and institutionalised structure of law is the general uncertainty of moral reasoning. Moral disputes tend to be endless. Often in social life a consensus cannot be achieved by discourse. For reasons of practical necessity an authoritative decision must, then, be substituted. This would, however, only be an argument for conceiving of moral reasoning as not belonging to law were it not possible to incorporate moral reasoning into legal reasoning without destroying the necessary authoritative elements of the latter. It is a main task of legal philosophy to consider whether or not this is possible.

A second problem is far more serious. It is the problem of whether moral knowledge or moral justification is possible at all. If the meta-ethical theses of subjectivism, relativism, non-cognitivism, or emotivism should prove to be true, the claim to correctness would have to be interpreted in terms of something like an 'error theory', as Mackie has suggested.[21] This shows that law, by incorporating morality *via* the claim to correctness, finds itself encumbered with the epistemological problems of moral knowledge and justification. This is not a small burden.

At the beginning of our deliberations we distinguished three main questions of philosophy: the ontological question of what there is, the ethical or practical question of what ought to be done or is good, and the epistemological question of what we can know. Our way through the fields of legal philosophy has shown that legal philosophy confronts all three kind of

[20] R Alexy (above n 16), 40–62.

[21] JL Mackie, *Ethics: Inventing Right and Wrong* (London, Pelican Books, 1977), 35.

questions. This already seems to be more than can be achieved by one person. But there is more. The reflective and systematic nature of legal philosophy demands that all these questions be connected in a coherent theory, which, for its part, must be as close to law as possible in order to guarantee that what it makes explicit really is the nature of law. In this way, our reflections about the nature of legal philosophy end with the exposition of an ideal.

4

Method in Law: Revision and Description

VERONICA RODRIGUEZ-BLANCO[1]

I. INTRODUCTION

THIS STUDY ARGUES that two views on metaphysics have been predominantly advocated by contemporary legal theorists. The first view is the abstinent one, which asserts that metaphysical judgements are either reducible to substantive claims or unintelligible. The second view is the descriptive one, which asserts that we should begin with conceptual analysis if we aim to do serious metaphysics. The abstinent view embraces an internal and evaluative point of view. By contrast, descriptive metaphysics embraces an external and descriptive perspective. I raise a number of arguments against both views and advance a positive thesis on metaphysics. The paper challenges Dworkin's abstinent view, according to which the neutrality and the austerity of metaphysical explanations in morality are rejected. The former is the idea that metaphysical theories do not take sides on substantive arguments. The latter means that metaphysical theories will not rely on very general or counterfactual arguments or positive moral judgements. It is argued, *contra* Dworkin, that conceptual analysis or descriptive metaphysics is not necessarily neutral and austere, and that, therefore, metaphysics as conceptual analysis is a substantive enterprise.

The idea that the rejection of 'factualism' does not entail a rejection of metaphysics is the second criticism raised against the abstinent view. Finally, it is argued that the abstinent view ignores the complexity of 'substantive' *a posteriori* arguments in law and morality. However, the paper argues that descriptive metaphysics or conceptual analysis also faces a difficulty: it explains the basic structures of thought and concepts at the pre-reflective level, but it cannot show that these structures are not the creation of the philosopher who explores them. In other words, it is difficult to make sense of its non-reflective status. Therefore, if descriptive metaphysics is not

[1] I am grateful to George Pavlakos and Sean Coyle for comments and suggestions on earlier drafts.

pre-reflective but reflective, there is room for a revisionist critique. This study argues that revisionary metaphysics enables us to dissolve the internal–external distinction and the evaluative–descriptive demarcation.

The essay is divided into four substantive sections. In Section II, the methodological debate in legal theory is discussed with special emphasis on the criticism raised by Perry against Hart's methodology, and the importance of an adequate understanding of the metaphysical presuppositions of Hart's methodology is shown. In Section III the two current metaphysical views in legal theory are explained and criticised. Section IV advances the view that legal theory should resort to revisionary metaphysics, and explains the relationship between revisionary and descriptive metaphysics. Section V raises some objections to the latter view and discusses possible replies to the objections.

II. THE METHODOLOGICAL DEBATE IN LEGAL THEORY

The methodological debate in legal theory is a hybrid of practical philosophy and reflections on the methodology of the social sciences. A number of legal theorists have focused on the problem of the double nature of law (Finnis,[2] Raz,[3] Simmonds[4]), within which law is conceived as a social phenomenon, but, it is argued, also creates reasons for actions that guide the conduct of its citizens. It seems, reasonable, according to this view, to reflect on distinctions between the internal and the external perspectives, the descriptive and the evaluative aspects of a legal theory, and between the theoretical inquiry of the law and the practical considerations that create the law. Other legal theorists prefer to focus on a more pure philosophical method and produce interpretations of contemporary legal theories in the light of philosophical debates. For example, Nicos Stavropoulos has offered an interpretation of Hart's methodology in terms of conceptual analysis;[5] Brian Leiter[6] an interpretation of American Realism in terms of naturalised epistemology; and Michael Moore[7] advances a methodology of law and legal theory that combines natural moral realism and Aristotelian functionalism. The purpose of the present essay is twofold: to

[2] J Finnis, *Natural Law and Natural Rights* (Oxford, Clarendon Press, 1980), 3–19.
[3] J Raz, *Practical Reason and Norms* (Oxford, Clarendon Press, 1999); *The Authority of Law* (Oxford, Clarendon Press, 1979); *Ethics in the Public Domain* (Oxford, Clarendon Press, 1994).
[4] N Simmonds, 'Protestant Jurisprudence and Modern Doctrinal Scholarship' (2002) 60 *Cambridge Law Journal* 271.
[5] N Stavropoulos, 'Hart's Semantics' in J Coleman (ed), *Hart's Postscript* (Oxford, Clarendon Press, 2001), 59.
[6] B Leiter, 'Realism, Positivism and Conceptual Analysis' (1998) 4 *Legal Theory* 533.
[7] M Moore, *Educating Oneself in Public* (Oxford, Clarendon Press, 2001).

show that metaphysics has a place in the methodology of legal theory and to rethink the distinctions that legal theory has inherited from the methodology of the social sciences.

Having these two purposes in mind, the study begins with Hart's methodology. This section discusses conceptual analysis as the fundamental method of Hart's legal theory and goes on to consider Perry's criticism of Hart's methodology. Perry argues that Hart's methodology cannot be descriptive, since Hart argues that the function of law is to guide the conduct of its citizens, and according to Perry this statement is an evaluative statement. Consequently, Perry argues, Hart is not faithful to his descriptive and externalist approach. This essay defends Hart's methodology and argues that when it is understood in terms of conceptual analysis, Hart's claim that the function of the law is to guide the conduct of its citizens is a conceptual claim. Perry's criticism has its origin in the distinction between evaluative and descriptive views in the social sciences. However, conceptual analysis aims to understand and explain through possible cases the structure of our concepts, including our normative concepts. Hart's claim is neither an empirical nor an evaluative claim. It is the outcome of the analysis of the concept of law. The point is to understand what conceptual analysis is. This debate illuminates the importance of descriptive metaphysics or conceptual analysis and invites us to reassess Hart's methodology in philosophical terms.

Perry's view can be summarised into four core arguments. First, he explains that there are features of a scientific-explanatory method in Hart. Second, Perry argues that the predominant methodology in Hart's book *The Concept of Law* is conceptual analysis. Hart's intention, according to Perry, is to analyse externally the concept of law. However, Hart also advocates the idea that law gives reasons for actions to its citizens, and therefore it is necessary to explain the reason-giving nature of the law. Because, according to Perry, Hart aims to explain the normativity of the law, Hart cannot engage in this kind of explanation successfully unless he is committed to an internal methodology. Consequently, Perry argues, Hart's methodology is internal conceptual analysis. Third, he asserts that there are resemblances between internal conceptual analysis and Dworkin's interpretivist methodology. Fourth, he concludes that Dworkin's interpretivist methodology is more satisfactory than Hart's internal conceptual analysis if the aim is to understand the reason-giving character of the law.

The first argument is not controversial and therefore I will attempt to undermine the second and the third arguments. The criticism focuses on two points. First, the idea that Perry's explanation of conceptual analysis is too narrow. Thus, I explain conceptual analysis as a wider research programme as understood by Frank Jackson and show the plausibility of an interpretation of Hart's methodology in these terms. Second, I show that conceptual analysis, when it is properly understood, can be reconciled with the reason-giving character of the law.

Perry claims that Hart invokes the explanatory power of a theory to elucidate concepts.[8] However, this explanatory power is not in the ordinary scientific sense, but lies in the fact that an elucidation of our concepts will clarify our social practices. Perry quotes Hart: 'We accord this union of elements [ie, primary and secondary rules] a central place because of their explanatory power in elucidating the concepts that constitute the framework of legal thought'.[9] Perry explains the notion of conceptual analysis and asserts that it is an inquiry into the manner in which we conceptualise our own social practices to clarify concepts and to come to a better understanding of the practices themselves. He then asserts that the notion of necessity is conceptual and not scientific.[10] I assume that he means that it is conceptual and not empirical. Perry defends both the view that Hart engages in conceptual analysis and that this explains the fact that Hart begins with an analysis of the salient features of a modern municipal legal system, the latter being the clear central case of our concept of law. Then, Perry tells us, once we have a better understanding of our concept of law, we will be in a better position to say whether various features of social practice are instances of law, according to our own light.[11] Perry also makes the following assertion:

> Hart's critique of Austin's theory of law as orders backed by threats is, in essence, that it does not have the internal resources to elucidate these concepts. However, the concepts of authority, state, legislation, etc. are our concepts, where 'we' must be understood as referring to participants in — or at least the subjects of — modern municipal legal systems. These are, in other words, the notions that we use to conceptualise certain of our own practices. This lends support to the suggestion that, when we speak of conceptual analysis, Hart has in mind the clarification of the conceptual framework that we apply to certain aspects of our own social behaviour. This is not, however, a standard goal of descriptive-explanatory theory. A radically external theory that transcended or ignored the participants' conceptualisation of their own practice might well have greater explanatory power in the usual scientific sense. Degree of conceptual clarification appears, in fact, to be the sole basis by which Hart would judge the success of particular theories of law.[12]

This claim conflates three different elements: the 'internal' point of view, an internal methodology, and conceptual analysis. A plausible interpretation of this paragraph is that we need the internal point of view to understand

[8] S Perry, 'Hart's "Methodological Positivism"' in J Coleman (above n 5), 321.
[9] HLA Hart, *The Concept of Law* 2nd edn (Oxford, Clarendon Press, 1994), 81.
[10] S Perry (above n 8), 314.
[11] *Ibid*, 316.
[12] *Ibid*, 322.

our concept of law and therefore to engage in conceptual analysis. Consequently, and not surprisingly, the only possible conceptual analysis is, according to Perry, internal conceptual analysis. We need then to elucidate the notion of conceptual analysis and to see whether Perry's interpretation of conceptual analysis is sound. Frank Jackson offers a well-argued and sophisticated study of conceptual analysis on whose basis Stavropoulos has advanced an interpretation of Hart's methodology.[13] In this section I will refer to both Jackson's work and Stavropoulos's interpretation.

The question of what conceptual analysis is, is already a controversial issue, although there is a set of common features which satisfactorily characterise the notion as a philosophical method which aims to clarify thoughts, concepts and propositions. The goal of conceptual analysis is to describe or define concepts in terms of other concepts, or perhaps to say certain things in one vocabulary in terms of a more fundamental vocabulary, for example, by using physical vocabulary to describe mental states, or non-moral vocabulary to describe moral issues. Conceptual analysis retrieves our intuitions, or what is familiar to us, or the things with which we are acquainted, and organises them. It uses verbal expressions, such as sentences and words, because this is the only way we can gain access to our concepts and propositions, but it should be noted that the subject of analysis is not the verbal expression itself.[14] Moreover whilst conceptual analysis seeks to access our intuitions and ordinary conceptions, the subject matter of the analysis is not our intuitions and acquaintances. Further, word usage

[13] N Stavropoulos (above n 5). I criticise Stavropoulos's interpretation of Hart's methodology and argue that Hart is committed to non-ambitious conceptual analysis. See my 'A Defence of Hart's Semantics as Nonambitious Conceptual Analysis' (2003) 2 *Legal Theory* 99–124. However, for the purposes of this paper and at this stage of the discussion, I will not make a distinction between non-ambitious and ambitious conceptual analysis.

[14] GE Moore in his reply to Langford clarifies the point that conceptual analysis is not about verbal expressions. He points out: 'Now I think I can say quite definitely that I never intended to use the word in such a way that the analysandum would be a verbal expression. When I talked about analyzing anything, what I have talked of analyzing has always been an idea or concept or proposition, and not a verbal expression; that is to say, if I talked of analyzing a "proposition" in such a sense that no verbal expression (no sentence, for instance) can be a proposition, in that sense.' (Moore, 'Reply' in *The Philosophy of GE Moore* (Evanston Northwestern University Press, 1942), 661.) Hart also rejects the idea that analysis is only about 'words' and quotes JL Austin, 'A Plea for Excuses' (1956-7) 57 *Proceedings of the Aristotelian Society* 33–4, in which he says at the end of the passage: 'A definition of this familiar type does two things at once. It simultaneously provides a code or formula translating the word into other well-understood terms and locates for us the kind of thing to which the word is used to refer, by indicating the features which it shares in common with a wider family of things and those which marked it off from others of that same family. In searching for and finding such definitions we are looking not merely at words ... but also at the realities we use words to talk about. We are using a sharpened awareness of words to sharpen our perception of the phenomena.' On the same topic see J Wisdom, 'Philosophy, metaphysics and psychoanalysis' in *Philosophy and Psychoanalysis* (Oxford, Basil Blackwell, 1953), 251–52, quoted by Hart (above n 9; hereinafter *CL*), 233n.

can lead to misunderstanding, since the ordinary usage and the technical one can come into conflict.[15]

Conceptual analysis sharpens the usage of our words. Another facet of conceptual analysis is that it is '*a priori*' because it aims to understand concepts before actual experience. For example, in order to analyse the concept 'negligence', we need to retrieve our intuitions and the familiar notions that we associate with this concept. We then look at the usage of the word 'negligence', because this is a way to gain access to our intuitions about the concept. Thus, we might say that 'negligence' is connected to the concept of 'duty', 'reasonableness' and 'intentionality'. We might consequently refine the use of the concept 'reasonableness' and find it obscure, and say that it is better to link the concept 'negligence' to the concept of 'objective standard of duty'. If we aim to analyse the concept 'law', we must first retrieve our knowledge of it. We know that it is connected to concepts such as 'morality', 'rule-governed behaviour' and 'obligation',[16] and following this connection may analyse its contextual usage in terms such as 'international law' or 'primitive law'. The former context is misleading[17] since users of this concept do not consider that international law is 'law'; however, the analysis reveals that the concept 'international law' shares some basic features with the concept 'law'. It is apparent then that the actual usage is mistaken.

It can be argued that in traditional conceptual analysis, the result of analysis is an analytic truth such as 'All bodies are extended'. Kant defined analytic truths as judgements in which the predicate is part of the subject:

> Analytic judgements (affirmative) are therefore those in which the connection of the predicate with the subject is thought through identity. If I say, for instance, 'All bodies are extended', this is an analytic judgment. For I do not require to go beyond the concept which I connect with 'body' in order to find extension as bound up with it. To meet with this predicate, I have merely to analyse the concept, that is, to become conscious to myself of the manifold which I always think in that concept.[18]

However, analytic truths say nothing about the world; they simply describe the relationship between the terms of a proposition. By contrast, according to Kant, judgements of experience are all synthetic. Kant tells us that the proposition that a body is extended is *a priori* and is not empirical. However,

[15] On this matter GE Moore argues: 'In other words, we may be able to use an expression perfectly correctly without being able to provide a correct philosophical analysis of the concept or proposition denoted by the expression' (GE Moore, 'Necessity' (1900) 9 *Mind* 289–304, at 290).

[16] Hart's *CL* begins saying that these three concepts are interrelated and that this relationship causes perplexity. This perplexity justifies the study of the relationship of these concepts (*CL*, 6–8).

[17] HLA Hart, *CL*, 3–4.

[18] I Kant, *Critique of Pure Reason* (London, Macmillan, 1992), B11, 48–9.

the judgement 'All bodies are heavy' is different from anything that I think in the mere concept of body in general.[19] Critics of conceptual analysis argue that it relies on the truth of the analytic–synthetic dichotomy and object to such a stark distinction.

These objections to conceptual analysis were mainly raised by Quine, Kripke and Hilary Putnam in the 1960s and 1970s.[20] Some describe *a priori* truths as conceptual truths on the basis that they are all true in virtue of the nature of the concepts they contain. Jackson, a recent defender of conceptual analysis, has incorporated Quine's, Putnam's and Kripke's criticisms[21] of the impossibility of a stark dichotomy between synthetic and analytic truths into his view of conceptual analysis. Jackson's defence of conceptual analysis lies in two core arguments: the argument that we need conceptual analysis to locate the subject matter of our theorising; and the idea that there is only one kind of necessity although there are two different ways of knowing it, namely '*a priori*' and '*a posteriori*'. In other words, he rejects the view that the '*a posteriori*'/'*a priori*' distinction produces more than one kind of necessity: the necessary '*a priori*' and the necessary '*a posteriori*'. Let us scrutinise these arguments.

The first argument constitutes the justification of conceptual analysis. Jackson tells us that metaphysics is about what the world is like, and that the questions we ask are framed in a language.[22] Thus, a metaphysician would be unable to engage in serious metaphysics by merely asking questions such as 'Are there Ks?', or 'Are Ks nothing over and above Js?'. The question 'what counts as a K or a J?' is prior to other questions that follow it. The metaphysician first needs to locate or identify the subject matter. According to Jackson, our starting point is our ordinary conception of K or J, and it can be extracted by appealing to our intuitions about possible cases. Let us suppose that I need to extract the ordinary conception of free action; to do this I appeal to my intuitions about free action. I am thereafter able to describe an action as free because I am guided by my intuitions about various possible cases, and can attempt to determine whether there are or not cases of free action.

My intuitions about possible cases reveal my theory of free action and your intuitions reveal your theory. *To the extent that our intuitions coincide, they reveal our shared theory. To the extent that our intuitions coincide with those of the folk, they reveal the folk theory.*[23] Jackson makes an

[19] *Ibid*, B11–12, 48–9.
[20] Brian Leiter has argued that conceptual analysis in jurisprudence is not immune from Quine's criticism. He claims, however, that analytical jurisprudence theorists have ignored the criticism of the analytic–synthetic distinction. See Leiter (above n 6), 546.
[21] WVO Quine, 'Two dogmas of empiricism' in *Clarity is Not Enough* (London, George Allen & Unwin Ltd, 1963); S Kripke, *Naming and Necessity* (Oxford, Basil Blackwell, 1972); H Putnam, *Mind, Language and Reality* (Cambridge, Cambridge University Press, 1975).
[22] F Jackson, *From Metaphysics to Ethics* (Oxford, Clarendon Press, 1998), 30. (Hereinafter, *ME*).
[23] *Ibid*, 32.

important disclaimer concerning the use of the word 'concept'. The purpose of conceptual analysis is to reach clarity about the cases covered by the words rather than the words *per se,* and Jackson differentiates conceptual analysis from word or sentence analysis.[24] The task that Jackson undertakes is to elucidate concepts by determining how subjects classify possibilities, and he emphasises that conceptual analysis is an hypothetical-deductive exercise. This can be understood as meaning that we are seeking the hypothesis that makes best sense of a person's responses to possible cases taking into account all the evidence.[25]

Jackson's second argument is the idea that there is only one kind of necessity and that the necessary '*a posteriori*' does not require acknowledging additional kinds of necessity. By contrast, critics of the '*a priori*' have argued that we might say that 'water = water' or 'H_2O = H_2O' are analytically or conceptually necessary, whereas 'water = H_2O' is metaphysically necessary. This means that there are two kinds of necessity. If this view is sound, then the necessity of water being H_2O is not available *a priori,* because what is conceptually possible or impossible is available to reason alone, and what is metaphysically possible and impossible cannot be known through reason alone. Therefore, the knowledge that water = H_2O can only be achieved '*a posteriori*'.

Jackson rejects this argument and claims that the necessity of 'water = H_2O' is not different from the necessity that water = water. His defence lies in two core arguments. First, he advocates an Occamist view and argues that we should not multiply the senses of necessity beyond need.[26] Thus, the necessary *a posteriori* can be explained in terms of one unitary notion of a set of possible worlds. Second, he advances the idea of the Twin Earth and states that to describe a counterfactual world, such as the Twin Earth, we need to look at the actual world. Moreover, the actual world plays an important role in determining the correct way to describe counterfactual possible worlds. Let us scrutinise both arguments.

There are two different ways of evaluating linguistic expressions relative to possible worlds. These, in turn, give rise to different intensions (and different extensions in non-actual worlds). The first way is the original way adopted by possible-worlds semanticists since the inception of the subject. Given the actual use of an expression — say the use of 'water' in the global presence of actual water, i.e. H_2O — its intension is just the function assigning an extension to the expression in every possible world considered counterfactually. The extension of the term in a possible world considered counterfactually is what Jackson calls the 'C-extension' of the term in that world. And the correlative intension is the 'C-intension'.

[24] *Ibid,* 33–4.
[25] *Ibid,* 36.
[26] *Ibid,* 70–71.

Now, it turns out that because of the rigidity of 'water', its C-intension is a constant function across water-containing counterfactual worlds in the sense that 'water' applies to water, ie, to H_2O, in any such world, and otherwise applies to nothing.

The second way of evaluating linguistic expressions relative to possible worlds is to consider possible worlds as actual contexts of use of the expression in question. The basic idea is that we do not consider 'water' as used in the actual world and then go on to consider what it applies to it in counterfactual worlds, given its actual use. What we do, rather, is consider what 'water' applies to as used in possible worlds considered as actual contexts of use. This generates different (non-actual) extensions and thus a different intension.[27] For presumably, in any world in which water is used in the global presence of a substance that plays the same role in the interactions of speakers with their environment as H_2O plays in our interactions with ours, 'water' will apply to that substance, whatever it is. Given a relevant world *x* and a relevant substance in that world, the substance in question is what Jackson calls the 'A-extension' of 'water' in *x*. And the 'A-intension' is just the function from possible worlds, considered as actual contexts of use of 'water', to A-extensions. So in possible worlds considered as actual, 'water' will pick out whatever substance in those worlds is relevantly superficially similar to water in the actual world. It will pick out whatever watery substance plays the same role vis-à-vis the everyday interactions of agents with their environment as the role played by water in the actual world.

What does all this have to do with conceptual analysis? Suppose we identify concepts with intensions. Conceptual analysis originally sought to uncover the nature of concepts, understood as C-intensions, by revealing their entailment-relations with one another. However, as Quine and Putnam have taught us, such an enterprise is hopeless to the extent that it relies on the contentious rendition of the analytic–synthetic distinction. It turns out that C-intensions depend on what the world is actually like, and no amount of analysis can reveal that all on its own. This hopeless project is what Jackson calls 'ambitious conceptual analysis'. *Non*-ambitious conceptual analysis begins by identifying concepts with A-intensions. These concepts, and their entailment relations, do not depend on what the world is like. They depend on the roles things play in agents' interactions with their environment, the folk theories they happen to uphold, etc. And Jackson considers conceptual analysis of the non-ambitious sort to be both immune from the usual criticisms of traditional conceptual analysis, and indispensable to metaphysics.

Jackson also points out that when a term's A-extension and C-extension differ, there is a difference between the epistemic status of a term's A-extension and its C-extension. He explains it as follows:

[27] *Ibid*, 49.

> The point is that in order to pick out water in a counterfactual world, we need to know something about relationships between the counterfactual world and the actual world that we could only know after discovering that in the actual world H_2O plays the watery role. By contrast, we did know the A-extension of water at every world, for its A-extension does not depend on the nature of the actual world. For the A-extension of T at a world *w* is the extension of T at *w* given *w* is the actual world, and so does not depend on whether or not *w* is in fact the actual world. What we can know independently of what the actual world is like can properly be called a priori. The sense in which conceptual analysis involves the a priori is that it concerns A-extensions at worlds, and so A-intensions, and accordingly concerns something that does, or does not, obtain independently of how things actually are.[28]

Furthermore, Jackson points out that we find our way around buildings by hearing or reading sentences that we understand, such as 'The seminar room is around the corner on the left'. There are many places and possibilities, but by reading or hearing the sentence, and by virtue of understanding it, we know which possibility is actual. He argues that we have a folk theory that ties together understanding, truth and information about possibilities, and that the obvious way to articulate this folk theory is by knowing in which possible worlds it is true or false.[29] However, he tells us, we understand some sentences without knowing the conditions under which they are true, in one sense of the condition under which they are true.[30] He gives the following example: I understand the proposition 'He has a beard', but I do not know the truth-conditions of this proposition, because I do not know who is being spoken of.[31] In other words, we can understand certain sentences by knowing how the proposition expressed depends on context, and it is not necessary to know the sentence's truth-conditions. Jackson asserts that *to know how the proposition expressed depends on context is to know truth-conditions in another sense of a sentences' truth-conditions.*[32]

Jackson argues that there are two superficially different, but essentially identical, accounts of the necessary '*a posteriori*', and he states this as follows:

> Thus, we have two superficially different but essentially identical accounts of the necessary *a posteriori*. One says a sentence like 'water = H_2O' gets to be necessary a posteriori because the proposition it expresses is necessary, but which proposition this is needs to be known in order to understand the sentence, and is an a posteriori matter depend-

[28] *Ibid*, 51.
[29] *Ibid*, 71.
[30] *Ibid*, 72.
[31] *Ibid*, 73.
[32] *Ibid*, 75.

> ing on the nature of the actual world. Little wonder then that it takes empirical work and not just understanding, to see that the proposition expressed and, thereby, the sentence, is necessary. The other says that there are two propositions connected with a sentence like 'water = H_2O', and the sentence counts as necessary if the C-proposition is necessary, but, as understanding the sentence only requires knowing the A-proposition, little wonder that understanding alone is not enough to see that the sentence is necessary. The important point for us is that both stories can be told in terms of one set of possible worlds.[33]

The former discussion illuminates and clarifies Jackson's distinction between ambitious and non-ambitious conceptual analysis. He advocates the idea that fallibility can be reconciled with the '*a priori*' and that conceptual analysis should be practised in its modest or non-ambitious role. In other words, analysis about possibilities should not play a big role in determining what the world is like, and thus, conceptual analysis cannot determine the fundamental nature of our world. Indeed, on the contrary, conceptual analysis is the activity of describing in less fundamental terms, given an account of the world stated in more fundamental terms.[34] This distinction will be elaborated further in the following section.

What is clear is that conceptual analysis is an '*a priori*' task, although this does not mean that the result is not informative. The aim of conceptual analysis is not only to understand, but also to explain properties, things, states of affairs and events in the world. If some of the things said in one vocabulary can be said in another, more basic or fundamental vocabulary, then the analyst is given a description in terms of new properties, state of affairs, events and so on of the concept subject to analysis. Conceptual analysis is, consequently, informational and it should not be, according to Jackson, ambitious.

This means that our intuitions alone should not determine the nature and properties of our concepts. In the past, criticism of conceptual analysis had its basis in the idea that conceptual analysis purported to know the nature and properties of our concepts by means of our intuitions alone. Conceptual analysis is not the trivial task of analysing the meaning of general terms and names in terms of other general terms and names; at the end of the analysis the analyst should have a better understanding of the concept.

Hart has frequently argued that word usage is either misleading, or insufficient to understand or explain the nature of legal concepts. He tells us that there are three recurrent issues in jurisprudence: How does law differ from, and how is it related to, orders backed by threats? How does legal obligation differ from, and how it is related to, moral obligation?

[33] *Ibid,* 77.
[34] *Ibid,* 44.

What are rules, and to what extent is law an affair of rules?[35] He then argues that one way to dispel doubts and perplexity about these issues is to resort to a definition through a typical use-based semantics, which provides an analysis of the day-to-day use of the word in question. However, he claims that even expert lawyers find it difficult to give a definition in this form of legal concepts. They *sense* important distinctions between, for example, morality and law, but they cannot explain these distinctions.[36] Similarly, we recognise an elephant when we see it, but cannot resort to our day-to-day usage to draw the necessary lines and define it.

Hart denies that the purpose of the analysis of legal concepts is to provide a rule by reference to which the correctness of the use of the words can be tested. His interest is in law, coercion and morality as types of *legal phenomena*,[37] and the purpose is to advance legal theory by providing an improved analysis of the distinctive structure of a municipal legal system.[38] Resorting to the usage of words, Hart tells us, in disputes such as that between natural law theorists and positivists on the legal responsibility of German officials during the Nazi regime, can disguise the nature of the disagreement and is usually verbally ill-presented:

> Neither side to the dispute would be content if they were told: 'Yes, you are right, the correct way in English (or in German) of putting that sort of point is to say what you have said'. So, though the positivist might point to a weight of English usage, showing that there is no contradiction in asserting that a rule of law is too iniquitous to be obeyed, and that it does not follow from the proposition that a rule is too iniquitous to obey that it is not a valid rule of law, their opponents will hardly regard this as disposing of the case. Plainly we cannot grapple adequately with this issue if we see it as one concerning the proprieties of linguistic usage. For what really is at stake is the comparative merit of a wider and a narrower concept or way of classifying rules, which belong to a system of rules generally effective in social life. If we are to make a reasoned choice between these concepts, it must be because one is superior to the other in the way in which it will assist our theoretical inquiries, or advance and clarify our moral deliberations, or both.[39]

Hart emphasises the usage of words, but the correctness of this depends on the phenomenon to be described or explained. Consequently, according to Hart, it is not necessarily the case that the phenomenon is correctly explained through a study of the usage of the words. For instance, Hart

[35] HLA Hart, *CL*, 13.
[36] *Ibid*, 13.
[37] *Ibid*, 17.
[38] *Ibid*, 17.
[39] *Ibid*, 204–5.

informs us that the starting-point of Austin's analysis is the concept of 'being obliged': a gunman orders his victim to hand over his purse and threatens to shoot him if he refuses; if the victim complies we say that the victim was 'obliged' to do so.[40] The use of this word is correct because it fits the phenomenon we aim to describe. As regards the main purpose of his book *The Concept of Law*, Hart claims that it is to elucidate the distinction between primary rules of obligation and secondary rules of recognition, change and adjudication, and the union of the two may be regarded as the 'essence' of law though they may not always be found together wherever the word 'law' is correctly used. Moreover, Hart asserts that the union has a great explanatory power.[41] Hart tells us that the use of the words justice and morality might be misleading. These words are used as coextensive. However, in his view, justice should have a more prominent place in the criticism of legal arrangements.[42]

Two examples used by Hart to exercise his conceptual analysis and show that word usage cannot help us in the task of elucidating the nature of our legal concepts are worth mentioning. First, he asks whether the common wider usage of the words 'international law' is likely to obstruct any practical or theoretical aim:[43] his response is positive. Hart argues that the word 'sovereign' is associated with the idea of a person above the law, but it is a bad guide to understanding the concept of 'international law', as it can cause confusion in the theory of international law.[44] Hart subsequently corrects the common usage of the word 'sovereign' and argues that it refers instead to independence, as in the sentence, 'a sovereign state is one not subject to certain types of control, and its sovereignty is that area of conduct in which it is autonomous'.[45]

Second, Hart uses conceptual analysis to elicit our intuitions through possible cases, rather than through our word usage, in his explanation of the concept of legitimate legislative authority. He considers the argument that, to the extent that participants of a community have the habit of obedience to a rule which comes from a particular authority, we can say that this person or body has an authority to legislate. Hart shows us through possible legal worlds that habit of obedience to a rule is neither a sufficient nor a necessary condition of legislative authority, and many legal theorists and lawyers agree with Hart's conceptual analysis of legislative authority because it fits our intuitions about what an authority to legislate is; their agreement is not due to our word usage.

[40] *Ibid*, 6.
[41] *Ibid*, 151.
[42] *Ibid*, 153.
[43] *Ibid*, 209.
[44] *Ibid*, 216.
[45] *Ibid*, 217.

Hart imagines a possible legal world, in which Rex I's rules are habitually obeyed and he may, therefore, be called a 'legislator'. Suppose, however, that a revolution takes place and that a society ceases to have a rule. This may happen during Rex I's lifetime or at the point of transition to a new Rex II, and as a result, either Rex I will lose, or Rex II will not acquire, the right to legislate. Hart argues that mere habit is not sufficient to guarantee Rex II's right to legislate. Rather, there should be a critical reflective attitude to certain patterns of behaviour as a common standard, and this should display itself in criticism, demands for conformity and acknowledgements that such criticism and demands are justified. Hart asserts:

> Even if we concede that a person, such as Rex, whose general orders are habitually obeyed, may be called a legislator and his orders, laws, habits of obedience to each of a succession of such legislators are not enough to account for the *right* of a successor to succeed and for the consequent continuity in legislative power. First, because habits are not 'normative'; they cannot confer rights or authority on anyone. Secondly, because habits of obedience to one individual cannot, though accepted rules can, refer to a class or line of future successive legislators as well as to the current legislator, or render obedience to them likely.[46]

This passage shows how Hart makes his case for eliciting our intuitions about legislative authority, and how his interest does not focus on word usage or on the rationale of conventional rules. You and I do not necessarily agree on shared criteria for applying the concepts of 'obedience' or 'authority'. You and I probably disagree on the criteria for applying the concepts 'habit' or 'obedience'. For example, I think that there are examples of 'obedience' such as the sacrifice of Abraham to God or Saint Therese to her conscience, whereas you might agree on the first and disagree on the latter example. We, nevertheless, are able to have a fruitful and 'genuine' disagreement. Thus the purpose of conceptual analysis, according to Hart, is to reach agreement on our common conceptions and not on our common usage.

Perry has purported to show that conceptual analysis is merely an analysis of our 'local' or 'internal' concepts to understand the central features of a municipal legal system. The generalisation of these features is possible, Perry tells us, because we analyse law in the light of our concept of law. By contrast, we have shown that conceptual analysis is a broader project with metaphysical implications and involves the study of the structure of legal thought.

The second point to be raised is the idea that the acceptance of a wider notion of conceptual analysis which involves the reason-giving character of

[46] *Ibid*, 58.

the law can be reconciled with Hart's conceptual analysis. Thus, Hart has argued that the function of law is to guide the conduct of its citizens, although this function can only be accomplished if the law gives directives that constitute reasons for action. The methodology of conceptual analysis enables the legal theorist to explore through possible cases and intuitions the reason-giving nature of the law. It is, initially, from the legal theorist's conceptual structure that the normative character of the law is explored in order to locate its subject matter. However, conceptual analysis aspires to generalise its insights to the structure of legal thought.

If Perry objects to this view and asserts that this analysis is evaluative, because the starting point is the internal point of view, the reply is that we are happy to accept this terminology and claim that it is an internal point of view. However, what we mean by an 'internal point of view' differs from Perry's understanding, which has a sociological or anthropological connotation. It is internal in the sense that it is from the conceptual structure of the legal theorist. This internal aspect does not make it, however, evaluative. Let us suppose that I would like to analyse the concept of 'legitimate authority', and analyse the different intuitions and possible cases in which we say that a rule has authority. I conclude that in the legal case there must be, according to our intuitions and possible cases, a rule of recognition accepted by the officials that enables us to explain the authority of the law. It is a description of the structure of our legal thought together with an understanding of the reason-giving character of the law. Hence the mistake lies in the idea that external conceptual analysis is a description of the law. On the contrary, conceptual analysis is a description of the structure of legal thought, and the metaphysical assumption is that there is only one structure of legal thought. A more fruitful attack on Hart's methodology should concentrate on this metaphysical presupposition. Sections III and IV will explore this route.

III. HART AND DWORKIN: TWO METHODOLOGICAL VIEWS

In this section the study discusses and criticises the two predominant metaphysical perspectives in legal theory. First, the abstinent view advocated by Dworkin. The Dworkinian attack on metaphysics might be formulated as follows: metaphysics in morality and law involves an Archimedean methodology, which means it is a methodology that aspires both to neutrality and austerity. This means that we need to scrutinize Dworkin's understanding of Archimedeanism. *Neutrality* means, according to Dworkin, that the theorist aims to ground his or her philosophical view without taking sides in substantive moral controversies.[47] *Austerity* involves the idea that the theorist

[47] R Dworkin, 'Objectivity and Truth: You'd Better Believe it' (1996) 25 *Philosophy and Public Affairs* 87 at 92.

will not rely even on very general, or counterfactual, or theoretical or positive moral judgements.[48] Consequently, there are sceptical and non-sceptical versions of Archimedeanism. The external or Archimedean sceptic challenges second-order opinions about substantive moral convictions. The sceptical Archimedean, Dworkin tells us, agrees with most people that genocide and slavery are wrong, for example; but he denies that these practices are 'really' wrong, or that their wrongness is 'out there'. The non-sceptical Archimedean also believes that genocide is morally wrong, but purports to ground morality on the existence of moral facts, which are independent of how we think about them.

Dworkin aims to show that the face-value of our moral judgements is not only expressed in external propositions (e-propositions), but also in internal propositions (i-propositions). Moreover, he challenges austerity and neutrality on the basis that the face-value of morality is expressed inaccurately in terms of e-propositions. The face-value view is the idea that our moral beliefs are true and that this describes our objective matter.[49] Consequently, according to Dworkin's claims, we only need to talk about objectivity and truth in terms of i-propositions.

The challenge to neutrality comprises two arguments. First, the idea that there is a plausible interpretation or translation of all external propositions, and consequently external propositions are really positive moral judgements. The purpose of external propositions, according to Dworkin, is to clarify, emphasise or re-elaborate internal propositions, and terms such as 'objective' or 'really' aim to differentiate qualified opinions from mere matters of taste. Second, Dworkin advances the idea that all interpretations or translations of our external propositions either are i-propositions or have no distinctively philosophical content. For example, a rejection of natural moral realism, which asserts that there are moral properties constituted by physical properties, has its basis in the idea that, according to Dworkin, these external propositions are not philosophical or metaphysical, but are a scientific discovery.[50]

A criticism of Dworkin's view involves an explanation of substantive truth. Substantive truth is very often opposed to conceptual truth, and the contemporary view maintains that substantive truths are discoverable *a posteriori* whereas conceptual truths are discoverable *a priori*. However, in both cases there is 'necessity', and the difficulty follows from understanding what kind of 'necessity' is involved in substantive and conceptual truths. Jackson has argued that there is only one kind of necessity, and that it is a mistake to think in terms of the 'necessary *a posteriori*' and the 'necessary *a priori*' as two different characterisations of reality. This study contends

[48] *Ibid.*
[49] *Ibid*, 93.
[50] *Ibid*, 100.

that this criticism is applicable to Dworkin's challenge to natural moral realism. The fact that substantive truths are discoverable *a posteriori* does not mean that there is not a necessity and a reality that can be explored in metaphysical terms. To oppose the latter view is to advocate the old logical positivist critique and its verificationist approach, which asserts that there are only two kinds of truths: logical or mathematical truths and empirical truths.

Dworkin also attacks natural moral realism on the basis that it cannot explain how natural moral properties impinge upon us and justify our moral convictions. It is a scientific nonsense, Dworkin tells us, to think that there is a direct impact between moral properties and human beings. Dworkin puts this as follows:

> The idea of a direct impact between moral properties and human beings supposes that the universe houses, among its numerous particles of energy and matter, some special particles — morons — whose energy and momentum establish fields that at once constitute the morality or immorality, or virtue or vice, of particular human acts and institutions and also interact in some way with human nervous systems so as to make people aware of the morality or immorality, or of the virtue or vice. We might call this picture the 'moral-field' thesis. If it is intelligible, it is also false. It is not even a remotely plausible thesis to attribute to anyone who might deploy any of the further claims, moreover, quite apart from its insanity as a piece of physics.[51]

Morality, Dworkin points out, fails to meet the test of the moral-field thesis, and therefore any reason we have for abandoning a moral conviction is itself another conviction.[52] We cannot do better, he tells us, and if you cannot help believing something, steadily and wholeheartedly, you'd better believe it.[53] In the beginning and in the end there is just conviction. However, it is arguable that there are other realist metaphysical views that are not undermined by Dworkin's criticism of 'factualism'. Factualism in morality is the view that there are moral facts, whose content are moral properties constituted by physical properties. The moral-field thesis aims to support factualism, but a practical realist such as Korsgaard cannot be classified as a factualist.

Korsgaard has developed an explicitly non-factual development of statements about freedom and responsibility in her piece 'Creating the Kingdom of Ends: Reciprocity and Responsibility in Personal Relations'.[54] The significance and epistemic value for us of statements of responsibility is explained in terms of some favoured role in thought and action. Regardless of its merit as a philosophical view, Korsgaard's view presupposes

[51] *Ibid,* 105.
[52] *Ibid,* 118.
[53] *Ibid,* 118.
[54] C Korsgaard, 'Creating the Kingdom of Ends: Reciprocity and Responsibility in Personal Relations' in *Creating the Kingdom of Ends* (Cambridge, Cambridge University Press, 1996).

a metaphysical conception of the concept of person and practical identity, and is an example of a realist metaphysics that does not involve factualism, and is not neutral either, since it departs from our moral convictions.

One has considerable evidence, Dworkin continues, of our own capacity to make moral judgements that are both durable and constitute convictions. These convictions agree with judgements of other people. Furthermore, he maintains that it is counterintuitive to assert that there is nothing wrong with genocide or slavery, or torturing a baby for fun.[55] Dworkin concludes that we cannot find reasons to justify moral convictions in Archimedean epistemology, since this is a hierarchical epistemology that tries to establish standards for reliable beliefs *a priori*, *ignoring the differences in content between different domains of belief, and taking an account of the range of beliefs we already hold to be reliable.*[56]

This study contends that Dworkin's criticism of hierarchical or Archimedean epistemology is not at odds with descriptive metaphysics or conceptual analysis. The conceptual analyst relies on counterfactual propositions, or moral intuitions or convictions to locate their subject matter and to understand the structure of legal or moral thought, therefore he or she does not aspire to advance a neutral and austere view of morality. It is a view of morality *within* the structure of moral thought. However, whilst conceptual analysts are entitled to believe that the structure of moral thought is part of the reality of morality, this metaphysical presupposition should be challenged.[57] But Dworkin is not in any better position than the conceptual analyst; and like the conceptual analyst, he resorts to counterfactuals and convictions to make his case and to ground moral substantive arguments. The fact that he calls these propositions i-propositions does not make them less metaphysical. We conclude that Dworkin has not shown that a rejection of Archimedeanism entails a rejection of metaphysics.

Interim Conclusions

The study has so far advanced three criticisms of Dworkin's ametaphysical view. First, the argument that substantive truths are necessary and '*a posteriori*'. However, there are not two kinds of necessity: *a posteriori* and *a priori*. It is arguable that there is just one kind of necessity, and therefore substantive truths do not escape metaphysical scrutiny. Second, the idea that a rejection of factualism does not entail a rejection of metaphysics. Third, the argument

[55] R Dworkin (above n 47), 118.
[56] *Ibid*, 119.
[57] Not surprisingly, Perry has argued that there are resemblances between the methodology of conceptual analysis and Dworkin's interpretivism. See Perry (above n 8); also 'Interpretation and Methodology in Legal Theory' in Marmor (ed), *Law and Interpretation* (Oxford, Clarendon Press, 1995), 100–1.

that descriptive metaphysics or conceptual analysis is neither neutral nor austere, since it resorts to counterfactuals and moral convictions to understand the structure of moral thought. The burden of proof is on Dworkin to show the differences between conceptual analysis and his interpretivist view. The conclusion is that Dworkin underestimates the complexity of meta-ethical and metaphysical claims, and that neutrality and austerity are not necessarily standard features of contemporary metaphysical claims in morality and law.

The study so far has shown the weaknesses of Dworkin's abstinent view and has argued that Hart's methodology might be understood as conceptual analysis or descriptive metaphysics. In the light of the weaknesses of Dworkin's abstinent view, are we forced to conclude that Hart's methodology and its metaphysical presupposition is the most appropriate for analysing normative concepts such as the ones contained in law? This conclusion is not endorsed, and it is argued that conceptual analysis or descriptive metaphysics faces a dilemma, which might be formulated as follows: if conceptual analysis is pre-reflective, there is no reason to think that our basic categories and concepts are changeless and not subject to a revision. Moreover, there is no guarantee that the convictions and intuitions at the pre-reflective level are not the creations of the philosopher. On the other hand, if conceptual analysis is neither pre-reflective nor constituted by revisable basic categories, and to the extent that it entails another metaphysical view, then there is no reason to maintain either that revisionary metaphysics is subsidiary to descriptive metaphysics, or that any metaphysics presupposes conceptual analysis.[58] Consequently, basic categories of analysis are either revisable by other basic categories, or represent a metaphysical view that competes with other metaphysical perspectives.

A closer examination of the role of metaphysics and the relationship between revisionary and descriptive metaphysics is required to assess the soundness of this dilemma and its possible solution. The following section discusses the interplay between these two metaphysical approaches.

IV. REVISIONARY AND DESCRIPTIVE METAPHYSICS: INTEGRATION IN LEGAL PHILOSOPHY

Logical Positivists in the 1930s and 1940s thought that metaphysics was a nonsense. It was the target of attacks by Carnap, Ayer and other participants of the Vienna Circle. Aristotle referred to metaphysics as a discipline that studies 'being' as being, and Kant gave a view of metaphysics as an attempt to use pure reason to arrive at an account of a reality which transcends those presuppositions of human understanding. But there must be

[58] In the next section I will explain the distinction between descriptive and revisionary metaphysics.

more to metaphysics. In what follows I will give a view on metaphysics and its relevance to our understanding of the question of what law is, and of possible answers to this question.

With Strawson's work *Individuals*,[59] metaphysics re-gained its place in analytical philosophy. He proposed there a distinction between 'descriptive' and 'revisionary' metaphysics. The latter aims to present the structure of human thought in a better way and to give the 'possibilities' of this structure, whereas the former pursues a description of the basic categories of human thought. I argue both that the sound methodology is to reach a reflective equilibrium between the two metaphysical enterprises and that to progress in the Hart–Dworkin dispute we need to reflect on metaphysical issues. I therefore advance a revisionary metaphysics that could show us the 'possibilities' of our concept of law. However, I further propose both that these 'possibilities' should be revised in terms of 'basic' features of our concept of law and that these 'basic' features are not definite and are subject to change in virtue of our revisionary views.

The key issue is whether there are other philosophical methods to explain or understand the normative aspect of the law together with its social character. It is argued that the concept of law is part of what the law is, and that an elucidation of our concept of law is merely a partial understanding of the law. In other words, the structure of legal thought and the concept of the law is part of the reality of the law. This section is accordingly divided into two parts: a scrutiny of descriptive metaphysics and revisionary metaphysics, and an examination of the interplay between these two kinds of metaphysics.

Descriptive and Revisionary Metaphysics

In this essay, the terms 'conceptual analysis' and 'descriptive metaphysics' have been used interchangeably. Now it is time to justify this terminology. In Section II, we offered an interpretation of Hart's methodology in terms of conceptual analysis, which we also referred to as 'descriptive metaphysics'. Strawson explains the differences between conceptual analysis and descriptive metaphysics as follows:

> The idea of descriptive metaphysics is liable to be met with scepticism. How should it differ from what is called philosophical, logical, or conceptual analysis? It does not differ in kind of intention, but only in scope and generality. Aiming to lay bare the most general features of our conceptual structure, it can take far less for granted than a more limited and partial conceptual inquiry. Hence, also, a certain difference in method. Up to a point, a reliance

[59] PF Strawson, *Individuals* (London, Methuen, 1959).

> upon the close examination of the actual use of words is the best, and indeed the only sure, way in philosophy. But the discriminations we can make, and the connexions we can establish, in this way, are not general enough and not far-reaching enough to meet the full metaphysical demand for understanding. For when we ask how we use this or that expression, our answers, however revealing at a certain level, are apt to assume, and not to expose, those general elements of structure which the metaphysician wants reveal. The structure he seeks does not readily display itself on the surface of language, but lies submerged. He must abandon his only sure guide when the guide cannot take him as far as he wishes to go.[60]

Hart was interested in something more than the mere description of the usage of the words. He points out that his book *The Concept of Law* is concerned with the clarification of the general framework of legal thought,[61] and on a number of occasions affirmed that a mere analysis of words cannot shed light on the legal phenomena. Hart endorses JL Austin's claim for 'a sharpened awareness of words to sharpen our perception of the phenomena'.[62] In his reply to Cohen, he asserts that his methodology is committed to the description of categories and not to the mere description of its usage.[63] Moreover, Hart refers to the linguistic phenomenon as a means to uncover the phenomenon, ie, the existence of a social rule,[64] and he believes that there are general features of law present at all times and places.

As previously noted, there are, according to Hart, three recurrent issues which may be observed:[65] how does law differ from, and how it is related to, orders backed by threats?; how does legal obligation differ from, and how it is related to, moral obligation?; and what are rules, and to what extent is law an affair of rules? Hart subsequently claims that dispelling doubts and perplexities about these three issues has been the main aim of theoretical thinking about the nature of law.[66] He tells us that it is possible to isolate and characterise a central set of elements which form a common part of the answer to all three,[67] and concludes that the purpose of his book is 'to advance legal theory by providing an improved analysis of the distinctive structure of a municipal system and a better understanding of the resemblances and differences between law, coercion, and morality, as types of social phenomena'.[68]

60 *Ibid.*
61 HLA Hart, *CL*, iv.
62 *Ibid.*
63 HLA Hart, 'Reply to Cohen' in 'Symposium: Theory and Definition in Jurisprudence,' (1955) Suppl. Vol XXIX, *Proceedings of the Aristotelian Society*, 245–47.
64 Hart, *CL*, 9.
65 *Ibid*, 7–8.
66 *Ibid*, 13.
67 *Ibid*, 16.
68 *Ibid*, 17.

Descriptive metaphysics faces a dilemma: if conceptual analysis is pre-reflective, there is no reason to think that our basic categories and concepts are changeless and not subject to a revision. Moreover, there is no guarantee that the convictions and intuitions at the pre-reflective level are not the creations of the philosopher. On the other hand, if conceptual analysis is neither pre-reflective nor constituted by revisable basic categories and to the extent that it entails another metaphysical view, then there is no reason to maintain either that revisionary metaphysics is subsidiary to descriptive metaphysics, or that any serious metaphysics presupposes conceptual analysis. Consequently, basic categories of analysis are revisable by other categories or represent a metaphysical view that competes with other metaphysical perspectives.

The first horn of the dilemma considers that there are pre-reflective and basic categories; however, these basic categories are not changeless, so how should we interpret the fact that there are basic categories but that they can change? Let us scrutinise the idea that descriptive metaphysics aims to reveal basic categories of thought. It is arguable that descriptive metaphysics, to some extent, marks a return to Kant; a revival not exactly of his doctrines but of his method of approach.[69] Descriptive metaphysics is the view that it is impossible to test any theory directly, as it were, against the facts, it is only within a structure that any meaning can be given to the concepts which are under review; and the only conceivable structure in which they could operate is that which actually does govern human thinking about the world. It is assumed that no other categorial structure is possible if human beings are to be the kind of beings that they are. In what sense are these basic categories pre-reflective?

Basic categories are prior to any thinking and any theory. The way human beings think about themselves or their world is something so natural and inevitable that it would never occur to them to call this way of thinking a theory. Thus, no person is in a position to alter the fact that he or she is a person who exists in a spatio-temporal world amongst other objects and persons.[70] It can be argued that it is not that ordinary usage sets any kind of philosophical standard, but rather that because these concepts can be used successfully in practice, it is not open to the philosopher to charge their ordinary use with being right or wrong.[71] This means, to paraphrase Kant and Wittgenstein, that the limits of human knowledge are set by the categorical structure of human thinking as it is.

McDougall, in his article 'Descriptive and Revisionary Metaphysics', has raised the point that although these concepts are central to human

[69] AJ Ayer, 'Philosophy and Language' in *The Concept of a Person and Other Essays* (London, Macmillan, 1963), 33.
[70] D McDougall, 'Descriptive and Revisionary Metaphysics' (1973) 34 *Philosophy and Phenomenological Research* 209–21, at 212.
[71] *Ibid*, 217.

thinking about the world, they do not in themselves determine in advance any particular theoretical framework which by itself can support a definite analysis of their meaning. He argues that they set general limitations on the possibility of human knowledge. The commitments are wholly general: no specific philosophical theory can be deduced from them in isolation. They do not specify any particular framework in which thought about the structure of human thinking should be carried out. This interpretation enables us to reconcile the two views, namely, that there are pre-reflective categories and that they change. It also explains Strawson's view:

> There is a massive central core of human thinking which has no history — or none recorded in history of thought; there are categories and concepts which, in their most fundamental character, change not at all. Obviously these are not the specialities of the most refined thinking. They are the commonplaces of the least refined thinking; and are yet the indispensable core of the conceptual equipment of the most sophisticated human beings. It is with these, their interconnexions, and the structure that they form, that a descriptive metaphysics will be primarily concerned. Metaphysics has a long and distinguished history, and it is consequently unlikely that there are any new truths to be discovered in descriptive metaphysics. But this does not mean that the task of descriptive metaphysics has been, or can be, done once for all. It has constantly to be done over again. If there are no new truths to be discovered, there are old truths to be rediscovered. For though the central subject-matter of descriptive metaphysics does not change, the critical and analytical idiom of philosophy changes constantly. Permanent relationships are described in an impermanent idiom, which reflects both the age's climate of thought and the individual philosopher's personal style of thinking. No philosopher understands his predecessors until he has re-thought their thought in his own contemporary terms.[72]

A plausible interpretation of this passage is that the subject matter of metaphysics, which is the structure of thought, does not change, only our critical and analytical idiom changes. Strawson also argues that there is room for a revisionary critique, but that the merits of revisionary metaphysics should be assessed in terms of descriptive metaphysics:

> Certainly concepts do change, and not only, though mainly, on the specialist periphery; and even specialist changes react on ordinary thinking. Certainly, too, metaphysics has been largely concerned with such changes, in both the suggested ways. The productions of revisionary metaphysics remain permanently interesting, and not only as key episodes in the history of thought. Because of their articulation, and the intensity of their partial vision, the best of them are both intrinsically admirable and of enduring philosophical utility. But this last merit can be ascribed to them only because there is another kind

[72] PF Strawson (above n 59), 10–11.

> of metaphysics which needs no justification at all beyond that of inquiry in general. Revisionary metaphysics is at the service of descriptive metaphysics.[73]

Is Strawson saying that if the views of revisionary metaphysics persist and are shown to be of utility, it is because the revisionary critique has revealed the structure of our thought and that it has therefore become descriptive metaphysics? In this sense, revisionary metaphysics is subsidiary to descriptive metaphysics. Moreover, in a less modest interpretation of Strawson's view, revisionary metaphysics collapses into descriptive metaphysics. Yet there is no test that will guarantee that we are revealing the structure of thought; since we cannot resort to facts, we cannot say which one of two competing philosophical views is the true structure of thought. The only test is their 'enduring philosophical utility'.

Descriptive Metaphysics vs Revisionary Metaphysics

I will focus now on the second horn of the dilemma: that descriptive and revisionary metaphysics are two competing metaphysical views. How are we to choose between them? One cannot refer to facts, and it is not possible to resort to basic notions such as 'intuitions' or basic categories. In any case, if there are basic categories, they are categories such as time, space and causality, and it is difficult to make a case about essential features of the law on the basis of these categories. It is arguable that descriptive and revisionary metaphysics should stand in reflective equilibrium with each other. Nevertheless, any revisionary critique needs to face the difficulty that the theoretician cannot stand outside the world and can only revise within his conceptual scheme. On the other hand, the conceptual analyst needs to explain and give a complete story of our thought, the world and the relationship between them, and this is the task of revisionary metaphysics.

Methodologies in legal theories tend either to have focused on a description of the structure of legal thought, or have claimed that because we cannot explain the relationship between legal and moral thought and the world, we need to reject both the structure of the legal thought and the world. Consequently, we can only interpret our practices and be guided by our moral convictions. For good or for bad, we cannot do better.

However, there is an interesting insight in Dworkin's critique of Hart's methodology: the idea that the structure of our legal thought is not the only subject matter of theoretical reflection in law. The legal theorist might begin with the ordinary use of our concepts, but he still needs to make something of that. The structure of our legal thought establishes the boundaries of

[73] *Ibid*, 9–10.

legal knowledge, but these boundaries leave many possibilities open, and it is the task of revisionary metaphysics to explore these possibilities. It is argued here that there should be a reflective equilibrium between revisionary and descriptive metaphysics. Thus, we need to suspend our judgements about the ordinary use of our concepts and consider the array of possibilities that can explain the nature of law; at the same time, these possibilities should be considered in the light of our intuitions about the law, and these intuitions should be tested against our revised intuitions. The legal theorist is entitled to revise his or her intuitions and to balance these changes against other possible and actual concepts.

In the context of legal theory, the proposal is faithful to the view that the 'internal point of view' is not a social fact or a conceptual truth that the legal theoretician merely discovers and describes; rather, the internal point of view is a set of conceptions and changing views about the value, or point, of law. The 'internal point of view' is neither an evaluative point of view that interpretivism constructs according to the two criteria of fitness and appealing. The methodology that I advance tries to understand and explain the best structure of law, rather than to describe our concept of law. However, it also supports the idea that the best structure of the law is true.

V. CONCLUSION

We have criticised the two metaphysical views that have been advanced in contemporary legal theory, and argue that an examination of the role of revisionary metaphysics might enable legal theorists to overcome the difficulties and distinctions encountered in recent methodological debates. There is still much to revise and to describe, and issues such as whether there is a relationship between morality and law, or whether there is plausible explanation of features such as objectivity and indeterminacy, or the understanding of notions such as 'authority' and 'obligatory', need to be scrutinised in the light of a different methodology. It is not reasonable anymore, it seems to me, to argue that there are features of the law because they are revealed by the structure of our legal thought, or that we can only resort to interpretation to make sense of what the law is because we cannot do better. The aim of the article has been rather modest: to show that both to revise and to describe cannot be done without metaphysics.

5

Normative Knowledge and the Nature of Law

GEORGE PAVLAKOS[1]

1. INTRODUCTION

IN THE OPENING pages of *The Concept of Law*, Herbert Hart argued for the pressing need to offer a fresh account of the nature of law (or the concept of law) for earlier and contemporary legal theories had merely amounted to a partial account of law's nature, upon which remark he set out to offer a full account of 'the concept of law'.[2]

Although Hart did not expand much on what a partial account of law may consist in, a useful way to read his observation is in the light of the concept of *knowledge*. Incontrovertibly, any theoretical inquiry aims at the increase of knowledge with respect to the object of the inquiry. To that extent, it is meaningful to ask whether any particular legal theory succeeds in generating knowledge with respect to law (*legal knowledge*). Succinctly put, this shall be the case when a theory manages to elucidate the conditions — or, to follow an established term, the 'grounds' — that render propositions of law true. Seen in this light, Hart's observation amounts to the criticism that

[1] For valuable comments I would like to thank the participants of the workshop in analytical jurisprudence that took place in October 2002 at the Queen's Law School, and in particular Sean Coyle for his splendid editorial comments. Carsten Heidemann, Veronica Rodriguez-Blanco and Ian O'Flynn spent a considerable amount of time on earlier drafts of the chapter, their comments leading to considerable improvements in the structure and clarity of the argument. I would further like to thank the participants of the 2002 annual meeting of the Irish Philosophical Club where a very early version of this paper was presented; Robert Alexy and the members of his *Doktorantenseminar* at the Kiel Law School; and the audience of a lecture reflecting the main ideas of the chapter which I gave in CIRFID at the University of Bologna. Last but not least, I am greatly indebted to Professor Martha Fineman who made possible a two-week visiting fellowship on the Gender, Sexuality and Family Project at the Cornell Law School, during which a substantial part of this essay was completed.

[2] HLA Hart, *The Concept of Law,* 2nd edn (Oxford, Clarendon Press, 1994). That Hart's analysis is much broader than a semantic account of legal meaning is something that I will take for granted here. This view seems to be a commonplace in the contemporary literature. But see M Moore, *Educating Oneself in Public: Critical Essays in Jurisprudence* (Oxford, Oxford University Press, 2000), especially chs 1 and 3.

legal theories, up to the time he was writing, had failed to pick the appropriate grounds regarding the truth of legal propositions and, hence, had failed to offer a full account of law's nature.

The concept of legal knowledge is particularly apt for evaluating legal theories (including Hart's own), or so I will argue. Its aptness lies in the fact that it is an especially demanding concept, for it requires that any theoretical account of law meet certain conditions in order for its findings to relate to law's nature. Although a full story of knowledge escapes the scope of this essay, I offer a brief account in part 2 of the essay. Once the requirements for legal knowledge have become relatively clear, I move on to a classification of legal theories with respect to their ability to meet these requirements (parts 3 and 4). There I distinguish between two types of legal theory: *Jurisscientia* and *Jurisprudentia*. I take the former to comprise legal theories which fail to generate legal knowledge, whereas the latter are those that are successful in doing so. In conclusion, parts 5 and 6 of the essay attempt to consolidate the distinction between *Jurisscientia* and *Jurisprudentia* by way of relating it to the meta-ethical discussion with respect to the nature of the evidence that amounts to normative knowledge. Although legal theory is not always conscious of that debate, it is nonetheless of great value in illustrating the potential that various legal theories have for generating normative knowledge.[3] What is more, the meta-ethical discussion is particularly apt in clarifying our views with respect to the potential of legal theories to produce knowledge (and to prompt a classification that is more surprising than one ever thought).

2. KNOWLEDGE AND LEGAL THEORY

The concept of knowledge refers to the relation between minds and the environment.[4] Things, however, are more complicated than that. Knowledge is a demanding concept, and not just any link between the mind and the environment will do: if I believe that something is the case and it turns out that my belief is true, it is far from certain that I also *know* that that thing is the case. To put it in a more technical language, not every true proposition p amounts to knowledge but, instead, in order to know p I need to stand in a special relation to the content of p. The special character of the relation relates to the *evidence* I associate with the truth of the proposition in question. It is only by picking those facts that actually make proposition p true that I come to know p. In contrast, reference to any other fact that

[3] An implicit assumption of the chapter is that legal and moral knowledge are two species of the same kind: normative knowledge.

[4] Here I allude to the view that knowledge is a truth-entailing mental state. This view has found its best expression in T Williamson, *Knowledge and its Limits* (Oxford, Oxford University Press, 2000).

merely appears to ground the truth of *p* amounts to a failure to produce knowledge, for *random truth does not constitute knowledge.*

The standard demonstration of this failure is to be found in Gettier,[5] who argues that even if one has reasons to believe that *p* and *p* turns out true, one might still fail to know *p*. Suppose I am visiting my friend David and minutes after my arrival someone delivers at his door a bottle of Scotch. David takes the bottle into the kitchen and seconds later reappears with a glass containing an ochre liquid in his hand. Given my evidence, I am perfectly justified in believing that David is having a glass of Scotch. However, my justified belief is not sufficient for knowledge, even if the liquid in David's glass is indeed the same Scotch. For suppose that David had actually poured himself a glass of Scotch from a different bottle earlier that day and left it, forgotten, in the kitchen. In this case the truth of my belief is not grounded on the facts that constitute my evidence but on a different fact which I ignore. Here, my belief is only randomly true, and random truth is insufficient for knowledge.

The discrepancy between evidence and truth is of particular significance in the case of theory. Theories aim to increase our knowledge with respect to a domain of inquiry. If a theory fails to refer to the evidence (facts) that ground the truth of the propositions it advances then it fails to generate knowledge with respect to its propositions, with a handful of undesirable consequences.[6] Consider, for instance, that I am putting forward a theory regarding the contents of glasses in David's apartment. If I limit my inquiry either to facts that support justified true beliefs or to irrelevant facts (say, facts about David's emotional states), I will fail to generate knowledge with respect to my subject. What is more, if I rely on such a line of inquiry that falls short of knowledge, I will soon end up making wrong assumptions about the environment and will have a hard time in matching coherently my beliefs with the environment (eg, if I conclude that 'the man who is drinking the Scotch just delivered at his door is my best friend' my belief will be false, for either it would fail to depict David or it would depict somebody else — say David's flatmate who, unbeknown to me, opened the new bottle).

Things are, of course, more complicated in the domain of law. Be that as it may, the main point holds here too: a legal theory that fails to pick the appropriate evidence falls short of generating knowledge regarding its subject matter (law's nature). This is not hard to imagine: a theory might hold a proposition of law to be true on grounds that do not relate properly to the truth of the proposition, thus failing to generate legal knowledge (eg, by arguing that proposition *p* is legal on the grounds that it is stated in a work

[5] The *locus classicus* is E Gettier, 'Is True Justified Knowledge Belief?' in (1963) 23 *Analysis* 121–3.

[6] See A Bird, 'Progress and Knowledge' (unpublished manuscript, read on 17 July 2003 at the British Society for the Philosophy of Science Annual Conference in Belfast). Many thanks to Alexander Bird for passing on the manuscript to me.

by Shakespeare). Ordinary cases of failure of legal knowledge tend to be far less extravagant than the one just mentioned. Setting aside the details of an exact typology, such cases are generally associated with legal theories that capture truth conditions of legal propositions through the formula '*P* is legal if and only if contained in a statute or decided case'. The resulting failure of legal knowledge, sooner or later, amounts to erroneous statements regarding various aspects of the law: the existence or non-existence of gaps in the law, the correctness of an interpretation or the question which norms should be included in the legal system. In contrast, the chances of legal knowledge increase when a theory expands its understanding of the grounds of legal propositions by including into them practical reasons for action: '*P* is legal only if it is justified in the light of all relevant reasons for action'. Bearing this rough categorisation in mind, I shall now briefly turn to sketch two ways in which a legal theory may fail to produce legal knowledge.

3. FAILURES OF LEGAL KNOWLEGDE

The first way in which a legal theory might go wrong is by limiting its inquiry to the internal mental states of the members of a linguistic community (*the objection of internalism*). The objection of internalism has been chiefly directed against legal theories that attempt to illuminate law's nature by way of referring to a set of criteria for the use of legal expressions.[7] These criteria may be stated through an analysis of the conceptual requirements of legal meaning (*conceptual analysis*)[8] and subsequently grouped together into a convention for the correct use of legal expressions (*legal conventionalism*).[9] To the extent that such criteria are treated as exclusive evidence with respect to the truth of legal propositions, conventionalist theories fail to generate proper knowledge; in the best case they may amount to justified true beliefs in the sense explained earlier. Instead, the objector continues, a proper check of the truth of legal propositions should involve facts outside the usage of legal language, facts that are usage-independent

[7] This is the standard accusation directed by Dworkin and, more recently, Stavropoulos, against semantic or conventionalist legal theories. See R Dworkin, *Law's Empire* (London, Fontana Press, 1986), especially chs 1–2 and 4, and N Stavropoulos, *Objectivity in Law* (Oxford, Clarendon Press, 1996). See also Stavropoulos, 'Hart's Semantics' in J Coleman (ed.), *Hart's Postscript: Essays on the Postscript to the 'Concept of Law'* (Oxford, Oxford University Press, 2001), 59–98.

[8] The most credible account of conceptual analysis in recent years comes from F Jackson, *From Metaphysics to Ethics* (Oxford, Clarendon Press, 1999). For a defence of his ideas in the realm of law, see V Rodriguez-Blanco (this volume).

[9] Hart's theory is taken to be the standard instance of conventionalism in law. See R Dworkin, (above n 7), ch 4. Theories like Austin's may also be included under the conventionalist heading, albeit they represent a cruder form of empiricism, for they offer an all-purpose formula containing a set of necessary and sufficient criteria of legality that may be ascertained on empirical grounds.

and pertain to the substance of law, which they take to be mind-independent and, hence, objective.[10] It is only against the background of this type of fact that we may accommodate the possibility of error and the need for revising our beliefs in the light of new evidence about 'how law actually is', a revision that is necessary in order to arrive at legal knowledge proper.

Admittedly the merit of the objection depends on what kind of fact the objector assumes conventionalism takes to underpin the criteria of legal meaning. Most critics allege that conventionalism (even in its sophisticated versions)[11] takes conventional criteria to consist of 'shallow' facts about the behaviour of the linguistic community, thus *reducing* law's normativity to non-normative aspects of the (social) environment. As a result, in order to accuse conventionalism of promoting reductionism, it is not enough to say that conventionalist accounts pick out criteria that are internal to legal practice but, more crucially, that these criteria consist entirely of descriptive facts.[12] It follows that internalism and conceptual analysis amount only *contingently* to a reduction of conventional criteria to brute behavioural facts and that, otherwise, they are perfectly compatible with accounts that accept the autonomy of the legal domain as one with a distinct normative character.[13] Thus, the objection of internalism meets its target only if it is topped up with reductionism and/or empiricism. What really undermines legal knowledge, then, is not internalism but a deficient explication of the evidence that underpins legal propositions as non-evaluative, descriptive facts. This explication is not necessarily connected to either internalism or conceptual analysis. In fact, as I am going to argue in the course of this chapter, the possibility of legal knowledge requires a certain form of internalism, one that acknowledges that normativity cannot be conceived of independently of our thought and its constructions.[14]

The second way legal theory may go wrong with respect to legal knowledge is by committing a category error, or by picking out facts that are *metaphysically* inert for grounding the truth of legal propositions. This is the case when a theory reduces law's normativity and takes *non-normative*

[10] Theories of this kind are often labelled *substantive*. Typical example of a substantive theory is Dworkin's, *Law's Empire* (above n 7). In addition, most natural law theories would count as substantive given their interest in law's normative nature. See for instance M Moore (above n 2) and J Finnis, *Natural Law and Natural Rights* (Oxford, Clarendon Press, 1980).

[11] See above n 8.

[12] Whether every conventionalist account necessarily collapses into reductionism, is a different story. A positive answer would require that conventional criteria be necessarily defined as value-free descriptive facts. There is no good reason to support such a view. Far from being necessary, the association of conventionalism with reductionism has a historical explanation. Despite the fact that conventionalism grew within the positivist camp in order to resist naive reductionist accounts of law, it never managed to escape the framework posed by the positivist insight for the separation of law and morality. Given the centrality of this insight for positivism, conventionalist accounts of law would always confine themselves to descriptions, albeit much more elaborate ones that those of the early positivists.

[13] But see N Stavropoulos, 'Hart's Semantics' (above n 7).

[14] See this chapter, at 6.3, below.

facts to ground the truth of legal propositions (*the objection of reductionism*). Reductionism can be seen as cutting across the issue of internalism, for even if a theory switches from criteria for the use of legal language to usage-independent facts about the law, it may still fail to generate legal knowledge if it chooses to limit itself to evidence that is value-free or empirical. One word of caution should be added: reductionism pertains not only to straightforward empiricist legal theories but, what is more, to theories that advocate the existence of evaluative entities that exist in the environment (independently of our minds) and can be perceived in a sensorial or quasi-sensorial way. (We can call these entities and the theories that postulate them *platonic.*) It is often the case that, once they discover that there is nothing out there to tease our senses, platonic theories end up replacing platonic entities with value-free empirical entities or facts, thus evoking anew the objection of reductionism.[15]

Given these types of failure of legal knowledge, legal theories can be taken to fall under either of two kinds, depending on what they consider as evidence for legal knowledge. The first I call *Jurisscientia* (or simply *scientia*). Roughly speaking, *scientia* has it that our knowledge as regards law is not very different from our knowledge about tables, chairs, mountains and the other entities that compose our physical environment. This similarity is suggested on the grounds that both sorts of knowledge rest on the same type of evidence, ie, phenomenal evidence[16] and, hence, legal knowledge is deemed a species of *phenomenal knowledge*. In contrast, the second kind of legal theory, *Jurisprudentia* (or simply *prudentia*), maintains that legal knowledge is of a different kind altogether, because it involves entities that are inherently practical, or action-guiding (eg, statutes, contracts, rights and so on), about which we cannot have (non-trivial) phenomenal evidence. Mere reference to things such as acts of will or enactment, commands, sovereigns, sanctions and so on is insufficient for grounding the truth of legal propositions. Instead, what is required is reference to norms, rules, principles, chains of valid inferences, argumentative schemata and, in general, things that are non-perceptible. To the extent that these entities are not phenomenal, *prudentia* solicits a kind of knowledge that is *noumenal*.

Alternatively, the difference between *scientia* and *prudentia* can be illustrated by the asymmetry in cognitive content between *prudentia*-propositions and *scientia*-propositions. True *p*-propositions convey knowledge that is not equivalent to the one conveyed by true *s*-propositions. Moreover, the asymmetry is more than a mere change of viewpoint, in that *p*-propositions denote entities that are more basic for an account of law than those denoted by *s*-propositions. Hence any account of law that is limited to *s*-propositions will

15 See this chapter, 6.2.1, below.

16 As already noted, the concept of phenomenality captures both evidence that is value-free or empirical, and evidence that is evaluative and perceptible.

fail to capture essential aspects of legal phenomena. The asymmetry between the two types of propositions springs from law's normative (or action-guiding) character, and reflects the idea that there are better and worse ways of accounting for it. Despite the fact that most legal theories would agree that law is action-guiding, not all manage to account for this fact successfully (theories that dispute the normative character of law altogether shall remain outside the scope of this paper). *Prudentia*-type theories succeed in capturing law's normativity by demonstrating how legal propositions generate reasons for action (below 4.2). *Scientia*-type theories, on the other hand, fail at precisely this point: they either eschew any reference to the reason-giving function of law (some crude forms of empiricism, below 4.1) or, alternatively, fail to account for the reason-giving function of law, despite purporting or proclaiming to do so (conventionalism but even interpretivism, below 4.1). On the face of it, the asymmetry in cognitive content between *p*-propositions and *s*-propositions stems from their respective ability to generate normative knowledge by picking the appropriate evidence (ie, by referring to the relevant reasons for action).

Before fleshing out *scientia* and *prudentia*, a short comment is needed on the meaningfulness of metaphysical inquiries into the nature of law. This type of inquiry has been repeatedly stigmatised as a sterile version of Archimedeanism, for it assumes that there is a privileged viewpoint outside any particular practice from which one can study the law.[17] To concede such criticism would amount to questioning the possibility of inquiring into the nature of law in a general way. This would, however, undermine the possibility of maintaining some critical distance from any practice and reflecting upon its most general characteristics. Rejection of the latter possibility would be far too hasty. This should be deemed true even if this type of reflection would eventually lead to the conclusion that there is very little to say about law's nature once we have stepped outside legal practice. For even then, theoretical inquiry will have clarified the focus or the point of the practice, a clarification that is absolutely essential for determining what counts as part of the practice. The truth of this statement can be illustrated on the example of theories that vehemently reject the meaningfulness of any general philosophical enquiry about the law, condemning it as a form of sterile Archimedeanism. On a closer look, such theories appear to be working as general metaphysical theories themselves: the most characteristic example is here Dworkin. Dworkin is entitled to conclude that (Hartian) positivism is Archimedean only *ex post facto*, ie, after he has argued in detail about the nature of the things that make legal propositions true and

[17] The *locus classicus* for a powerful rejection of any detached, metaphysical inquiry into the nature of law is R Dworkin, 'Objectivity and Truth: You'd Better Believe It' (1996) 25 *Philosophy and Public Affairs* 87; and very recently his, 'Hart's Postscript and the Character of Political Philosophy' (2004) 24 *OJLS* 1.

on the basis of this discussion has dismissed all rival theories as erroneous. Law, he announces then, is not about value-free facts that deliver the formula of legality, but about the realisation of integrity within the normative practices of a political community. Yet his 'attached' conclusion is heavily determined by his prior 'detached' analysis.

4. *SCIENTIA* AND *PRUDENTIA*

4.1 *Scientia*

Scientia comprises all legal theories that study law as a causal phenomenon. The main feature of these theories is that they ground their knowledge of law exclusively on phenomenal evidence about certain aspects of the environment that pertain either to external properties of legal entities, or to facts about the practice of the legal community (social facts). Under the first category falls evidence about the role of the law-creator (sovereign), the expression of a will (command), as well as evidence about sanctions.[18] On the other hand, social facts are increasingly complex and refer to more comprehensive aspects of the legal practice than do simple features of legal entities.[19] In addition, the idea of a social fact is alleged to incorporate certain normative elements that elude the rather thin notion of isolated features of legal entities, as is illustrated, for instance, by Hart's criticism of Austinian jurisprudence with respect to the latter's inability to account for the notion of obligation. Be that as it may, social facts are still treated as being part of the environment and, hence, are regarded as constituting phenomenal evidence for legal knowledge,[20] a fact that might seriously compromise the purported account of law's normative or action-guiding nature. Associated with this failure are, in particular, two features of *scientia*: observation and externality.

Typical for *scientia* is the use of the vocabulary of *observation*. Hart envisages the role of the legal theorist as that of the social scientist who *observes* the participants of a social practice from a distance and gathers (phenomenal) evidence in order to reconstruct that practice.[21] This applies

[18] This type of *scientia* roughly depicts Austin's legal theory.

[19] An example of a social fact is the use of the language of obligation on behalf of a group of officials with respect to some pattern of behaviour of the same group. This form of *scientia* characterises Hart's theory of law.

[20] Stated in terms of the so-called fact-value dichotomy, social facts still fall on the fact side. See also below.

[21] See especially Hart's claim that his legal theory is descriptive sociology. See HLA Hart (above n 2), v. The insistence on observation goes hand in hand with the fact-value dichotomy that pertains to the positivist philosophy of the 20th century and whose roots are to be found in the work of the representatives of the so-called Vienna circle. In order to sustain a sharp distinction between fact and value, the movement of positivism identified a fact with 'something

not only to the non-normative aspects of the practice, but also to the normative aspects thereof, ie, those aspects that render the practice capable of obligating actors. For instance, in order to state the Rule of Recognition, his version of the master-rule for a legal system, Hart asks the theorist to consider evidence that pertains, first, to the behaviour of officials and, second, to the external demonstration of the officials' belief that they are obligated, be it through the uttering of certain words or the performance of certain actions.[22] As a result, the evidence that the theorist considers does at no instance extend beyond the external, phenomenal features of actors' individual or collective behaviour. What is more, these features are considered sufficient in inferring the internal, normative aspects of the practice. In a nutshell, the condition of observation states that a careful recording of social facts, on behalf of the legal scientist, exhausts the available evidence regarding legal phenomena.

In addition, *scientia* aims to be an *external* legal theory.[23] This is in particular the claim that knowledge with respect to the phenomenal aspects of law exhausts all there is to know about the normativity of law. Externality underpins the belief in the observational character of *scientia*, in that it expresses the deeper metaphysical thesis for the reducibility of normative facts to facts that are value-free and phenomenal.[24] Accordingly, to refer specifically to Hart, the legal theorist, in accounting for law's normative nature, is not required to consider actual reasons for action but, instead, facts about the behaviour of certain actors who take themselves to be obligated. It follows that knowledge about law's normativity is reduced to knowledge about the *appearance of law's normativity*, the latter consisting in sets of descriptive facts.[25] The success of the reduction depends heavily upon stating a corpus of theoretical sentences that would illustrate the connections between phenomenal propo-

that could be certified through mere observation or even a mere report of a sensory experience', see H Putnam, *The Collapse of the Fact/Value Dichotomy* (Cambridge Mass, Harvard University Press, 2002), 22; and his very recent, *Ethics without Ontology* (Cambridge, Mass, Harvard University Press, 2004), where he discusses the futility of 'neutral' ontological discussions of ethics.

22 See HLA Hart (above n 2). But see M Moore (above n 2) and R Dworkin (above n 7).

23 For an illuminating discussion of the possibility of Hart's external account, see M Moore (above n 2), ch 3.

24 Reductionism differs from non-cognitivism in that it endorses the possibility of normative knowledge via phenomenal evidence, as opposed to the latter's complete denial of normative knowledge. However, to the extent that non-normative evidence might fail to generate normative knowledge, the line that separates reductionism from non-cognitivism is not particularly sharp. See the discussion of normative knowledge, below.

25 This point that has been developed over the last two decades by Gerald Postema in a series of essays. See GJ Postema, 'Coordination and Convention at the Foundations of Law' (1982) 11 *Journal of Legal Studies* (1982) 165; 'The Normativity of Law' in R Gavison (ed), *Issues in Contemporary Legal Philosophy* (Oxford, 1986), 81–104; 'Legal Theory as Practical Philosophy' (1998) 4 *Legal Theory* (1998) 329; and 'Norms, Reasons and Law' (1998) 51 *Current Legal Problems* 149–79. Many thanks to Sean Coyle for drawing my attention to this connection.

sitions about appearances of obligation and higher-order normative propositions about actual obligating reasons. Besides being unlikely that legal theorists will ever spent any time on such a task, an enquiry into its viability escapes the scope of this paper. A more modest task that can be undertaken at present is to suggest that external propositions about appearances of obligation are true of law's normative nature only contingently. However, if external propositions tell us something true about law's normative nature only by chance, then they fail to generate any knowledge regarding this nature, and the project of *scientia* is thrown into question.[26]

Scientia-type legal theories may be further distinguished in two categories: empiricist or conventionalist. A third category, interpretivist theories, will be explored towards the end of this section. (The reader should be warned that the inclusion of interpretivism[27] in *scientia* is not straightforward: interpretivism constitutes an instance of legal science not because it reduces law's sing normativity.)

Empiricism is the archetypal case of *scientia*. This is roughly the view that the study of certain facts about the environment (be they natural or social) will amount to a full account of legal phenomena. An obvious implication of this proposition is that any legal theory that solicits it must also hold that law is essentially empirical. It is useful to remark that empiricism in legal theory may come in two forms: a closed, static form and an open-ended, dynamic form. The static form corresponds roughly to John Austin's understanding of law as amounting from a closed set of conditions. Here legal phenomena are explained as complex empirical phenomena that can be reduced to a set of more basic empirical phenomena which, if taken together, amount to a universal formula of legality. In other words, to the question 'what evidence elicits our knowledge of the law (legal knowledge)?' Austin's answer points to the conjunction of a sovereign, a command and an adjacent sanction, that is, to a relatively small set of empirical facts that fully determines the essence of law. Thus, in order to affirm the existence of a legal rule all the lawyer needs to do is to check

[26] A claim in the opposite direction is raised by sophisticated forms of *scientia* like Hart's, which argue that they can actually offer an external analysis of law's normativity, as opposed to naive versions that may do so only contingently. In Hart this claim is famously formulated as the juxtaposition between the concepts of 'being obligated' and 'being obliged': although sophisticated *scientia* manages to offer an account of obligation by selecting the appropriate external facts, naive *scientia* amounts to crude descriptions of patterns of behaviour that cannot discriminate between 'being obligated' and 'being obliged'. Despite raising this claim, sophisticated *scientia* fails to fulfil it. For a detailed demonstration of the failure see G Pavlakos, 'Book Review of Michael Moore *Educating Oneself in Public*' (2003) 54 *NILQ* 201.

[27] For a succinct, albeit authoritative, discussion of interpretivism, see N Stavropoulos, 'Interpretivist Theories of Law' in *The Stanford Encyclopedia of Philosophy (Winter October 2003 Edition)*, (Zalta, ed), <http://plato.stanford.edu/archives/win2003/entries/law-interpretivist/>.

whether the facts of the formula obtain. To that extent, Austin's theory is a paradigmatic instance of legal theory as a science, or *scientia*.[28]

Once the circle of the evidence relevant to legal knowledge is broadened in order to include empirical facts of a wide variety (psychological, sociological, economical and so on), *scientia* loses its static character and becomes dynamic. Instead of relying upon a rigid definition, dynamic legal science departs from a variety of factors that can causally affect human behaviour and uses the quantifying laws of social sciences in order to produce nomological predictions about the law. What the law is (ie, its nature) is what the laws of social sciences tell us it is. Once again legal phenomena are thought of as being essentially empirical.[29] All in all, empiricist legal theory, be it static or dynamic, rests on the implicit assumption that there is nothing special about legal phenomena, and that in order to achieve a full account of law we need to reduce legal phenomena to some kind of empirical phenomena that can be studied through the established methods and laws of the social sciences.

Conventionalism is the view that the environment normatively determines law's nature, where 'environment' is understood as the social environment that is constituted by our social practices (institutional theories of law fall under this category too).[30] Here the nature of law (manifested in the meaning of legal propositions and the content of legal concepts) is exhausted by a social convention. Provided that speakers understand the convention, they can partake of (know) the meaning of legal expressions. Two problems may arise in this context: the first has to do with the requirements for understanding the convention. Conventionalists have traditionally assumed that all it takes to understand the content of the convention is to check whether certain value-free, descriptive facts obtain. This understanding does not derive from a conceptual necessity but has been the contingent product of a historical association of conventionalism with positivism. Along these lines Hart seems very often to argue that the fundamental convention of any legal system (the so-called Rule of Recognition) is usually asserted on the basis of a series of brute facts. Such an understanding, however, makes social validity not very different from the empiricist conceptions mentioned earlier. Once again the concern is reiterated that any explication of social

[28] Of course Austinian scholars would deny that Austin's account of law is exhausted by such a formula and argue that there is a lot in Austin's work that suggests that lawyers must employ utilitarian reasoning alongside the general formula of legality. To the extent that this is true Austin's theory is here taken to signify the paradigmatic instance of *scientia* only as far as the identification of law is concerned.

[29] Theories of this kind include most versions of legal realism both in its traditional and contemporary variants. This is the type of legal theory defended by P Leith and J Morison, 'Can Jurisprudence without Empiricism Ever be a Science?' in this volume.

[30] See N MacCormick and O Weinberger, *An Institutional Theory of Law* (Dordrecht, D Reidel Publishing Company, 1986).

conventions via value-free entities may become problematic when it comes to accounting for law's normative nature.

Ronald Dworkin launched his most influential attack on conventionalism with respect to a different problem, one that arises from the disagreement with regard to legal concepts: on the conventionalist understanding, any failure on behalf of the members of the linguistic community to understand the content of the convention would have to lead to a so-called *conceptual disagreement*, namely, disagreement about the content of the linguistic conventions that regulates (fixes) legal meaning. The immediate effect of any conceptual disagreement is failure of communication: the parties who engage in it are talking past each other. All it would take, however, to dissolve this kind of disagreement would be to explain to the disagreeing party the convention on which law 'works', which is to say, the relevant Rule of Recognition. Dworkin argued, however, that this is not the case, for disagreement usually persists even after the facts of the convention have been fully explained to the disagreeing parties. Thus, the parties may continue to disagree about whether something is a valid contract even after the conventional definition of 'contracthood' has become fully transparent to them. In so far as this is true, Dworkin claims that when people disagree about the law their disagreement extends further than the (linguistic) conventions of the legal community, thus encompassing the very *nature* of law (*theoretical* or *substantive disagreement*)[31] which includes much more than just the facts of a convention; in fact, Dworkin tells us, it embraces the essence of the things legal language refers to, an essence that is located *outside* the conventions of the community in the legal phenomena themselves.

Relying on these premises, Dworkin proceeds to specify the nature of law: once we focus on the phenomena themselves we *discover* that law is not about accurate descriptions of facts (pertaining to the conventional pedigree of rules) but about best possible justifications of action-guiding standards (rules) that constrain the freedom of individuals within a political community. These justifications are embedded in interpretative claims that are put forward by anyone who partakes of the legal practice of the community. The soundness of interpretative claims depends on whether they can attain to the demands of integrity, that is, are capable of realising a coherent and equal application of the same set of substantive principles for everyone, in a manner that would guarantee the ideal of a viable community. The important idea introduced by the Dworkinian line of argument was that law is essentially evaluative, for it is the outcome of an interpretative process that aims at presenting the legal system in its best light, one emitted by a set of substantive principles that realise the idea of integrity.

[31] For the concept and example of substantive disagreement see, R Dworkin (above n 7), ch 2, and SL Hurley, *Natural Reasons* (Oxford, Clarendon Press, 1989), chs 2 and 3.

Why, then, include Dworkin's theory (and more generally *interpretivism*) within the discussion of *scientia*? The reason for this is that, despite its critical claim to want to avoid some crude form of *scientia* (where legal theory is supposed to consume itself in a fruitless fact-finding with respect to the external behaviour of social agents), interpretivism seems to be fostering a different, perhaps more obscure, kind of fact-finding. This is the result of a move aiming to explain law's evaluative nature by advocating a kind of *essentialism*. On this view, all evaluations that are to be found in any legal system are part of the ontological structure of the legal phenomena themselves, where those are conceived of as forming parts of the natural environment that surrounds us, ie, externally to our linguistic practices and the conventions those rest upon. As will become apparent through the meta-ethical discussion in section 6 below, essentialist explications[32] of normative entities (values, reasons, principles or rules) end up defending either of two claims: that either normative entities are *sui generis* evaluative entities that can be perceived through a sixth sense, or that it is possible to grasp them through a full description of the non-normative facts of each and every particular case. To that extent, either case alleges that normativity has a phenomenal aspect that can be 'sensed' and that, consequently, normative (legal in particular) knowledge is the outcome of a scientific activity of collecting a certain type of data.

4.2 *Prudentia*

Prudentia understands legal practice as a genuinely practical activity in which the members of a legal community synthesise the law through a combination of fact and value. On this explication, law neither consists of the external features of the participants' past behaviour, nor can it be read off the particular fact-situations the community runs into. Instead, law amounts from a creative process in which legal actors exercise their practical wisdom by evaluating fact-situations in the light of substantive, action-guiding principles. These principles cannot be known on the basis of a study of the phenomenal aspects of the environment, but need to be conceived of as necessary conceptual conditions for making sense of any legal practice as a practice that gives rise to obligations.[33] To the extent that this evidence

[32] I mention only interpretivism here owing to its widespread influence in contemporary theoretical debates. Other essentialist programmes would include most of the current natural law theories (see above n 10 and 6.2.1 below).

[33] For a legal practice to aim at generating obligations it is sufficient that its participants require that the demands of the law be legitimate or justified. Moreover, the fact that these claims are raised by everyone, implies the form of legitimacy required: laws must be sufficiently legitimate to everyone through a process that involves everyone (this is close to Kant's idea of autonomy). Recently, Carsten Heidemann has rejected the necessity of the claims and instead opted for a less substantive principle of legislation conceived of along the lines of the

does not exist in the environment independently of our thought, the type of knowledge solicited by *prudentia* may be labelled *rational or noumenal.*[34]

In virtue of being the conceptual boundaries of an obligation-generating practice, these principles fulfil a double function: aside from determinants of legal meaning (semantic rules) they are also substantive-normative, ie, they themselves spell out criteria of normative correctness. This they achieve by refusing to delegate normative authority to anything outside legal practice itself. Thus, determination of legal meaning takes place *not* by relating propositions to entities that either are normatively inert (as is the case with empiricism and conventionalism) or exist outside the legal practice all together (interpretivism), but, instead, by prescribing a particular *process* that involves the projection of the practice onto specific fact-situations (such as a process of universalisation). With this move *prudentia* secures a notion of normativity that is still rooted in social practices, as well as a notion of objectivity that derives from conceptual necessity (hence it is *a priori* knowable).

5. THE FACT/VALUE DICHOTOMY

Many of the issues regarding the differences in philosophical opinion between *scientia* and *prudentia* draw their force from a range of different views on the metaphysics (and the epistemology) of normative discourse.[35] Amongst them, the view that has mostly influenced this area of philosophy is the thesis that no ought-proposition can be derived from an is-proposition,

Kelsenian Grundnorm. See C Heidemann, 'Law's Claim to Correctness', this volume; and his more detailed *Die Norm als Tatsache. Zur Normentheorie Hans Kelsens* (Baden-Baden, Nomos Verlag, 1997).

[34] Two meanings can be associated with 'noumenal': first, it may stand for 'rational', thus denoting any entity that is abstract (eg, norms, numbers, facts and so on) as opposed to concrete (eg, trees, tables, rocks and so on); second, it may stand for 'practical'. This meaning derives from the Kantian idea of freedom as a necessary condition for understanding the self. The term is here used as combining both meanings. A note of caution is needed here: states of affairs (or facts) are structured entities whose parts are objects and concepts or relations. States of affairs are themselves always noumenal entities, even if their constituents are not. To that extent, any knowledge that is grounded on facts is noumenal. However, the distinction I draw here focuses on a different point: noumenality and phenomenality refer to the constituents of facts; whether *they* are noumenal or phenomenal, as opposed to facts themselves. A different distinction is the one drawn between theories of knowledge depending on what they take to be the most elementary truth makers: those that take them to be facts could be labelled noumenal. In contrast, those that take them to be the constituents of facts, could not be readily classified as either phenomenal or noumenal: one would have to further investigate into the nature of each constituent before passing the relevant judgement (thus a name that denotes an abstract object, say a number, would give rise to noumenal knowledge, as opposed to the name of a fruit that would clearly generate phenomenal knowledge).

[35] I use 'normative' throughout as meaning 'action-guiding' rather than as referring to the normativity of rationality.

which is widely known as the *fact/value dichotomy.*[36] The story of this thesis is long and intriguing; however, there are two moments that decisively shaped its content: Hume's philosophy and the writings of the Logical Positivists.[37] Roughly speaking, the fact/value dichotomy began its life as the realisation that moral propositions cannot be rationally known. Hume took the realm of reason to comprise factual truths, as well as analytic truths, and argued that moral propositions cannot amount to either, as there is no matter of fact or analytic truth ('relation of ideas' is the term he used) to make them true.[38] This realisation, however, was for Hume not a reason for denouncing morals but, instead, an incentive for restructuring and reconstructing the moral realm. As a result, and given the semantic and metaphysical views Hume held at the time, he turned to emotions as the key item in the explanation of moral discourse.

On the other hand, the contribution of Logical Positivism and, in particular, Rudolf Carnap, to the evolution of the fact/value dichotomy had some more devastating results for the domain of normative discourse, along with a sharpening of the dichotomy. In the language of Logical Positivism, a proposition is factual only if it can be reduced to propositions of physics, which in turn are verifiable through observation or sensory experience.[39] More importantly, this formulation of facticity was taken to be a criterion for cognitive meaningfulness for any proposition. Given this strict test, normative language was deemed meaningless, and the realm of morality nonsensical.[40] To a certain extent the conclusion about the meaninglessness of morals that Positivism drew seems to have been the result of ideological bias rather than rational argument, considering that the Humean vocabulary of emotions could easily have been recast in the language of physics (relating to brain states, etc), a task that many contemporary empiricists undertake.[41] In any event, cast in the sharp formulations of Logical Positivism, the fact/value dichotomy acquired the status of a criterion for distinguishing between cognitively meaningful discourse that pertains to science and the theoretical philosophy one the one hand, and cognitively

[36] For the purposes of the following few paragraphs the notion of 'fact' is being used as the opposite of 'value'. To that extent, 'fact' is here taken to refer only to those facts that are empirical and observable through the senses.
[37] For a brief, albeit accurate, survey of the history of the fact/value dichotomy, see H Putnam (above n 21).
[38] See D Hume, 'Of Morals' in LA Selby-Bigge (ed), *A Treatise of Human Understanding,* 2nd edn (Oxford, Clarendon Press, 1978), 463–7.
[39] See H Putnam (above n 21), 7–27.
[40] To that extent, the empiricism of Logical Positivism is radically different from that of Hume, as the former amounts to a rehabilitation of morality while the latter to a rejection thereof.
[41] The ideological bias is illustrated by the fact that Hume's language of emotions could have been accommodated within what Carnap calls theoretical terms. In his later work Carnap distinguished between *observation terms* that readily refer to observable properties and *theoretical terms* that serve the purpose of a heuristic device with respect to those sentences that really state the facts. For a reliable summary of Carnap's distinctions see H Putnam (above n 21), ch 1.

empty discourse that pertains to the activity of inquiring into morals on the other. As a result, accepting the dichotomy should *prima facie* commit one to non-cognitivism regarding value, given that there is no matter of empirical fact that is value-laden.

However that may be, the fact/value dichotomy did not manage to impose the sharp distinctions Logical Positivism intended. The pressure to account for the reality of normative discourse was too high as to allow for the luxury of rendering normative language inert, with the result that, at the end of the day, very few philosophers came to accept a full-fledged non-cognitivism. Yet Logical Positivism's bad publicity against the value end of the dichotomy resulted in a reiteration of the fact/value dichotomy within the cognitivist camp: even philosophers who did not wish to question the cognitive value of normative vocabulary were still ready to accept that respectable knowledge is only knowledge that derives from empirical evidence. Hence, in a somewhat ironic way, many cognitivists attempted to ground knowledge of value on evidence that related more to the 'fact' than to the 'value' end of the dichotomy.[42] The main consequence of this move was to generate a pretension of *scientism* within normative philosophy, which stood even in opposition with Hume's original intention to rehabilitate/reconstruct the realm of morals.

Attendant to scientism is an increased commitment to reductionism that, even nowadays, dominates large areas of normative philosophy. By restricting the evidence of the philosophical enquiry of value to what the fact end of the dichotomy prescribes, one subscribes to a caricature and fails to generate normative knowledge. The caricature is the idea that all firm knowledge is based on purely perceptible evidence, in other words, that all knowledge is phenomenal.[43] There is a widespread view that this idea fails even in the area of theoretical philosophy because of an inadequate understanding of 'fact'.[44] However, if this is true there, it is *a fortiori* true in normative/practical philosophy: even if a purified conception of 'fact' were tenable, it would only serve the purpose of grounding too thin a knowledge with respect to the realm of value. On such a thin conception of knowledge we would know a lot about various phenomenal aspects with respect to the activity of normative judgement, but we would *still* fail to know what is right and wrong, what ought to be done and what ought not. For, to know the latter, we need to expand our notion of evidence and, connectedly, to depart from a strict distinction between fact and value.

An expanded view of evidence is one that integrates fact and value in a manner that brings about the collapse of the fact/value dichotomy. The collapse involves adhering to the idea that declarative evaluative propositions

[42] See 6.2, below.
[43] More accurately, that all *a posteriori* knowledge is based on phenomenal evidence, given that most philosophers would accept the existence of *a priori* principles of rationality.
[44] See H Putnam (above n 21).

are made true in virtue of evidence that is neither purely evaluative nor purely factual, but instead derives from 'interpretations' of phenomenal fact in the light of noumenal value (evaluative propositions). Consequently, the evidence that generates knowledge with respect to any declarative evaluative proposition does not consist of either just 'fact' or just 'value', but instead involves both as making up an organic whole. To that extent, the collapse of the fact/value dichotomy can be compared to the collapse of another dichotomy: the analytic/synthetic dichotomy. Famously, Quine debunked this dichotomy by showing that there is no single moment in the process of acquiring knowledge, where fact and analytic truth can be separated. In his characteristic own words:

> The lore of our fathers is a fabric of sentences. In our hands it develops and changes . . . It is a pale, grey lore, black with fact and white with convention. But I have found no substantial reasons for concluding that there are any quite black threads in it, or any white ones.[45]

In this statement Quine's point seems to be less that all sentences are synthetic, and therefore that no distinction between analytic and synthetic is possible, and more that the sentences upon which our knowledge is premised are neither purely synthetic nor purely analytic. Similarly, with respect to normative knowledge, the evidence that supports it need not be exclusively factual or exclusively evaluative, in the sense that it might be not possible to judge which of the two ingredients contributes more to the foundation of our knowledge, but merely that both are present in indiscernible proportions while acquiring knowledge. Once again, it is not the case that all there is, is 'fact', but merely that 'fact' and 'value' complement each other.

Obviously, a question arises as to the ontological status of evaluative evidence: that value intertwines with fact, in order to generate normative knowledge, is true enough. However, to the extent that it is possible to distinguish conceptually between two different items, it is important to say something about the grounds of the distinction. These grounds can be revealed by pressing further the analogy between evaluative and analytic sentences: both types of sentences can be taken to depict constructions of reason, be it in the form of analytic truths or evaluative entities (norms). On the face of it, and in contrast to factual evidence, which is best described as phenomenal, evaluative evidence lies closer to the evidence embedded in analytic sentences and is best described as noumenal (ie, abstract and reason-dependent). Taking on board this line of argument has a distinctly rationalist or Kantian (and certainly anti-Humean) flavour, given the commitment it entails to rational abstract entities as grounding (even partially) normative knowledge. On this conception, normative knowledge derives from the

[45] WVO Quine, 'Carnap and Logical Truth', quoted in H Putnam (above n 21), 12.

interpretation of factual evidence in the light of normative propositions that denote rational abstract entities. As I am going to argue towards the end of the chapter,[46] this conception has the great advantage of explaining normative knowledge as *specifically* being of propositions that pertain to agency as opposed to propositions about aspects of the environment that relate only externally to normative practices. An alleged shortcoming of the Kantian conception is its adherence to a minimum amount of *a priori* noumenal knowledge with respect to the supreme principle of morality: the Categorical Imperative. To refer again to the analytic/synthetic dichotomy, this could be a problem if and only if it could be shown that all *a priori* knowledge is, on closer examination, *a posteriori*. In the absence of such a general demonstration, adherence to *a priori* knowable propositions is not outlandish and, provided that it does not amount to the simplistic dichotomy targeted by Quine, it can illuminate the way normative knowledge works.

But why favour the Kantian/Rationalist account over other explications of normative knowledge? Roughly speaking, there are two alternatives to rationalism and, as will be indicated in the next section, both end up embracing scientism and the attendant fact/value dichotomy. For now, suffice it to make a short comment on the reasons why they fail: the first alternative for explicating 'value' is to perform a reduction of it to fact by, coarsely, arguing that factual evidence exhausts all there is to know about value. In this context, normative (legal, moral and so on) philosophy is expected to operate on a strict fact/value dichotomy, by recording the phenomenal evidence that pertains to the external, perceptible aspects of normative phenomena. This scientistic conception of normative knowledge underpins the kind of legal theory that was earlier labelled *scientia*.

On the other hand, the second alternative aims to preserve the autonomy of 'value' vis-à-vis 'fact' by postulating the existence of special *evaluative kinds* that exist as part of the 'fabric of the world', along the lines of something like GE Moore's ontology of values (Platonism, etc). To the degree that the postulation of special normative kinds aims at grounding a new order of quasi-phenomenal evidence, which substantiates independently of rational (noumenal) constructions, it faces two problems. First, it falls prey to metaphysical exaggeration, as John Mackie argued with his 'argument from queerness'.[47] Secondly, given that talk of normative kinds is usually accompanied by the requirement of a special sixth sense, tuned into perceiving value, the second alternative appears to model itself after the scientistic ideology pertaining to the fact/value distinction. To that extent, the strong presumption arises that the second alternative assumes that the only way to establish the autonomy of 'value' is by postulating categories which are

[46] See below, at 6.3.
[47] J Mackie, *Ethics: Inventing Right and Wrong* (Harmondsworth, Penguin Books, 1990).

ontologically as solid as the natural kinds and, as a result, can compete with them.[48] In so far as the presumption is true, the second alternative fails to associate itself with *prudentia* and, instead, amounts to a peculiar kind of *scientia* that is dysfunctional, due to an awful lot of metaphysical luggage that it carries. In contrast to this view, this chapter's central contention is that *prudentia* rather relies on a rationalist (Kantian or quasi-Kantian) explication of normative knowledge and not just any theory that postulates autonomous (or anti-reductionist) normative knowledge.

6. THE META-ETHICAL DISCUSSION

So far, our conspectus of legal knowledge has made it possible to draw a distinction between *scientia* and *prudentia*. More needs to be said, however, in defence of the distinction and the way each of the two types of legal theory was framed. In particular, three points shall be taken up in this section: first, to the extent that legal knowledge is normative, why does *scientia* fail to generate it? A lot of the theories that have been described as instances of *scientia* will protest that they are epistemically fit to generate such knowledge. As regards this claim, it has to be demonstrated exactly why they fail. Adjacent to this task shall be, second, to show why a rationalist legal theory is much better suited to underpin normative knowledge. Finally, while both *scientia* and *prudentia* depart from the conviction that it is possible to have normative (as in legal) knowledge, a significant number of philosophers have questioned its possibility *tout court*. A discussion of the various views on the possibility of normative knowledge shall serve as an introduction to a number of key metaphysical issues that underpin the distinction between *scientia* and *prudentia*.

Discussions of normative knowledge traditionally fall under the area of meta-ethics and mainly revolve around the nature of the evidence that generates normative knowledge. At this level, distinguishing between law, morality and other areas of normative discourse is not too important, all the more so because the metaphysical issues involved are common to all these areas. On the other hand, the meta-ethical discussion is appropriate in underpinning the proposed distinction between *scientia* and *prudentia* by illuminating their respective views on the nature of legal knowledge and, hence, on the nature of law. The discussion opens with an outline of non-cognitivism, as the meta-ethical view that more than any other is closely connected to the idea of a strict fact/value dichotomy. In many respects non-cognitivism is the meta-ethical position that underpins *scientia*. Despite the

[48] If, however, talk of 'normative kinds' is merely a figurative way of picturing the intellectual process of interpreting portions of the phenomenal environment in the light of normative propositions (norms), then no special provision for it is needed, but it can be accommodated within the rationalist account.

fact that *scientia* affirms the possibility of normative knowledge and attempts to offer an account of law as constituting a normative domain, it does so only after having internalised the lesson of scientism. Thus, embarking on the view that only knowledge of fact is possible, *scientia* proceeds to explain normative knowledge as resting on the same type of fact as the one advocated by the strict fact/value dichotomy. To that extent, the amounting species of cognitivism is beset from the start with the metaphysical prejudices of scientism and non-cognitivism, and can hardly perform its task to generate normative knowledge.

6.1 Non-cognitivism

Non-cognitivism can be explained as comprising a twofold thesis: the *relativity thesis* and the *queerness argument*. Neither rebuts resolutely the possibility of normative knowledge: the latter leads to some version of minimalism about truth which, however, does not pose any devastating threat to cognitivism; the former leads to anti-reductionism, but this is a useful qualification for a more refined understanding of normative knowledge. The starting point for non-cognitivist considerations is usually some form of relativity or disagreement thesis (DT):[49] 'two or more people (groups, communities, cultures and so on) can agree on all the facts there are to agree on and yet disagree as to what is right to do'.[50] Shifting from the level of disagreement to the level of language, the same idea can be phrased as the inability of descriptive language to account for evaluative judgements ('what is right to do'). This can be formulated as the open question argument (OQA):[51] 'no amount of information couched in purely descriptive terms seems to exhaust the question of what is right to do'.

Moving away from the level of disagreement and language, non-cognitivist considerations further aim to provide a metaphysical argument that accounts for both the inadequacy of descriptive language and the normative disagreement that survives a full description of environmental facts. In simple terms, the metaphysical argument directly addresses the reasons that block objectivity in normative discourse by focusing on the asymmetry between the levels of description and evaluation. The explanation of this

[49] See F Jackson, 'Non-Cognitivism, Normativity, Belief' in (1999) XII *Ratio* 420–35. See also J Mackie (above n 47).

[50] This is basically Mackie's argument from relativity re-phrased in the light of some thoughts on the asymmetry between the ethical and the descriptive, advanced by Frank Jackson. Jackson's proposal is more precise as it takes non-cognitivism to reject knowledge only in the domain of ethics but not in that of description. Indeed most ethical non-cognitivists are cognitivists with respect to empirical knowledge. This is better captured when one says that relativity/disagreement prevails in ethics because of the asymmetry between ethical and descriptive knowledge (and the concomitant impossibility to transfer 'certainty' from the domain of the descriptive to that of the ethical).

[51] See F Jackson (above n 49), 421.

asymmetry seems to lie in the fundamentally different ways in which descriptive and evaluative judgements 'match' the environment. Whereas descriptions of the environment are correct or wrong depending on whether objects satisfy the relevant descriptive properties, there is nothing such as satisfying a normative property, simply because normative properties do not exist as a matter of fact. And anything that does not exist as a matter of fact cannot be objectively known (and agreed upon).

What is more, insisting on the existence of normative properties would require one to admit into the fabric of the world entities that are metaphysically odd (entities that have a 'to-be-doneness' built in themselves). Along these lines the open question argument and the disagreement thesis are backed by the metaphysical thesis (MT): 'there is no such thing as having or failing to have a normative property because this would involve the existence of queer properties' (this is more or less Mackie's *argument from queerness*). Frank Jackson makes the same point in slightly different terms:

> Non-cognitivism is precisely the view that, although the language of normativity is meaningful, there are no properties corresponding to normative predicates . . . non-cognitivism about normativity is the view that normative predicates when attached to subject terms do not serve to make claims about how the subjects are; in consequence, there is no such thing as being how things are claimed to be by normative predicates and normative language in general.[52]

Adapted to ethics this is the familiar position of emotivism/expressivism: just as utterances like 'hurrah' and 'yuck' do not refer to anything, equally there is nothing to satisfy 'being good', 'being right', 'being under an obligation', etc (and that these properties point to a different domain: expressions of emotions or the kingdom of norms)

A danger lurking in attending closely to non-cognitivist metaphysics is that one might end up dismissing large portions of normative talk as meaningless:[53] if there is no such thing as satisfying a normative property, what then do normative judgements mean? In order to avoid this reef, a standard move taken by non-cognitivism is to opt for the view that evaluative properties ascribed by normative judgements satisfy a modest semantic notion of property ascription, without presupposing the existence of full-blooded entities. This is the position tendered by *minimalist theories of truth and property ascription*. Minimalism contends that it is wrong to think that when we have a meaningful sentence which ascribes a predicate to the subject term and which carries all the marks of truth-aptness, there is then still

[52] See F Jackson (above n 49), 422.

[53] As indicated earlier, this was the view of the so-called *logical positivists* who argued that meaning should be related to our ability to verify sentences. See J Skorupski, 'Meaning, Use, Verification' in B Hale and C Wright (eds), *A Companion to the Philosophy of Language* (Oxford, Blackwell, 1999), 29–59.

a further question as to whether the predicate ascribes the property. This mistake, minimalists argue, is committed when people wrongly assume that a predicate like 'is wrong' behaves differently from predicates like 'being round', '. . . square' etc, in that only the latter properly ascribe a property when attributed to a subject term. Instead, the minimalist position submits that a meaningful sentence, which is syntactically well-formed and carries all the features of truth-aptness, exhausts the issue of property ascription in respect of both types of predicates. By subscribing to minimalism, non-cognitivism hopes to address in the best way the queerness argument without sacrificing the meaningfulness of normative language: in view of the fact that there are no such things as queer moral entities, the issue of property ascription is exhausted by semantics.

However, the minimalist gloss of non-cognitivism does not entirely succeed in demarcating it from the rival meta-ethical positions of cognitivism and, in particular, subjectivism, the latter being the view that moral sentences actually depict persons' psychological/emotional states. Let me explain briefly why. On a closer look, (minimalist) non-cognitivists attack subjectivism and cognitivism for the same reasons: *first*, on the ground that both hold that a complete description of the relevant facts exhausts the question of 'what is right to do' (the only difference being that subjectivism evokes attitudinal facts, cognitivism environmental facts).[54] *Second*, on the ground that ascribing normative properties to individuals *goes beyond* attributing predicates to subjects within well-formed sentences that carry the marks of truth-aptness. However, minimalism about truth does not readily perform the demarcation for which it is employed. The reason is that minimalism merely addresses the second ground, or else the (semantic) question of how robustly we should think of truth and property ascription. Still, it does not take issue with the first: it may still be the case, under the minimalist cupola, that 'what is right to do' can be sufficiently reported on the basis of (the fullest possible) description of either attitudinal or environmental facts. This is the more so, once property ascription is understood in the minimalist way, as then normative predicates could not be readily accused for picking out robust queer entities.[55]

That normative knowledge remains an open possibility within minimalism can be read into the further attempt of some non-cognitivists to block it by

[54] To keep the discussion simpler I assume that cognitivism in ethics encompasses some version of the view that ethical sentences are truth-apt owing to the fact that normative properties are descriptive properties. For the moment I disregard more robust versions of cognitivism which hold that ethical sentences are true in virtue of the existence of full-blooded normative properties, as they would be straight incompatible with the argument from queerness. See the discussion below.

[55] This points to the fact that the minimalist position is not a sceptical position but one for epistemic modesty, as it does not deny the possibility of knowledge in the various domains but merely our ability to determine the metaphysical status of the entities involved in our knowledge (or the possibility to gain insight into the *Ding an Sich*).

arguing that normative sentences have all the marks of truth-aptness but are not actually truth-apt. (This move is in particular made vis-à-vis the fear of subjectivism.)[56] To begin with, this distinction strikes one as rather implausible: the reason is, roughly, that if a sentence carries the marks of truth-aptness then there is some kind of fact (perceived as less or more minimalist) that will (or will not) make the sentence true. Given that most forms of non-cognitivism take normative sentences to *express* emotional states (as opposed to *reporting them — pace* subjectivism), the required facts will be of the same kind as those postulated by subjectivism. To that extent non-cognitivism will collapse into subjectivism as no distinction between *expressing* and *reporting* will be easy to sustain, particularly within a minimalist context.

More generally, irrespective of the specific difficulties involved in distinguishing between 'carrying the marks of truth-aptness' and 'being truth-apt', the rationale of the very distinction is strictly incompatible with the very idea of minimalism: minimalism does not deny truth-aptness. As it has already been pointed out, it merely denies that truth-aptness has to be understood in a robust language-independent way but, in doing so, it captures both descriptive and normative properties. Hence, normative language interpreted as referring to either attitudinal facts or environmental facts, could be deemed appropriate for capturing 'what is right to do', without pointing to any robust property ascription.[57] Along these lines any non-cognitivist project that is couched in minimalist terms has equal chances of collapsing into (minimalist) subjectivism or cognitivism. Hence, instead of sharpening the differences between non-cognitivism and its metaethical rivals, minimalism works in the direction of neutralising differences across the border: normative predicates can be presented as picking out properties in a minimalist fashion.

To sum up so far: it seems that minimalism about truth is not sufficient for grounding the argument from queerness and in effect blocking normative knowledge, be it subjective (based on attitudinal facts) or objective (based on environmental facts). Perhaps there are other forms of non-cognitivist argument that could effectively demonstrate reasons for adopting a metaphysical position on the impossibility of normative knowledge. I am not going to spend more time on looking for such arguments, mainly because I think that non-cognitivism cannot plausibly aim at more radical forms of rejection of normative knowledge (to the extent it does, it threatens to restrict meaningful normative sentences to a degree that is untenable).

Given that normative truth and knowledge cannot be doubted beyond the limits of minimalism with much hope for convincingness, it remains to investi-

[56] In particular, *expressivism* holds that bearing the marks of truth-aptness coarsely means that normative judgements are merely *expressions* of subjective attitudes rather than *reports* of fact with respect to those attitudes (as in the case of subjectivism).

[57] In this case subjectivism/cognitivism can either attain to a full reduction of 'what is right to do' to reports of facts or, alternatively, evoke some form of supervenience and retain an anti-reductionist outlook. For the issue of reductionism, see the discussion that follows.

gate the conditions for a moderate or tenable non-cognitivism regarding normative knowledge. For that I will turn to the key thought that informs the *open question argument* and the concomitant *disagreement thesis*: namely, that agreement on what is factually the case cannot settle the issue of what is right to do. Of course non-cognitivism takes the fact of disagreement as a proof of the impossibility of normative knowledge. Be that as it may, I suggest that this fact be interpreted as pointing to a constrain applicable to any tenable conception of normative knowledge. This is the constrain that normative knowledge has to be perceived as lying on a different level from descriptive/empirical knowledge and that, for that reason, it cannot be inferred from the latter.

Couched in these terms non-cognitivism puts forward the *anti-reductionist* thesis that no description of facts, either with respect to persons' attitudes or in respect of the environment, can exhaust the problem of how things normatively are (should be). Anti-reductionism, as a critique advanced by non-cognitivism,[58] poses a much more serious challenge to both subjectivism and cognitivism than any crude rejection of normative knowledge. (The more so because it need not be incompatible with the idea of normative knowledge.) Instead anti-reductionism offers itself as a tool for refining different conceptions of normative knowledge. Along theses lines, I shall assume the anti-reductionist thesis to pose a test for *tenability or reasonableness* with respect to various views on the possibility of normative knowledge. However, for brevity, I will primarily focus on two such views which I will assume to comprise, in an ideal-typical way as it were, the main conceptions of normative knowledge that exist in the current philosophical market.[59] Following this, I will offer a rough sketch of a third alternative which I take to accommodate better the anti-reductionist challenge and, hence, to underpin successfully normative knowledge.

6.2 The Possibility of Normative Knowledge

6.2.1 Essentialism

This is the thesis that no description of the world is sufficient for settling the issue as to 'what is right to do' for normative language refers to distinct

[58] However not exclusively; see GE Moore, *Principia Ethica* (revised edition) (Cambridge, Cambridge University Press, 1993).

[59] As mentioned earlier, there is another conception of normative knowledge, subjectivism. This can be captured as the thesis that a (complete) description of certain persons' attitudes exhausts the issue of 'what is right to do'. The assumption is here that normative language depicts/reports speakers' attitudes. It follows that normative knowledge comprises descriptions of subjective facts (the Humean view). In what follows I am going to skip a discussion of the Humean view for two main reasons: first, because it is straightforwardly rejected by non-cognitivism as incapable of generating objective normative knowledge; second, because the issue of subjectivism and the related issue of the impact that agents' standpoints have on normative judgements, are addressed under the second conception of cognitivism (the Lockean view).

normative properties that are part of the essence of things. The first complete expression of normative essentialism is to be found in GE Moore's seminal work *Principia Ethica,* which argues that normative properties are *sui generis* and cannot be analysed in anything more basic.[60] To begin with, the Moorean view is compatible with anti-reductionism. In fact, it is often cited as the archetypal anti-reductionist view in moral philosophy. The obvious problem of Moore's view is that it straightforwardly pronounces the existence of robust normative entities of the sort that non-cognitivists reject as queer; hence it falls directly under the objections of MT (the queerness argument). For sure, it is possible to avoid some or most of the problems linked to its rampant ontological assumptions if we reconstruct the Moorean view in the light of a minimalist explication of property ascription. Leaving this problem aside, there is an aspect of the Moorean view that retains its momentum within contemporary moral and legal theory. This is the idea that the possibility of normative knowledge presupposes that normative properties are mind-independent for they are part of the make-up or the essence of moral (and legal) phenomena themselves. There are a number of influential contemporary moral and legal theories that — more or less explicitly — go down the essentialist path of thought without purporting to commit themselves to Moore's ontology. These theories are not so much interested in blocking the reduction of normative properties (as Moore was) but more in the idea of mind-independence as a condition of objective normative knowledge. As regards the distinction between *scientia* and *prudentia* in legal theory, essentialism's attempt to ground legal knowledge on mind-independent entities amounts to *scientia*, for any entities that are normative and exist as part of the environment will connote phenomenal evidence, be they some kind of 'queer' Moorean properties or some reduced physical properties which are assumed to be offering a firm footing of normativity on the physical environment. Following a demonstration of the shortcomings of the Moorean option, I shall look in more detail into the reductionist version (below, at 6.2.2).

Contemporary versions of essentialism build heavily upon recent theoretical work in the philosophy of mind and language. In the late 1970s and early 1980s a group of philosophers, in particular Hilary Putnam and Saul Kripke, forcefully argued that the meanings of our words are 'not in our heads' but in the environment. Their argument was chiefly directed against internalist theories of meaning, then dominant in the philosophical landscape. Those theories took concepts to refer to whatever was stipulated by appropriate definitions that contained necessary and sufficient conditions (ie, so-called definitions *per genus et differentia*) and could be arrived at independently of the environment. It is not difficult to see some form of radical scepticism associated with such an idea: should meaning be rooted

[60] See GE Moore (above n 58).

in speakers' heads, one would end up believing in the existence of a well-defined conceptual universe that has no relevance whatsoever with the actual environment.[61] Putnam and Kripke set out to undermine this particular understanding of meaning by demonstrating that the meaning of natural kind concepts is causally determined by the actual properties of the entities referred to, rather than any properties of our mental states.[62] On the face of it, the importance allocated to the *intention* (conventions of use or definitions) and the *extension* (actual referents) of (natural kind) concepts is being reversed: conventions and definitions are rendered subordinate to actual referents. Moreover, conventions and definitions may retain their value as guidelines for speakers only to the extent that they remain open to revision in the light of new (empirical) discoveries vis-à-vis the environment. Thus, our language and the ways we employ it cease to be constitutive in our understanding of the environment, and instead the latter becomes the measure for a successful employment of language that leads to communication. This new explication of meaning makes it possible for a speaker correctly to employ a concept (say 'water') without having a complete understanding of the conventions or the definitions that determine its use within a linguistic community, for stability in communication relies on the properties of the actual referent (the fact that it is H_2O) rather than any facts about the linguistic practice.

This notion of a standard of meaning that lies outside our practices opens up a gap between the practice and its referent, a gap that makes room for the possibility of error and, hence, the idea of objectivity. Objectivity is intertwined with the possibility that we might be wrong in our understanding of the world precisely because the world may actually be different than what we take it to be. To put it in a different way, what determines how the world is, is the world itself rather than our linguistic practices. To that extent, Putnam's and Kripke's thought experiments demonstrated the limits of our understanding (thought) by pointing to the actual criteria of meaning. At the same time they showed that, in so far as our expressions tell us anything about the world, meaning is a dynamic idea, one that evolves constantly, indeed proportionally to the increase of our knowledge with respect to the environment.

[61] This should be the case if the meaning of, say, 'water' should be determined by a linguistic convention as opposed to the actual stuff it refers to (H_2O). This is not an extravagant thought: just think of speakers in classical Athens using 'water' without knowing much about its actual chemical composition. In their case it would be very easy to confuse water with some other stuff that superficially resembles it.

[62] Roughly speaking, their argument runs as follows: suppose there are two parallel universes: Earth and Twin-Earth. Two thirds of Earth's surface is covered by some colourless and odourless liquid stuff whose chemical composition is H_2O. Equally, Twin Earth is covered for two thirds of its surface by some superficially identical stuff, whose chemical composition is XYZ. Now the inhabitants of Earth use 'water' to depict H_2O, whereas the inhabitants of Twin-Earth use 'water' to depict XYZ. Suppose also that both groups of speakers refer to the same definition or conventional rule when they use 'water' (that is, there is an identity of *intention*).

It is not difficult to see why moral and legal philosophers were mesmerised by those ideas.[63] Considering that problems of scepticism and relativism are much more intense in the domain of evaluative (moral, legal or ethical) language, these philosophers were very happy to be given a new theory that set meaning free from conventions and definitions, the latter two being particularly prone in substantiating the suspicion of relativism. In contrast, the new theory would allow an explication of normative meaning as depending on the actual properties of normative (moral, ethical or legal) kinds, properties that exist independently of a community's linguistic practices and the conventions they give rise to.

However tempting the analogy with natural kinds may sound, it is in fact unworkable, the main reason concerning the different nature of the kinds depicted in each case. Normative kinds (rights, contracts, norms and so on) lack the essential underlying microstructural property[64] of natural kinds that allowed Putnam and Kripke to develop their theory of meaning.[65] The microstructural property of natural kinds (which, incidentally, can be discovered by science) is responsible for causally determining meaning from the outside, ie, independently of any convention or definition and irrespective of our knowledge of the microstructural property itself. This is not the case with normative kinds. Unless one postulates something like an *underlying microstructural property* for normative kinds, the option of casual determination of normative meaning from the outside is not available. In other words, there is nothing in the environment that is essentially normative and is capable of causally determining the reference of our normative expressions irrespective of our knowledge of it. Be that as it may, interpretivism in law (and other similar theories from the field of moral philosophy) seems to rely on such a microstructure and to look for entities of the

Be that as it may, 'water' as employed by Earthians has a different reference (or *extension*) than 'water' as employed by Twin-Earthians. It follows that the difference in extension must cause some difference in meaning. Hence 'water' has a different meaning in each case, one that is determined by the actual stuff the concept depicts. See H Putnam, 'The Meaning of "Meaning"' in H Putnam, *Mind, Language and Reality* (Cambridge, Cambridge University Press, 1975), 215–71, and his more concise 'Meaning and Reference' reprinted in Moore (ed), *Meaning and Reference* (Oxford, Oxford University Press, 1993), 150–61.

[63] The way to such work in the area of normative philosophy was paved by the writings of Tyler Burge, who developed a sophisticated externalist theory of meaning for concepts that denote 'social' and 'artefact' kinds (eg, 'arthritis' and 'sofa' respectively). See T Burge, 'Intellectual Norms and the Foundations of Mind' (1986) 83 *Journal of Philosophy* 697. And for an explicit reliance on Burge's work see Stavropoulos, *Objectivity in Law* (above n 7), esp chs 2 and 6.

[64] The term connotes the fact that such kinds exist *qua* the elementary particles of matter (atoms and electrons).

[65] Similar criticism has been developed with respect to Tyler Burge's externalist theory of meaning for artefact kind concepts. See the recent discussions of J Brown, 'Critical Reasoning, Understanding and Self-Knowledge' (2000) LXI *Philosophy and Phenomenological Research* 659; ÅM Wikforss, 'Externalism and Incomplete Understanding' (2004) 54 *The Philosophical Quarterly* 287.

appropriate kind. To that extent, and despite declaring the opposite, interpretivism fosters a new kind of *scientia*, albeit different from the one presupposed by conventionalism. What the new *scientia* is after are *sui generis* evaluative particles[66] that (causally) determine the meaning of legal expressions.[67] How these properties are individuated, and by which means we access them cognitively, must remain a mystery.

So far essentialism falls prey to the exact same objections as Moore's own philosophy. The metaphysical extravagance of normative properties that are mind-independent and belong to the essence of things gives rise to a conception of normative knowledge so demanding that can not be met. On the face of it, it is not uncommon amongst essentialist philosophers to resort to a physicalist version of essentialism, one that attempts to reclaim mind-independence through a correspondence between normative properties of things and their physical (micro)structure. By switching to physicalism, however, essentialism fails to reclaim normative knowledge, for it employs evidence that is normatively inert. With respect to legal theory this move amounts to an empiricist *scientia* that attempts to ground legal propositions on things such as commands and sovereigns or the behavioural components of a practice of recognition (see above, part 4).

6.2.2 *The Lockean View*

This is the thesis that a complete description of the facts of the environment exhausts the question 'what is right to do'. The assumption here is that normative language depicts descriptive properties, and to that extent normative knowledge can be reported by descriptive language.[68] From a systematic standpoint the Lockean view is a highly successful move vis-à-vis the metaphysical accusation of queerness of normative discourse. To that accusation

[66] In the 20th century the first to postulate such entities was the Cambridge philosopher GE Moore, who argued that evaluative concepts are unanalysable because they refer to basic moral universals that can be perceived through intuition. Intuitionism, as Moore's theory came to be known, has been attacked on many occasions for its metaphysical extravagance, the most distinctive attack being the one by John Mackie, who famously accused Moore's metaphysics of being queer. See GE Moore (above n 58) and J Mackie (above n 47).

[67] Many philosophers evoke the notion of supervenience in an attempt to avoid both the reduction of evaluative properties to physical properties, as well as the idea of some robust evaluative realm that would be independent of the natural environment and whose appreciation would require that agents be equipped with some kind of sixth sense, see 6.2.2 below.

[68] This is the view associated with moral theories that aim to provide a naturalistic explication of normative judgements by relating their truth to the *empirical* circumstances of particular situations (moral particularism). For an overview of particularist views, see B Hooker and M Little (eds), *Moral Particularism* (Oxford, Clarendon Press, 2000). Interpretivism in legal theory should be interpreted as a variant of particularism to the extent that its proponents argue that the 'substance' of law, and hence the truth of legal propositions, lies in a mind-independent objective reality. There are numerous passages to suggest this interpretation in both R Dworkin (above n 7), chs 1 and 2, and N Stavropoulos (above n 7), chs 3 and 4.

the Lockean view replies that no metaphysically queer entities need to be presupposed because the totality of our normative judgements applies to one kind of thing only: the entities that constitute our environment. Furthermore, these entities are what they are in virtue of their descriptive properties. It follows that normative properties exist *qua* descriptive properties. One should distinguish between two at least directions into which the Lockean view could be further developed. The first is the *eliminativist* direction: as normative properties do not, strictly speaking, exist we would be much better off to forget about them altogether (eliminate them) and stick to those properties that actually do exist. In doing so it would make more sense to favour descriptive language over normative as the latter might give rise to confusions and support metaphysical illusions. This conclusion is exactly what the anti-reductionist reasoning aims to oppose: the fact that normative disagreement outlasts any description of the environment agreed upon by all parties, shows that the level of normativity cannot be eliminated without causing serious misrepresentations of the way we talk and act.

In response to this problem, the second direction taken by the Lockean view suggests a more level-headed solution. Instead of eliminating normative properties the second strategy takes them to be distinct properties that sit on top of, or *supervene* upon, descriptive properties. Leaving aside the theoretical complexities pertaining to the notion of supervenience,[69] the basic idea here is that normative properties do not exist independently of descriptive properties (or the way objects are) but are still discernible as distinct properties by perceivers. Usually an analogy between normative properties and secondary qualities of objects (colour, smell, sound, etc) is evoked in this context: the property of being violet (melodic, smelly, etc) exists as an experience-dependent property that, however, is a genuine property of objects that look violet. As such, secondary properties have two aspects: a *subjective/perspectival* aspect (they depend upon human perception); and an *objective* aspect (they are perceived according to how objects actually are, where the latter is determined by the primary qualities of objects). On this account normative properties, like secondary qualities, are intrinsically phenomenal *and* genuine properties of objects.[70] This elaboration of the Lockean view is not free from objections either. In particular two pertain to it: the *objection of subjectivism/perspectivism* and the *objection of justification*.

[69] For the notion of supervenience in general see F Jackson (above n 8); J Kim, *Supervenience and Mind: Selected Philosophical Essays* (Cambridge, Cambridge University Press, 1993); EE Savellos and ÜD Yalçin (eds), *Supervenience: New Essays* (Cambridge, Cambridge University Press, 1995); in moral philosophy see RM Hare, *The Language of Morals* (Oxford, Clarendon Press, 1952), 80n and 153n; RM Hare, *Freedom and Reason* (Oxford, Clarendon Press, 1962), 19n; in legal philosophy see R Dworkin, 'On Gaps in the Law' in P Amselek and N MacCormick, *Controversies about Law's Ontology* (Edinburgh, Edinburgh University Press, 1991), 84n; N Stavropoulos (above n 7).

[70] See eg, P Benn, *Ethics* (London, UCL Press, 1998), 42–3.

The objection of perspectivism rests on the fact that normative judgements are true only relative to perceivers. It is possible, the objection submits, that this fact outbalances any objective aspect of normative properties, with the effect that normative qualities will always be relative to the perceiver's viewpoint. However, unlike secondary qualities, in the case of normative qualities the viewpoint will depend on the perceivers' attitudes as they are shaped by the social and historical context in which perceivers are embedded. Accordingly depending on the viewpoint, the judgement that 'slavery is wrong' could be equally deemed true (classical Greece) or false (modern constitutional democracies).

Before commenting on the special nature of the viewpoint that pertains to normativity, a quick word on the second objection. The objection of justification[71] says that unlike judgements on colour (descriptive properties), judgements on normativity are usually underpinned by reasons. Indeed it is the case that when we make normative judgements we tend to support them with reasons, aiming thus to produce *justifications* rather that merely give *evidence* for them. To that extent the analogy with secondary qualities breaks.

Both objections, if taken seriously, seem to compel a distinct understanding of the viewpoint from which normative judgements are made. It seems that this viewpoint, to say the least, comprises more things than merely perceptual capacities (as the viewpoint with respect to colour and other secondary qualities does). Not too long from now, I will argue that those extra things consist of our capacity for *reason*, but for now it is worthwhile pressing a connection between the nature of the viewpoint of normativity and the idea of anti-reductionism. I said earlier that the most interesting aspect of non-cognitivism might be its anti-reductionist tendency. And although I often referred to the difference between the levels of description and normativity, I have not, so far, said anything about what, in positive terms, this difference consists in. Now the discussion of the two objections against the Lockean view gives me the opportunity to attempt to do so for the first time: I assumed that the reason why normative disagreement outlives any agreement on facts, is because the level of normativity cannot be reduced to that of description. Now, I can say that the reason for this is that the level of normativity relates to the standpoint of those who make normative judgements. But this should not be taken to constitute any concession to subjectivism.[72] Remember that I extracted non-reductionism from the tenet of non-cognitivism, and the latter categorically opposes

[71] See also P Benn, *ibid*, 45.

[72] Subjectivism, as was explained earlier *ibid*, argues that normative judgements are true in virtue of there being facts with respect to attitudes and other psychological states, and that to that extent normativity can be reduced to description. Hence subjectivism is a form of reductionism.

subjectivism, as it was argued earlier.[73] It follows that the standpoint of those who make normative judgements will have to be reconstructed as precluding subjectivism.

The task of clarifying the standpoint of normative judgements points toward a third, and to my view more successful, conception of cognitivism within which the balance between the objective and the subjective aspects of normative properties can be restored. In attempting a rough outline of that standpoint, I will take seriously the objections of perspectivism and justification and use them as guidelines for my construction.

6.3 Rationalist Normative Knowledge

The discussion so far has pointed to the key ingredients for a fresh look at the tenet of normative knowledge. We need to take seriously the idea that normative properties are perceiver-dependent, however without succumbing to subjectivism. At the same time we need to appreciate the fact that normative properties are objective properties of things, albeit without importing any claims for queer metaphysical entities. Let me attempt to reconcile those two aspects.

A valuable idea deriving from the perspectivist objection is that the objective aspect of normative properties is not self-standing. As in the case of secondary qualities, normative properties are genuine properties of objects to the extent that perceivers perceive them. This perceiver-dependent aspect is what I earlier referred to as the perceiver's standpoint. Obviously it is a very delicate issue what this standpoint consists in. In the case of secondary qualities, the standpoint of the perceiver comprises his/her perceptual powers so far as secondary qualities are intrinsically phenomenal. That is to say, those qualities substantiate in virtue of their being directed at perceivers' perceptual powers. Despite resembling secondary qualities, normative properties *are not* intrinsically phenomenal.[74] This is not very difficult to realise: no normative property is in any way perceived directly by our perceptual apparatus. To that extent normative properties and secondary qualities share merely the feature of being something like 'composite' properties, ie, of being held together by two components, one subjective and one objective. However, beyond this shared feature they should not be thought of as having very much in common.

To be sure, secondary qualities are intrinsically phenomenal; however, we need to conduct some investigation before passing any judgement with regard to the nature of normative properties. A good starting point is to ask

[73] Besides, subjectivism is anyway targeted by the objection of perspectivism, as explained above.
[74] *A fortiori* they are not extrinsically phenomenal either, for this would make them primary qualities.

how these properties are 'perceived', and subsequently to try to see what the subjective aspect of normative properties consists in. Strictly speaking, normative properties are not perceived. In passing a normative judgement one might perceive a lot of things, but none among them will be a normative property. (In contrast, in judging the colour of an object the relevant colour-property will count among the things perceived by the person who makes the judgement.) It follows that normative properties are not perceived in the strict sense of the word, and for that reason they should not be deemed to be phenomenal. Instead it should be enough to say that normative properties are *depicted* by those who use normative language.[75]

The next point to clarify is about the locus of *normative cognition*. Given that normative properties do not stimulate our perceptual apparatus, one is left with two *prima facie* possibilities: *first*, that normative knowledge rests on emotions and other psychological attitudes of those who are involved in normative judgement. This option is deemed unattractive on the grounds of the critique advanced by the objection of perspectivism. As argued, normative properties are composite in the sense that they comprise an objective and a perspectival side. Once the perspectival side is interpreted as consisting of emotions and other attitudes, the balance between the two sides is disturbed to the extent that the perspectival side cannot anymore accommodate the objective aspect of normative properties: if normative properties are known along the lines of the attitudes people develop toward certain facts, then normative judgements become radically indeterminate and no room is left for considering them as depicting genuine properties. However, if the perspectival side is constructed as comprising some objective element then the whole edifice of normative properties survives, indeed with surprisingly promising results. This brings me to the second alternative.

On the second alternative, the standpoint of normative understanding can be positioned in the realm of reason, where reason, for present purposes, may be understood as comprising those *a priori* propositions that are necessary conditions for knowledge. Given the fact that normative properties are dual-natured, any tenable cognitivism with respect to them has to maintain that the perspectival aspect of normative knowledge does not call off the fact that normative properties are genuine properties. One such strategy, already mentioned, is the Lockean view. There the perspective or the standpoint from which normative properties are cognised is the perceptual apparatus of perceivers. This apparatus constitutes, by and large, a common denominator to all human experience, and therefore can be accepted as constituting an objective standpoint from which we perceive the environment. Unfortunately, as was argued earlier, normative properties are

[75] Clearly, in recognising normative properties one will at the same time perceive a handful of other descriptive properties (primary and secondary) in virtue of which the environment is thus and so.

not (or at least not primarily) phenomenal and, to that extent, cannot be registered by our perceptual apparatus. The rationalist conception takes this last point seriously and contends that it is possible to have objective normative knowledge that is not (exclusively) perceptive.[76]

This is enabled on the ground of the Kantian idea of a *noumenal world* that exists alongside the *phenomenal world* (the physical environment). Strictly speaking the two Kantian worlds are merely two different standpoints for considering one and same world.[77] The phenomenal standpoint comprises all the phenomena that our senses report and which can be explained within the framework of succession of cause and effect (the principle of causality); the knowledge we form when we take this standpoint is perceptual/empirical. Contrapositively, the noumenal standpoint comprises the normative relationships that pertain to actions between agents. From this standpoint our actions are not subjected to the principle of causality, but to a principle of autonomy (the Categorical Imperative), hence our actions need to be *justified* as opposed to explained. The knowledge we form when we take this standpoint is rational (Kant says that it can be arrived at through *a priori* reasoning).

The strong *a priori* character of normative knowledge that Kant postulates can be relaxed.[78] The two standpoints should not be thought as being mutually exclusive. Rather, the idea is that we are at the same time phenomenal and noumenal beings, and therefore our actions are subjected to both principles (causality and freedom). However, the two principles address different levels of knowledge in a way similar to the idea of supervenience. An action can be explained by its causal antecedents to the extent that it is a phenomenal event. However, the question of whether it is justified or not refers to — indeed makes sense only via — the action not as a phenomenal but as a normative event, and hence needs to be answered on a different level (think of the following analogy: a copy of Kant's *Grundlegung zur Metaphysik der Sitten* occupies space in my briefcase not in virtue of its being a work in metaphysics, but in virtue of its volume). Accordingly, a successful or failed explanation of any action in casual terms cannot yet determine whether the same action is justified or not.

[76] It is worth noting that Kant never takes our perceptual apparatus to be sufficient in directly producing any sort of knowledge (not even phenomenal). Instead, both in the case of normative and phenomenal knowledge, perceptual input is subjected to interpretation, the difference between the two kinds of knowledge consisting in the fact that the interpretation is subjected to different standpoints: in the case of phenomenal knowledge the standpoint is that of the principle of causality, and in the case of normative knowledge the principle is that of the Categorical Imperative.

[77] For a general introduction see P Benn (above n 70), 99n. See also PF Strawson's classic, 'Freedom and Resentment', (1962) 48 *Proceedings of the British Academy* 1, for an analysis of the two standpoints with respect to questions of moral responsibility and determinism.

[78] By strong apriority I mean the idea that an action *qua* phenomenal event cannot be associated to any action *qua* normative event (that there is no correspondence between the level of description and the level of justification/prescription).

This conspectus of the phenomenal/noumenal distinction underpins a fresh look at the issue of normative knowledge. Primarily, on the Kantian view, normative properties (NP) cannot be known through perception. This is so because NP are neither intrinsically nor extrinsically phenomenal and, hence, cannot be perceived directly. Yet it is possible to acquire knowledge about NP through acquiring knowledge about norms (and the Categorical Imperative), by presupposing the noumenal point of view. This is not to say that normative knowledge is unadulterated by phenomenal elements, but merely that, unless one presupposes the noumenal point of view, normative knowledge cannot be substantiated as specifically referring to states of affairs pertaining to action/agency.

Explaining normative knowledge along these lines allows for understanding it as the outcome of a composite *interpretative process*: any phenomenal object/event will become normatively relevant in the light of a noumenal norm (or a cluster of such norms). On this understanding, any *judgement* that ascribes a normative property to some portion of the (phenomenal) environment will be like the conclusion of an argument that comprises two kinds of premises: an *noumenal premise* (*a priori* or *a posteriori*) and a *phenomenal premise* (an empirical judgement about the environment). It follows that the ascription of the normative property (the conclusion) will standardly be a *synthetic* judgement.[79] Synthetic judgements of that sort may refer either to the normative characterisation (or evaluation) of some aspect of the environment (an act's being right or wrong, good or bad, etc), or to the designation of a set of phenomenal items as amounting to the existence of a norm. In the vocabulary of properties, the latter can be represented as the ascription of the property 'being a norm' to a series of factual evidence: 'X, Y, Z is a norm'.

The noumenal point of view contains *a priori* as well as *a posteriori* norms. As *a priori* norms count a general principle of normative validity (one that is akin to Kant's Categorical Imperative) plus any other norm that can be grounded through the general principle in a more or less direct way, that is by a simple test of reason (akin to the Kantian test of universalisation).[80] As *a posteriori* norms count all other norms that feature as conclusions in normative (deductive) schemata whose major premises are either *a priori* norms or other *a posteriori* norms. Any contingently chosen maxim, or fact about the expression of a will, or about an emotional state can be inserted into the minor premise of the argument and eventually be 'upgraded' to a valid norm appearing in the conclusion of the argument. It follows that not any piece of noumenal knowledge is *a priori*: as remarked

[79] If the noumenal premise is analytic and the phenomenal is synthetic then the conclusion is synthetic. If the noumenal premise is synthetic then the conclusion is also synthetic. It follows, the conclusion will always be synthetic.
[80] One may include under this category *human rights* norms.

incidentally to the phenomenal/noumenal distinction, norms constitute merely the standpoint from which we interpret the environment in a normative way (if we do not take this standpoint it does not make sense to talk about normativity and justification). Be that as it may, the standpoint of normativity still relates to one and the same environment. It is, as it were, a distinct interpretation of the phenomenal environment. To that extent any ascription of NP on the ground of a specific norm will have to take into account what is the case (phenomenally speaking).

On this understanding the relevance of a norm, or even the need to introduce a (new) norm (exception from a norm, etc), will depend on the way things are; nevertheless, the norm taken on board will always be ultimately subjected to a test of rationality. Thus, the question about which states of affairs amount to the existence of a norm (in other words the question about the grounds of a normative proposition) will be the subject of a *synthetic judgement*, which, however, will be part of a chain of judgements that ultimately refer to an *a priori* norm of agency (it is like saying that our normative objectives or interests have to be reconciled with the way the world turns out to be).

In the context of legal theory, the rationalist explication of normative knowledge amounts to *prudentia*. Legal knowledge is noumenal and involves both *a priori* and *a posteriori* elements. A series of events is sufficient for grounding a proposition of law, if and only if it is interpreted in the light of another norm: the expression of the will of a party in a contract, the fact that a command is issued by someone who is the sovereign, or the fact that judge X demonstrates an attitude of commitment towards a pattern of behaviour, all these events count as grounds for a proposition of law (rule or principle; precedent or statute) only within a noumenal framework that ultimately refers to an *a priori* principle of normativity. As was the case with moral knowledge, also in law the rationalism of *prudentia* does not imply the neglect of factual evidence. Given the inherent weakness of a general principle of normativity in specifying more particular standards of correctness, rationalism looks into the way legal practice interacts with the environment (call this the *factual aspect of law*). What is of interest here is to illustrate in what ways a general normative principle that underpins legal practice is capable of determining more particular legal principles.[81] Indeed it is possible to demonstrate that an infinite number of legal principles that apply to particular cases amounts from the subsumption of an infinite number of factual situations under the general principle of legislation. Along

[81] This problem, which can also be understood as the relation between normative universals and particulars, has currently revived in the debate between moral universalists and particularists. For an authoritative source of reference, see B Hooker and M Little (above n 68). An interesting version of particularism, one that affirms the existence of universal principles, is solicited by R Holton, 'Principles and Particularisms' (2002) *Proceedings of the Aristotelian Society*, Suppl. Vol 126, 191–209, with a brief discussion of law.

these lines, and despite its thinness, the general normative principle is capable of explaining the passing from factual to evaluative knowledge without presupposing any kind of 'queer' entities, as John Mackie's notorious accusation goes.[82] As a consequence, rationalism amounts to the view that through a series of subsequent 'projections' of the normative point of view (*a priori* knowable) onto infinite fact-situations of the world (*a posteriori* knowable), it is possible to arrive at knowledge of particular legal principles (also *a posteriori* knowable) by avoiding the disadvantages of *scientia*, be it in the form of empiricism, conventionalism, or even interpretivism.

7. CONCLUSION

In this chapter I set out to investigate the conditions under which a legal theory may increase our knowledge in regard to law (legal knowledge). This investigation was deemed important in the light of a distinction drawn between theoretical propositions that amount to legal knowledge and those that are only randomly true. On the face of it, it was argued that not any legal theory is capable of producing legal knowledge but, instead, that there are specific conditions to be met by any theoretical account of law. Such conditions relate mainly to the quality of the evidence that a theory considers as relevant in making judgements regarding law's nature. In other words, a true judgement shall amount to an increase in legal knowledge if and only if it depicts those properties that are essential to law.

In a further step, it was claimed that law's essence is normative or action-guiding. This claim seems to be a commonplace amongst contemporary legal philosophers and has served also in this case as a working assumption for the entire chapter. Once normativity was identified as the key element of law's nature it has been possible to pin down the conditions for legal knowledge: *a true judgement of legal theory amounts to an increase of legal knowledge if and only if it depicts law's normative essence.*

Using law's normative essence as the compass for an investigation into legal knowledge, the remainder of the chapter undertook an inquiry into the conditions for depicting law's normative essence. The inquiry unfolded in two parts: the first part took on a classification of legal theories according to the way each of them understands and attempts to uncover law's normative nature. The second part underpinned the classification of the first part by drawing upon contemporary discussions in meta-ethics. There, the focus was on examining whether the different representations of law's normativity make coherent sense, metaphysically speaking.

Following on from that inquiry, the next part of the essay compiled the profile of two rival ideal-typical legal theories: one that fails to attend to

[82] J Mackie (above n 47).

legal knowledge, labelled *scientia*, and another that succeeds in doing so, labelled *prudentia*. In drawing the distinction, the emphasis was placed not so much on whether a legal theory treats law as normative (most do anyway) but, instead, on how it actually casts this claim. Accordingly, *scientia*-type theories try to understand law's normativity as corresponding to properties that are thought- or mind-independent and, hence, *phenomenal*, ie, capable of impinging upon our sensorial apparatus. On the other hand, *prudentia*-type theories conceive of normative properties as emanating from certain categories of thought in whose light we interpret the environment. To that extent, normative properties possess a constitutive *noumenal* component, one that cannot be depicted through experience.

Finally, the paper demonstrated the extent to which the two opposed representations of normativity, those of *scientia* and *prudentia*, manage to produce legal knowledge. *Scientia* was accused of falling short in this task for, metaphysically speaking, there are only two ways for making sense of mind-independent entities as bearers of normativity (Platonism or essentialism, and reductionism), both of which fail to generate normative knowledge. On the other hand, it was argued that *prudentia* lives up to the task of producing normative knowledge when it is coupled with a rationalist account of normativity. The latter makes possible an understanding of normative properties as projections of mind-dependent entities (norms) on the environment. Despite being mind-dependent, norms are not subjective, for they exist as objective constructions of reason.

Finally, it is noteworthy that the discussion throughout the chapter has rested on the author's belief that a general theoretical enquiry into law's nature is both desirable and possible.[83] Admittedly, this belief runs against one current of contemporary jurisprudential thought, which thinks that law's normative nature cannot be revealed on the basis of a neutral inquiry into the metaphysics of law but, instead, that legal theory has to engage directly with the substantive legal arguments of the various domains of legal discourse. To the extent that the arguments of this chapter have succeeded, it turns out that law's normative nature is not compatible with just any understanding of normativity, but only with one that is metaphysically capable of amounting to normative knowledge.

[83] In this, I fully concur with Robert Alexy. See R Alexy, 'The Nature of Legal Philosophy, this volume.

6

Law's Claim to Correctness

CARSTEN HEIDEMANN[1]

THE SUBJECT OF this paper is the plausibility of the thesis that law necessarily raises a claim to (moral) correctness, and that this establishes a connection between law and morality. At first glance, this does not seem to bear on the question whether legal science is *prudentia* or rather *scientia*. But this is not quite true. As will be shown, the thesis that law raises a claim to correctness is convincing at least in so far as legal dogmatists and members of the legal staff, ie, those engaged in finding out what ought to be done according to the law, utter normative assertive sentences and regularly raise a claim to truth. This means that they are talking about facts. Facts are a paradigm case of 'objective' entities, so — obviously — legal norms are objective in this sense.

It might seem as if this qualified legal science as *scientia*, not as *prudentia*. But *scientia* seems to deal with mind-independent objects. It is, however, not at all clear what it would mean to say that something is 'mind-dependent', thus the question whether legal norms are mind-*independent* (besides being objective) is not easily answered. It is a fact that thieves ought to be punished if (if-and-only-if) the sentence 'Thieves ought to be punished' is true. There is no way of capturing facts other than by true sentences; and language seems indeed to be mind-dependent (or, vice versa, mind to be largely language-dependent). So one *might* conclude that legal norms are in a way mind-dependent. But this applies to *all* kinds of facts and does not seem to have any impact on the status of legal science at all. For even an adherent of the thesis that jurisprudence is more 'prudence' than 'science' will probably grant that any dispute about norms where a rational disagreement is possible at all is a dispute about facts. Therefore, the alternative 'science or prudence' concerns less the character of the object of legal cognition than it does the *methods* by which normative or non-normative facts are ascertained.

It is obvious that empirical sciences, moral sciences and legal science employ different methods in determining their respective objects. Whether

[1] Warm thanks are due to Stanley L Paulson for help in matters of English style and grammar.

this suffices to hold that the institutionalised systematic attempt to find out what one ought to do according to the law is more 'prudence' than 'science' is not necessarily dependent on the status of the norm *qua* normative fact and is, to a certain degree, a matter of taste. It follows that this paper does *not* attempt to solve the problem whether legal science is *prudentia* or *scientia*; it simply tries to focus on one necessary precondition of the possibility of its being *either prudentia or scientia*, namely, the objectivity of law as a system of norms.

I. PROBLEMS CONNECTED WITH THE ARGUMENT FROM THE CLAIM TO CORRECTNESS

The Argument from the Claim to Correctness

According to Robert Alexy, a special type of argument called the *Richtigkeitsargument* (argument from the claim to correctness, in short 'ACC') serves to establish a necessary connection between law and morality. It is of central importance in his theory; at one place he even maintains that the 'connection-thesis' 'stands and falls with the thesis that the law necessarily raises a claim to correctness'.[2]

Alexy holds the ACC to be valid from the internal perspective, ie, from the point of view of someone who contemplates what ought to be done according to the law. In a compressed version, the ACC runs as follows:

> [According to the ACC,] individual legal norms and individual legal decisions as well as legal systems as a whole necessarily lay claim to correctness. A system of norms that neither explicitly nor implicitly makes this claim is not a legal system. In this respect, the claim to correctness has a classifying significance. Legal systems that do indeed make this claim but fail to satisfy it are legally defective legal systems. In this respect, the claim to correctness has a qualifying significance. An exclusively qualifying significance is attached to the claim to correctness of individual legal norms and individual legal decisions. These are legally defective if they do not make the claim to correctness or if they fail to satisfy it.[3]

In an initial step, the problems posed by this argument and the way Alexy tries to deal with them will be examined. In a second step, Alexy's claim that the argument establishes a necessary connection between law and morality will be scrutinised.

[2] R Alexy, 'My Philosophy of Law: The Institutionalisation of Reason' in LJ Wintgens (ed), *The Law in Philosophical Perspectives* (Dordrecht, Kluwer, 1999), 24.
[3] R Alexy, *The Argument from Injustice — A Reply to Legal Positivism* (Oxford, Clarendon Press, 2002), 35–6.

How Can Norms Raise a Claim?

Alexy's thesis that legal norms or legal systems raise a claim to correctness poses, initially, the question as to the source of the claim. For Alexy favours a 'semantic' conception of legal norms according to which norms are abstract normative meaning-contents.[4] Obviously, a meaning-content cannot raise a claim. Consequently, Alexy concedes that, strictly speaking, claims can only be raised by 'subjects having the capacity to speak and to act',[5] so that the claim is not raised by law itself, but by those persons who work 'in and for the law' like the legislator and the judge. This solution, however, gives rise to further problems.

How is the Act of Claiming Correctness Connected to the Legal Norm?

If we assume that the claim is raised not by norms but by participants in the legal procedures, the question emerges as to how the act of claiming correctness is connected to the legal norm as a normative meaning-content. When expounding the ACC, Alexy most often simply talks as if the legal norms themselves raise a claim to correctness, and this implies that if there is anything wrong with the claim, it directly affects the meaning-content of the speech-act.[6] But this is highly doubtful. Just imagine people in Galileo's times winking — thus implying that they are just making fun without raising any claim to truth — and 'asserting' among themselves:

> 'Oh yes, of course, the earth is moving around the sun!'

What they say, ie, the meaning-content of their utterance, is in no way faulty, even though they did not raise a claim to correctness.[7] This example, however, just concerns a special kind of speech-act, namely, the act of asserting something. This prompts the next question as to what kind of act is involved in raising a claim to correctness.

[4] R Alexy, *A Theory of Constitutional Rights* (Oxford, Oxford University Press, 2002), 20–28.
[5] Alexy (above n 2), 24.
[6] See R Alexy, 'Law and Correctness' (1998) 51 *Current Legal Problems* 206: 'Therefore it could be said that law raises this claim through persons who work for and in it.'
[7] This argument poses a problem that will not be pursued in this paper: Either the speech-act of asserting is necessarily connected to a claim to correctness; in this case, employing the form of this speech-act in 'opaque' contexts, like joking, being ironic or telling a fairy-tale, does not amount to making an assertion. Or even these special language-games presuppose that something is asserted; in this case, joking, being ironic or telling a story involves making an assertion, and this is *not* necessarily connected to a claim to correctness. A solution might be that these special language-games are 'secondary' ways of employing the speech-act of asserting. The first-level-act is an assertion with a claim to correctness that is embedded in a second-level-act qualifying this claim.

What Kind of Act is it by which the Claim is Raised?

Alexy is not entirely clear on this point. Both of his standard examples for faulty acts whose content denies the claim to correctness[8] imply that the claim is raised by means of acts through which legal norms are brought into existence. In those passages, however, where Alexy explicitly deals with the nature of these acts, he assimilates them to assertions. Thus, he maintains that

> claims to correctness do not exist only in law. They are also raised with moral value and obligation judgements. In their most general form they are connected to the speech-act of assertion.[9]

In other contexts he holds that 'only those speech-acts which raise a claim to truth or correctness are assertions',[10] and that 'anyone who asserts something raises a claim to truth or correctness'.[11] Thus, correctness seems to be somewhat like normative truth, and a claim to correctness is raised by anybody asserting a normative sentence.

This means that whatever else a legislator or judge may be doing in issuing a norm, he is asserting a normative sentence, and this constitutes his claim to correctness. Given the insight won by the example of Galileo's contemporaries, it follows — contrary to Alexy's intention — that it does not necessarily affect the validity of the norm as a meaning-content when the party to assert it does not raise the claim to correctness.

Who Raises the Claim to Correctness for Legal Norms or Legal Systems?

On this basis, it might seem as if it were not necessary to investigate the matter any further, for the thesis that any failure to raise the claim to correctness of those creating or asserting law renders the law defective has been shown to be wrong from the beginning. Still, if it really were the case that any assertion of a legal norm necessarily comprises the claim of being correct in a moral sense, this might be a sign for the indivisibility of law and morality. It is therefore worthwhile to continue examining the case.

Connecting the claim to correctness with the speech-act of asserting something gives rise to further questions. First, why should the function of raising law's claim to correctness be restricted to the legal staff? For if this claim accompanies *any* legal normative assertion whatever, the person who makes it should not then matter. To be sure, Alexy himself grants that the claim is also raised by any 'participant' in a legal system, for example, by a

[8] See below.
[9] Alexy (above n 6), 214.
[10] Alexy (above n 2), 27.
[11] R Alexy, 'Discourse Theory and Human Rights' (1996) 9 *Ratio Juris* 214.

citizen in a public debate about legal matters.[12] But, on the one hand, either this circle of possible claimants has to be circumscribed more closely, or anybody who utters legal normative sentences with a claim to correctness or truth must be regarded as a 'participant'. On the other, it seems obvious that the functions of just describing or interpreting norms and issuing norms should be distinguished with regard to the claim to correctness, but Alexy's theory does not offer sufficient tools here. Although Alexy, in his *Theory of Constitutional Rights*, makes a distinction on the pragmatic level between 'asserting a norm' and 'creating a norm' as different ways of using normative sentences,[13] he does not elaborate it. A possible solution may be that both the acts of describing norms and of issuing norms are based on the speech-act of asserting, but that issuing a norm — as a performative — demands a special institutionalised context and comprises the claim that the performance of the speech-act in this context brings about the truth of the asserted normative sentence.

The second question is: How is it possible to raise the claim to correctness for the whole legal system? There seems to be no member of the legal staff whose acts could be regarded as representative of the legal order as a whole. Do we have to assume that the judge who sentences someone raises a claim to correctness not only for his individual judgement but also for the general norm he applies, or even for the whole legal system? Or does a legal system as a whole raise a claim to correctness if the authors of the constitution raised a claim to correctness? Alexy's examples where law does *not* raise the claim seem to imply that every legal person raises the claim only for the act performed by that person. Recently, Alexy has maintained that legal systems lose their legal character only 'if such a large number of norms or decisions goes without the claim to correctness that one can say that the system as a whole abandons the claim'.[14] This implies that the legal order as a whole raises the claim to correctness where a certain number of individual legal acts are accompanied by the claim. Consequently, saying that legal systems raise a claim to correctness would simply be a 'double' figure of speech; for neither do norms raise a claim, nor is there anyone who raises the claim for the legal order as a whole. The claim can only be raised for individual norms.

What is Meant by the 'Claim' to 'Correctness'?

The central problem, however, has not yet been discussed: What exactly is meant by 'correctness' and by someone 'raising a claim' to correctness?

[12] Alexy (above n 2), 24.
[13] Alexy (above n 4), 28–30.
[14] R Alexy, 'On the Thesis of a Necessary Connection between Law and Morality: Bulygin's Critique' (2000) 13 *Ratio Juris* 142.

a) On the concept of correctness, Alexy is ambiguous. One reading is that correctness is nothing but truth applied to normative sentences, so that the claim to correctness is a claim to normative truth. This is implied by his thesis that the claim to correctness is raised by the speech-act of asserting. Moreover, Alexy explicitly appeals to Tarski's *Convention T* to explain the concept of correctness, by maintaining that 'the sentence "X ought to be done" is correct exactly if X ought to be done'.[15] This is a rather formal explanation of correctness as being truth-like.

At the same time, however, Alexy favours a more material conception according to which correctness in the legal sphere at least partly means being in accordance with justice or with a universal morality.[16] What is more, this substantial interpretation is in fact necessary to back his claim that the ACC establishes a connection between law and morality. But it gives rise to several difficulties. First, simply including justice in what somebody asserting a legal sentence claims is to beg the question; this is exactly what a positivist would deny. Second, Alexy stresses that 'it is a genuine characteristic of the claim to correctness that the criteria of correctness are open'.[17] In a similar way, he holds that 'in order to raise a claim to justifiability one must not refer to good but just to any reasons'.[18] But such formal concepts of correctness and justifiability seem to exclude defining correctness substantially as justice.[19] This problem will be reconsidered below when examining examples intended by Alexy to show that law raises a claim to substantial correctness.

b) According to Alexy, the 'claim' to correctness comprises three different elements:

> [Legal acts] are always connected to the non-institutional act of *asserting* that the legal act is substantially and procedurally correct . . . Correctness implies justifiability. Therefore, in raising a claim to correctness, law also raises one to justifiability. In recognising this claim it does not only accept a general obligation to justification on principle; it also maintains that this obligation is complied with or can be met. The claim to correctness therefore includes not only a mere assertion of correctness but a *guarantee* of justifiability. Moreover, there is a third element besides assertion and guarantee. It is the *expectation* that all addressees of the claim will accept the legal act as correct as long as they take the standpoint of the respective legal system and so long as they are reasonable.[20]

[15] R Alexy, 'Probleme der Diskurstheorie' in *Recht, Vernunft, Diskurs* (Frankfurt, Suhrkamp, 1995), 118.
[16] Alexy (above n 2), 25.
[17] Alexy (above n 6), 209.
[18] Alexy (above n 11), 214.
[19] This is all the more so because truth probably is not a matter of degree, whereas justice is.
[20] Alexy (above n 6), 208 (emphasis in the original).

This is a decidedly heterogeneous mixture. An assertion[21] is a linguistic element, a guarantee is a normative element, and an expectation is a mental element. Alexy does not go any further in setting forth how these elements are related to each other, and to assess the plausibility of the conception it is helpful to examine the speech-act of asserting by which the claim to truth or correctness is raised. This matter cannot be discussed in detail in this context, however, so I will simply mention the necessary features of asserting something in a rather apodictic way.[22]

Suppose someone asserts the sentence *p*. In analysing this, several levels may be distinguished. First, the meaning-content of his utterance implies — according to Tarski's *Convention T* — that *p* is true.[23] This is a matter of the semantics of the utterance. Second, the speaker, by performing the speech-act, points to several features of his attitude towards his utterance: that he believes that *p* and — though this is contestable — that *p* can be justified.[24] Third, by performing the speech-act he regularly implies or purports that he expects us — the attentive audience — to believe that *p* (and, perhaps, to believe that *p* can be justified).

Failures in some of these categories may have different consequences. If the content of the speech-act does *not* imply its own truth then, obviously, the speaker has failed to point to a fact from the beginning, so his utterance is no assertion at all. On the other hand, it does not matter whether the content of the speech-act is true or can be justified, it will be an assertion nevertheless. On the second level, there may be two kinds of mistakes. First, the speaker does not believe that *p* or that *p* can be justified, he only purports to believe it. This, however, does not count as a flaw in his utterance; he is just lying, and a successful lie even presupposes a successful assertion.[25]

[21] Note, by the way, the reduplication: asserting something comprises a claim to correctness, which in turn is partly made up of another assertion. The danger of an infinite regress is lurking (still, this need not be harmful in itself).

[22] For an interesting discussion of the relation between asserting and knowing, see T Williamson, 'Knowing and Asserting' (1996) 105,4 *The Philosophical Review* 489. I would differ from Williamson's conception, however, in that the rules he mentions which govern the speech-act of asserting are not constitutive for performing this speech-act but just part of its 'ethics'.

[23] See A Tarski, 'The Semantical Concept of Truth and the Foundations of Semantics' in Tarski, *Logic, Semantics, Meta-Mathematics*, 2nd edn (Indianapolis, Hackett, 1983). One might be inclined to say that asserting *p* not only implies that *p* is true but also that *p* can be justified. This, however, is contestable; a strict realist (in the philosophical sense) would not subscribe to this thesis.

[24] To cover all possible cases, the term 'justify' has to be understood in a broad sense: one can justify *p*, for example, by giving reasons which imply *p*, by 'pointing' to something which can be experienced or by referring to an authority. Saying that one must purport to believe that what one asserts can be justified does not, by the way, contradict the thesis that *p* possibly does not imply that *p* can be justified (see n 23); for asserting *p* implies that the truth of *p* is known by the speaker, and it is impossible that something be known without any justification. Thus, a realist may consistently hold that truth is independent of justification and that someone may assert *p* only if he thinks that he can justify *p*.

[25] It might be said, however, that the audience — in the absence of evidence to the contrary —

Second, the speaker even fails to purport that he believes that *p*, or that *p* can be justified. In this case, his utterance is no assertion at all, for his act does not involve pointing to a fact. On the third level, things are even more complicated. If the speaker fails to convince the audience of the fact that *p*, or if he succeeds in convincing his audience of *p* even though *p* is not the case, then his utterance is still successful in counting as an assertion. If he (simply) fails to purport that he wants or expects us to believe *p*, his utterance is an assertion as well, but it is a faulty one.

In these cases, the claim to truth is 'raised' (from the perspective of an 'objective recipient') as long as there is a successful, though perhaps faulty, assertion, ie, as long as the meaning-content of the speech-act implies its own truth and the speaker at least purports to believe that *p* and to believe that *p* can be justified.[26] Any other mistakes are irrelevant.

This can in fact be shown, as Alexy points out, by making the negation of what the utterance presupposes explicit. For the explicit negation of elements necessarily involved in making an assertion gives rise to — at the very least — a performative contradiction (being a logical contradiction between the contents of an utterance and what is necessarily presupposed by the performance of the utterance). An example of a sentence negating the first-level presupposition of its own assertion would run:

'Snow is white, but it is not true that snow is white.'

This, indeed, counts as being no less than a *logical* contradiction. Second-level examples would be:

'Snow is white, but I do not believe that snow is white.'

and

'Snow is white, but I do not believe that it can be justified that snow is white.'

The first sentence gives expression to a performative contradiction; the second one contestably[27] does as well. A third-level example would be:

regularly has to assume that the utterer really does believe that the content of his assertion is true. For unless a vast majority of those persons who assert something really believed what they say, the language-game of asserting could not work.

[26] For a similar conception see D Davidson, *Inquiries into Truth and Interpretation* (Oxford, Clarendon Press, 1984), 268.

[27] In what follows, when speaking of an assertion's implying its own justifiability, I shall drop the qualification that this is 'contestable'. The question whether someone who does not pretend that what he asserts is justified does not 'really' assert something is scarcely to be answered in a rational way. For anyone who favours — as I do — a non-realist conception of truth, the connection between truth and justifiability is obvious, and for someone defining

'The earth is moving around the sun, but I do not expect you to believe that the earth is moving around the sun.'

This involves *no* performative contradiction; the sentence is perfectly sensible if uttered by someone like Galileo before an uneducated audience, which shows that the purported expectation of acceptance is no necessary part of the assertion. But the utterance of the sentence would be faulty in so far as the point of an assertion is usually to 'inform' someone not only in the weak sense of uttering a truth, but also in the sense of trying to convince him, and the speaker explicitly negates this point of his utterance.

If we leave aside certain peculiarities of normative sentences[28] and transfer these results to the normative sphere (disregarding the question whether there is a significant difference between simply describing and issuing norms), we get the following thesis: A claim to correctness is raised by a speaker if the normative meaning-content O*p* of his speech-act implies its own correctness/truth and the speaker purports both to believe that O*p* and to believe that it can be justified in some way that O*p*.

This has the following consequences for the alleged three elements of the claim to correctness, namely, assertion of correctness, guarantee of justifiability, and expectation of acceptance. The 'assertion of correctness' is captured by the feature that the normative meaning-content of an assertion implies its own truth and that the speaker purports to believe in it (and in its justifiability). The (purported) 'expectation' that the audience will accept the uttered meaning-content as true, however, is *not* a necessary feature of the speech-act of asserting and is therefore not included in the claim to correctness. Finally, it is not easy to say what the normative element of the claim, the 'guarantee of justifiability', amounts to. For an answer, it is helpful to examine the conditions under which we are inclined to reprimand someone for making an assertion on the ground that he has not fulfilled the obligation undertaken by asserting something.

There are *prima facie* two different situations that might be regarded as fulfilment of the obligation: first, the speaker has done his best to ascertain the truth of what he utters and really *believes* that what he utters is true and can be justified; second, what he utters really *is* true and can be justified. In my estimation, the audience would not reproach the speaker simply if what he asserted proved to be wrong or unfounded; rather, they would reproach him only if he did not believe that what he had asserted was true and could

knowledge as 'justified true belief' it is likewise clear that asserting something comprises a claim to justifiability, for saying 'Snow is white, but I do not know that snow is white' obviously involves a performative contradiction.

[28] According to Alexy, two contradictory norms/normative sentences can both be relatively correct (*relativ richtig*), if both are possible outcomes of an ideal discourse: see Alexy (above n 15), 121.

be justified, or if he had been careless in ascertaining its truth. So the guarantee of justifiability amounts to an obligation to make an assertion only if one believes that what one says is both true and can be justified, and if one has not been careless in forming this belief. This obligation, however, is arguably not part of the claim to correctness but part of the 'ethics' of the corresponding language-game of asserting something — instead of being constitutive of it — ie, not fulfilling this obligation is not detrimental to the character of the assertion as such.

What Kind of Correctness is Claimed with Necessity?

It was demonstrated above that Alexy is not quite clear on the point whether the 'correctness' claimed by issuing or asserting a norm amounts to a Tarski-like formal correctness, or to something more substantial. When arguing for the necessity of the claim to correctness, Alexy takes correctness to be *substantial* correctness, ie, moral correctness, and he takes the necessity of the claim to correctness to be something akin to, though not identical with, *logical* necessity. It cannot be explained but only demonstrated by explicitly negating the claim in the assertion itself, for this negation results in a performative contradiction — a performative contradiction being a logical contradiction between the content of an assertion and the necessary presuppositions of its utterance. To illustrate this, Alexy brings forward two examples. The first example is an article from a constitution running:

> 'X is a sovereign, federal, and unjust republic.'

According to Alexy,

> neither the conventional nor the moral, nor the technical defectiveness explains the absurdity of the injustice clause. It results ... from a contradiction. Such a contradiction emerges because the act of giving a constitution encloses a claim to correctness which is mainly a claim to justice in this case. Claims comprise ... assertions. In the case of the claim to justice raised here, it is the assertion that the constituted republic is just. This assertion implicit in the act of giving a constitution contradicts the explicit content of the constituent act, the injustice clause.[29]

This example poses several problems. First, the authors of a constitution are not in the position of any participant in the legal system, rather, they are privileged: on the one hand, they are law-makers; on the other hand, in the act of law-making, they are not bound by any other positive legal norm. Second, 'X is an unjust republic' is neither expressive of a constituent act nor is it a normative sentence. It requires some interpretation. Somebody

[29] Alexy (above n 2), 25.

who defines the law-maker in terms of social power might interpret it non-normatively as meaning:

> 'We wish every member of the legal staff to act in an unjust way, and we are able to enforce this.'

To give a normative twist to it, it needs reformulation such as the following one:

> 'We hereby enact that every member of the legal staff ought to act in an unjust way.'

This sentence, however, is not at first sight absurd. There are two possible interpretations. On the one hand, taking a natural-law stand, we might interpret 'acting in an unjust way' as meaning, *inter alia*, acting in a way in which one categorically ought *not* to act. But then we would not have to recur to the figure of a performative contradiction to show the flaw. It would be — as far as the content of the enactment is concerned — a simple *logical* flaw, for the sentence, spelled out, would run:

> 'We hereby decree that all members of the legal staff ought to act in a way they ought not to act.'

On the other hand, keeping law and morality/justice apart, one might interpret the sentence as meaning:

> 'We hereby decree that every member of the legal staff ought to act in a way contrary to what material principles of justice demand.'

This, as a basic principle of law, is certainly strange, but not at first sight self-contradictory or absurd. This can be demonstrated by 'toning down' the sentence, as in the following version:

> 'We hereby decree that every member of the legal staff ought to act strictly according to the law, even if this contradicts fundamental moral principles or principles of justice.'

This formulation seems to be entirely satisfactory, at least from a logical point of view. (I will elaborate on this point in what follows.)

Alexy's second example is the judicial verdict:

> 'The defendant is (wrongly, because the valid law was interpreted incorrectly) sentenced to life imprisonment.'

This is an explicit act of issuing an individual norm, but its content still needs reformulation as a normative sentence. It is not quite clear what

Alexy means by an 'incorrect interpretation of the valid law', but the sentence might possibly be formulated as follows:

> 'I hereby decide that the defendant ought to be imprisoned for life, although this cannot be justified in terms of the valid law.'

Now, if we take the stance of a radical positivist, who says that all legal acts must be justifiable by means of the positive law (alone), there does indeed seem to be a performative contradiction, for the judge's act implies that the words 'the defendant ought to be imprisoned for life' can be justified by the positive law. But, ironically, the judge's decision need not be absurd for the *non*-positivist (depending on the interpretation of the terms 'valid law' and 'non-positivism').

In any case, the examples cannot be generalised. They simply concern the law-giver, not any participant in the legal system; the first example concerns the special case of enacting a constitution, where there usually are no legal criteria for the validity of the enactment, and the second example concerns the special case of a judge authoritatively interpreting the law. This failure of the examples to provide support for the point they are supposed to be making, namely, that any legal actor necessarily raises a claim to substantial correctness, is corroborated by the fact that in legal practice, it is not uncommon to encounter judges deciding in the following way (the example is from my own experience):

> 'I hereby dismiss the action of *A* against the immigration office demanding a residence permit. I think it is morally wrong to deny *A* the permit, but our strict laws leave me no other choice.'

This judgment certainly is not faulty from a legal point of view, and there does not seem to be any performative contradiction either. Consequently, if a judge consistently decides such that the content of his decision is in accordance with moral principles that are supposed to be objectively valid, and if by doing so he totally disregards the positive law, we might appreciate this, and — in some cases — even demand such behaviour from him; but we still would be inclined to think that somehow he abandoned the role assigned to him by the legal system.

It might be objected that even in the example given — the denial of a residence permit — the judge necessarily raises the claim that his decision is morally justified in so far as the legal system as a whole is correct and the wrong done to the plaintiff is not unbearable, and that if this be the case there is a duty even to observe unjust norms.[30] To a certain degree, this is plausible. It would probably capture not only the average stance of a mem-

[30] George Pavlakos has pointed out to me that this position might well involve a contradiction, based as it is on something like the following argument: '(1) Morally, we ought to act in

ber of the legal staff, but also what the judge in the example given had in mind. But the argument would force us to reformulate the claim to correctness: the judge would not claim that the issued norm is correct in the sense of being just, he would simply claim that it is part of a system which is just, or at least morally justified, as a whole, and that the decision is obligatory inside this system and, finally, the decision is not unjust in the extreme.

The argument, however, in this complex form will scarcely do without the presupposition that there *is* a very special connection between law and morality, so the possibility of a *petitio principii* looms large. But there are more significant flaws. On the one hand, an amoral or indifferent judge is neither a logical nor a psychological impossibility. On the other hand, the assertion:

> 'I sentence you to death, for our laws impose this as a duty on me, even though I think this is extremely unjust'

does not involve a performative contradiction. A rejoinder might take the following form: in a case like this, the judge at least implicitly claims that it his *moral* duty to obey every positive law, even if it is an extremely unjust one, without any exception, so that he claims a kind of moral correctness for his decision after all. This is probably true, but not really helpful. For the judge's position would imply that any legal norm that meets the positivist criteria of legal validity at the same time meets the criteria of moral validity, and this would result in the worst kind of positivism imaginable, actually excluding any questions directed to the substantive moral correctness of the positive law. Still, it is a conceivable stance. In fact, as is well known, Kant advocated a position somewhat like this.[31]

What is more, the claim to moral correctness raised by a judge would in the first instance not simply be the kind of claim to correctness which attaches to an assertion, but rather a claim that might be said — if we are inclined to metaphorical and metaphysical extravagance — to be 'implied' by *any* act that can be imputed to a responsible person: the claim that the act reflects moral standards. This thesis might be supported by a metaphysical conception of a Kantian hue according to which the concepts of 'will', 'norm', 'act', 'person' and 'imputation' are *gleichursprünglich*, ie, interdependent: any 'act' may be distinguished from an exclusively causal 'event' in

the way x. (2) Morally, we ought to obey the law. (3) Legally, we ought to act in the way ~x. (4) So, morally, we ought to act in the way ~x.' Still, the position is sound. Premise (1) contains what morality demands when disregarding the existence of positive law; conclusion (4) contains what morality demands taking into account the existence of law.

[31] I Kant, *Metaphysik der Sitten*, W Weischedel (ed) (Frankfurt, Suhrkamp, 1968), 437–43 (A 173–82/B 203–12).

that it is 'willed'; this means that it can be 'imputed' to a 'person', and this again means that it is regarded as being governed by (valid) norms. Thus, if anyone behaves in a way we call 'acting', we take him to aspire that his behaviour be in accordance with universally valid norms governing human conduct, ie, morality; and we therefore reproach him if his behaviour proves *not* to be in accordance with morality.[32] These, however, are matters which cannot further be discussed in this context.

A claim similar to the claim raised by acting might be said to attach — this much has to be granted — to any unconditional assertion of an Ought. If somebody asserts 'A ought to be imprisoned' instead of 'Legally, A ought to be imprisoned', he claims that A ought to be imprisoned *all-things*-considered (and not just *all-legal-norms*-considered). And claiming that A ought to be imprisoned all-things-considered certainly is a way of claiming that it is morally obligatory that A be imprisoned. If, however, someone takes it to be a moral duty to obey any positive law, then even extremely unjust measures might be morally obligatory in this sense, which is to say that the claim does not amount to much. What is more, this wide range of the claim to correctness would be a *symptom* of a justificatory connection between law and morality rather than *constituting* this connection; it presupposes the unity of the normative sphere. I will return to this point.

It might be objected that the cases dealt with in the last paragraphs just stand for one part of the range of possible permutations between law and morality, namely, the situation where legal demands are in conflict with moral demands, and that there is also a different kind of permutation, namely, the situation where the positive law simply does not determine that a certain legal act be issued by the legal authority.

No doubt this is true. But situations where morality comes to bear on legal procedures just because there are no legal constraints are comparatively uninteresting. To be sure, if we presuppose the conception of moral-claims-necessarily-raised-by-acts introduced above and/or take any unconditional normative assertion to claim that the asserted sentence can be justified all-things-considered, the authors of the constitution make several mistakes by enacting an unjust constitution and, moreover, explicitly saying that it is unjust. But these mistakes have nothing to do with the law itself, for they

[32] A similar conception can be found in Kant's philosophy: the will which governs conscious acts can only be thought of as an 'autonomous' will, ie, as a will necessarily subjected to normative moral laws. So any procedure which we would characterise as a conscious act must be regarded as governed by a will subjected to (normative) laws, and this state of affairs might well be expressed by saying that any willed act implies a claim to moral correctness. See I Kant, *Grundlegung zur Metaphysik der Sitten*, W Weischedel (ed) (Frankfurt, Suhrkamp, 1974), 81 (BA 98): 'Der Satz aber: der Wille ist in allen Handlungen sich selbst ein Gesetz, bezeichnet nur das Prinzip, nach keiner anderen Maxime zu handeln, als die sich selbst auch als ein allgemeines Gesetz zum Gegenstande haben kann. Dies ist aber gerade die Formel des kategorischen Imperativs und das Prinzip der Sittlichkeit: also ist ein freier Wille und ein Wille unter sittlichen Gesetzen einerlei.'

occur in a range of acts which are in no way legally determined. There is no reason why we should think that acts which do not raise or even deny a claim to moral justification, but which nevertheless are not legally determined and, therefore, do not conflict with positive law, are *legally* faulty. As long as an act is not determined by the law, it does not matter, from the perspective of law, whether the actor raises a claim to correctness; the act vis-à-vis the law is indifferent. The possible faultiness of such an act stems from its violating the rules of *morality* and of the language-game of *asserting* something, so that any failure to raise the claim can only lead to moral or linguistic faultiness.

How Can the Claim to Correctness be a 'Necessary' but only Qualifying Feature of Legal Acts or Assertions about the Law?

Another problem with regard to the 'necessity' of the claim to correctness arises from Alexy's thesis that, on the one hand, the claim is necessarily raised by legal norms but, on the other, a legal norm which does not raise the claim still is a legal norm. This — as Bulygin has pointed out[33] — is not tenable.[34] In his reply to Bulygin, Alexy defended his position by introducing the distinction between a 'subjective' and an 'objective' raising of the claim: a person raises a claim subjectively if he wants to raise it; an objective claim, on the other hand, is 'no private matter, but it is necessarily connected to the role of a participant in the legal system'.[35] Thus, all legal acts would be connected with two different claims to correctness: the objective claim would necessarily be raised as soon as the institutional act of law-giving is performed; the subjective claim would be raised only if the person performing the act shows that he 'agrees' with it. So it would be possible for law not to raise the claim 'subjectively', even though it is necessarily raised 'objectively'.

This, however, is not convincing. First, it is difficult to see how the distinction between a subjective and an objective raising of the claim might work. If some member of the legal staff consciously plays his official role *qua* norm-issuer by performing a certain legal act with an eye thereby to issue a legal norm, he can scarcely avoid raising the claim connected to this

[33] E Bulygin, 'Alexy und das Richtigkeitsargument' in E Garzón Valdés et al (eds), *Rechtsnorm und Rechtswirklichkeit, Festschrift för Werner Krawietz zum 60.* (Berlin, Duncker & Humblot, 1993), 21; E Bulygin, 'Alexy's Thesis of the Necessary Connection between Law and Morality' (2000) 13 *Ratio Juris* 134.

[34] The problem, of course, is easily resolved by appeal to the fact that there is no necessary relation between the validity of a normative meaning-content and the claim to correctness connected to the speech-act of asserting it: the claim is raised by asserting a norm, but failing to raise the claim only destroys the character of the speech-act; it does not (necessarily) affect the norm itself. This resolution, however, cannot be granted by Alexy, for — as was shown above — it undermines his version of the ACC.

[35] R Alexy (above n 6), 206.

role, so he 'wants' to raise it. Second, and more important, the distinction is not really helpful. For if any act meeting the formal conditions of a legal act 'objectively' claims correctness, then it is impossible, according to Alexy's conception, for the corresponding legal norm *not* to raise the claim. So it is not possible for anything to be a legal norm or a legal system and not objectively to raise the claim. And it could not really be to the detriment of legal norms or of the legal system as a whole if the participants in the law did not raise the claim 'subjectively' (whatever this means) or even deny it. There is nothing 'logically' wrong with a smoothly running legal system which is managed by a bunch of cynics who pronounce their decisions in the manner of:

> 'It's all humbug; there is no justice and no objective normativity either. Anyhow, hereby I sentence *X* to repair the damage done to *Y*, for the state is silly enough to pay me for this work.'

II. A NECESSARY CONNECTION BETWEEN LAW AND MORALITY

The first part of what has been said thus far can be summed up as follows: People who assert legal-norm sentences — be it that they describe legal norms, be it that they issue norms — raise a claim to correctness or truth. This means that the normative meaning-content of their utterance O*p* implies its own truth and that they purport to believe that O*p* and that O*p* can be justified. They are obligated to make an assertion only if they really believe that O*p* and that O*p* can be justified, and if they have done their best to ascertain this. If, however, the claim to correctness is not raised, or if the obligation is not fulfilled, this has no necessary consequences for the normative meaning-content of their utterance or its validity (as long as its character as a proposition is left untouched).

Moreover, legal actors or persons asserting legal-norm sentences do not necessarily claim that the content of their decision or assertion is morally justified. Still, by virtue of being actors, they might be said to claim that their act is in accordance with morality; what is more, any unconditional assertion of an ought-sentence contains the claim that this sentence is correct 'all-things-considered', ie, so long as we regard morality as an overarching system, *morally* correct.

The significance of this point is as follows. On the one hand, the fact that a claim to correctness is raised by any act or assertion does not constitute a necessary connection between law and morality, for the validity of the legal meaning-content of an utterance is not impaired by failing to raise the claim to — moral or legal — correctness. What is more, an act's or utterance's being faulty in a *moral* sense does not imply that it is faulty in a *legal* sense as well.

On the other hand, the fact that a claim to correctness is raised by normative assertions prepares the ground for a certain kind of 'soft' connection thesis. For the claim to correctness is linked exclusively to meaning-contents, which imply their own truth. So the thesis that law raises a claim to correctness may be reissued as the thesis that legal norms are 'normative facts' that are expressed by true normative sentences. This means that the ACC can be reformulated as the claim that legal-norm sentences imply their own truth, and that this connects law and morality. This thesis is *prima facie* plausible if we take a non-realist stance by assuming that the notion of truth implies justifiability,[36] and bestow a realist touch upon it by assuming that there can be just *one* truth. The former assumption might serve to connect legal and moral justification, the latter assumption amounts to postulating the consistency of all true normative sentences. This would mean, at the very least, that there can be no true assertive sentence expressing a legal Ought that contradicts a true assertive sentence expressing a moral Ought, and there would indeed be a necessary connection between law and morality.

But this solution, apart from being trivial, contains some flaws. First, the result reached by analysing the claims raised by the judge's 'justified-but-morally-wrong decision' points into a different direction. Obviously, it is possible that there are valid legal and moral norms that contradict each other. This problem, however, might be tackled by formulating moral norms with some exception-clause like:

> 'You ought to do *x* — unless a valid norm of a legal system which is correct as a whole says otherwise and is not extremely unjust.'

Second, the ACC would just be a preliminary to establishing a necessary connection between law and morality by showing that normative sentences are true-or-false; the actual burden is borne by the thesis that the set of all true normative sentences is consistent. And this is rather more an explanatory formulation of the connection thesis than its justification. Third, arguing that there is a unity of the normative or practical sphere makes it in a way meaningless to say that the law is correct if it is 'in accordance' with morality or justice, for law, just like morality, would be part of the normative sphere, which — to preserve its unity — must not allow for any substantial

[36] This is a contestable assumption, for a 'hard-core realist' would deny that there is any necessary connection between truth and justifiability (see above nn 23 and 24). Note, too, that this 'semantic justification' of a sentence is not necessarily the same as the justification we demand of someone who is making an assertion: obviously, a sentence *p* as such is not justified by the sentence 'Mr A, who is — as we all know — a person competent in these matters, said so', whereas a speaker may well be said to 'justify' his assertion that *p* by uttering this sentence about Mr A. The semantic justification would probably be more or less what the competent Mr A would say to justify *p*.

subdivisions.[37] Fourth, it is by no means obvious that there is just one normative truth. Even in mathematics and natural sciences there are mutually exclusive theories, which are still 'correct' in that they offer a coherent explanation of the same kind of phenomena (presupposing that one can speak of 'the same' phenomena where there are different ways of conceptualisation).

Over and above that there are good reasons for regarding positive law as an independent subsystem of the normative sphere. That need not be developed in this context, but it is a main function of law to offer more or less clearly defined criteria for what one ought to do, and it is plausible that the overarching moral question of whether one 'really' ought to act according to the law[38] is sensible only after it has been determined what law, according to its own clearly defined criteria, demands. And this is possible only if law is seen as an independent subsystem that, though stating what ought to be done legally, does not yet determine what ought to be done all-things-considered.[39] This, by the way, would not be a matter of the 'nature' of law, but rather a question of a reasonable stipulation.[40]

Although Alexy anticipates the objection that the legal justification of a normative assertion might be confined to the positive law,[41] his rejoinder is not really convincing. He maintains that in cases where the open texture of the law does not determine a certain decision, the guarantee of justifiability ensures that justification 'must go on' as far as possible, and this necessarily involves moral argumentation. But, first, the necessity of going on further with one's reasoning once it is clear the positive law does not determine a certain solution, is not obvious. For Alexy concedes that in moral questions there can be situations where there is no 'one right answer', as well;[42] in these cases the solution has to be found by a decision, or by simple agreement. This might well be transferred to the situation in law once a positive

[37] For a similar argument see U Neumann, 'Review: Robert Alexy, Begriff und Geltung des Rechts' (1994) 6 *Protosoziologie* 246.

[38] It is worth noting that the question of whether one really ought to act according to the law is not meaningless, whereas the question of whether one really ought to act according to morality obviously is.

[39] A similar relation obtains between morality and other normative systems, too. Eg, we saw that the language-game of asserting comprises the regulative rule not to lie when asserting something. Yet (contrary to Kant) morality might demand from us to lie in certain situations (imagine the terrorist asking us which switch he is to turn to set off an explosive); and this might clearly 'overrule' the norm belonging to the specific language-game of asserting.

[40] To avoid any mistakes, a note on the expression 'necessary connection between law and morality'. Of course, saying that it has to be established and taken into regard what the positive law demands before deciding whether one 'really' ought to act according to it implies a connection between law and morality too. For it is (arguably) a non-contingent part of any morality to take into regard what the positive law says. But this is not what Alexy means; according to Alexy, the connection thesis says that moral considerations are necessary in determining what the *law* demands. It is on just this interpretation that the connection thesis (probably) fails.

[41] Alexy (above n 9), 214–6.

[42] See above n 28.

legal norm does not determine a certain solution. Second, even if we concede — and this is plausible — that it is a general postulate of rationality that true sentences must be justifiable 'absolutely' (meaning that their justification transgresses all subsystems), it would not follow that a justification which sticks to the criteria of positive law alone is *legally* faulty or leads to a result that is not *legally* valid. This, however, need not be taken up here, for it is beyond the scope of the ACC.

In any case, perhaps even an argument for the unity of the normative sphere would not be enough to establish a necessary connection between law and morality. This is shown by the fact that one of the paradigm representatives of legal positivism, Hans Kelsen, would subscribe to almost everything that has been said so far. He holds that sentences expressing — or rather describing — legal norms are true-or-false,[43] such that anyone who utters such a sentence in an assertion raises a claim to correctness, meaning that he claims that the norm meets the validity criteria of the legal system. At the same time, Kelsen holds that in the realm of Ought, there can be just one system of norms. But this does not induce him to say that law and morality are interconnected; instead, he maintains that it follows that there can be no morality for the jurist and no law for the moralist.[44]

III. SUMMARY

That legal norms raise a claim to correctness cannot be taken literally. Someone issuing or describing a norm raises a claim to correctness or normative truth — ie, he asserts a norm using a normative sentence — if the normative meaning-content of his utterance O*p* implies its own truth, and if he purports to believe that O*p* is true and to believe that O*p* can be justified. In the case of a speaker issuing a norm there is the additional claim that his performance of the speech-act in its institutionalised context brings about the truth of the asserted normative sentence. The speaker is obligated to make the assertion only if he really believes that O*p* and that O*p* can be justified, and if he has done his best to ascertain this.

But not raising the claim to correctness, or not fulfilling the obligation one undertakes when asserting a norm, has no necessary consequences for the meaning or validity of the normative content of the assertion (as long as this meaning-content implies its own truth); it simply destroys the character of the speech-act as an assertion, or renders it a faulty one.

[43] H Kelsen, *Reine Rechtslehre,* 2nd edn (Vienna, Deuticke, 1960), 82. Strictly speaking, things are a lot more complicated. In his impressive neo-Kantian phase, which peaks around 1923, Kelsen even identifies legal norms with judgements in a logical sense.

[44] H Kelsen, *Die philosophischen Grundlagen der Naturrechtslehre und des Rechtspositivismus* (Charlottenburg, Pan-Verla, 1928), 27.

Moreover, it is highly doubtful whether participants in the legal system, by asserting a legal norm, necessarily raise a claim to substantial correctness in the sense that the content of the asserted norm is morally justified *as such*, ie, just as if it were not the content of a legal norm. There is some evidence, however, that those engaged in issuing norms by doing so implicitly 'raise the claim' that their acts meet the demands of morality. This kind of 'claim', however, may be said to be attached to every conscious act of responsible persons and is not a feature peculiar to legal acts. What is more, any unconditional assertion of a normative sentence might be said to contain the claim that the normative sentence can be justified all-things-considered — so long as we presuppose that there is a unity of the normative sphere.

Even though raising or not raising the claim to correctness does not directly affect the normative meaning-content that is being asserted, the argument from the claim to correctness may be understood as an opaque way of expressing that norms are 'normative facts' and that normative sentences are true-or-false.[45] This is a plausible basis for an argument for a necessary connection between law and morality, but it needs — at the very least — one further argument for the unity of the normative sphere, ie, an argument showing that there is just *one* consistent set of all true normative sentences.

A tentative version of the connection thesis that is consistent with the results reached thus far might be that morality is an overarching normative system that determines what one ought to do all-things-considered, law is a closed subsystem determining what ought to be done legally, and morality arguably contains a norm demanding that one ought to do all-things-considered what one ought to do legally unless this results in gross injustice. This, however, is not a question for the jurist, but for the moral philosopher.

[45] For an attempt to give a minimalist and non-realist account of norms as normative facts along the lines of Kelsen's Pure Theory of Law, see C Heidemann, *Die Norm als Tatsache* (Baden Baden, Nomos, 1997).

7

Can Jurisprudence Without Empiricism Ever be a Science?

PHILIP LEITH AND JOHN MORISON

INTRODUCTION

This contribution is very different from the others in this collection. Our thesis — essentially critical — is concerned with the lack of involvement of the empiricist tradition in jurisprudence and should be read as a negative perspective on the approach which suggests that analytical jurisprudence is 'the way forward'. While we accept that within the field of jurisprudence (formally defined) the analytical seems to be more favoured than the empiricist, we will seek to counter this by developing vignettes which show how analytical jurisprudence misses the most interesting elements of legal reasoning and law in action. Our approach is not to carry out a detailed critical survey of analytical jurisprudence but to suggest that in the 1960s there was an opportunity for jurisprudence to look outwardly rather than inwardly — to become part of the wider movement using empiricism to attack formalism — but this opportunity was wasted. The wasted opportunity is one which put Herbert Hart and his *Concept of Law*[1] in a central location in jurisprudence. Further, that for reasons that these authors still find hard to understand, we note that jurisprudence continues to pay tribute to Hart and the fundamentally flawed perspective he brought to the discipline, rather than move on and participate in a more coherent and compelling intellectual framework.

It is ironic that at the same time that jurisprudence in the sense of a formal subject for study seems to be vanishing from the sight-line of the law school, theory has become more and more important to the legal academic. There are several reasons for this growing importance. One is obviously that the structure of employment within the law school (related to assessment of research) has meant that non-theoretical approaches to law (the simple case

[1] HLA Hart, *The Concept of Law,* 2nd edn (Oxford, Clarendon Press, 1994).

note, perhaps) are less valued than those which attempt to look in depth at legal developments, legal systems or law in a social context. However, it may also be that this increased importance of theory has come about due to the changes in law school employment. Now PhDs have become the norm for recruitment, replacing a model where a (sometimes unsuccessful) barrister would turn his (or, less often, her) hand to teaching. Also, the increasing number of law students means that not everyone can find a career in legal practice, and so law degrees are now less wedded to professional demands and the curriculum in law schools is increasingly required to deliver on promises that law provides an excellent general liberal arts training in how the world works.[2] Further, and important to our argument, there has been a move away from the formalist tradition in law to one where law is seen as part of the social world, and has to be judged as coherent and systemic not purely within its own terms, but whether it actually has the effect upon the world that it desires — perhaps amounting to a move from the 'law library' to at least the 'law commission'. This latter anti-formalist movement has developed particularly since the 1960s and that unparalleled period of intellectual change within the university system generally.

Yet this anti-formalism seems to have missed out on jurisprudence — at least in its most traditional sense. Jurisprudence has become narrow and, in our view, of reduced interest and limited impact to other legal scholars and to scholars in related fields. Take, for example, the debates over the changing nature of government in terms of the political and structural change that is captured in ideas of new technology, globalisation, the rights revolution and, most of all, 'governance'. Where is the impact of jurisprudential thinking about this? It is not visible at all in the current discourse of analytical legal philosophy.

We see ourselves as jurisprudents/jurisprudes/jurisprudential scholars, or whatever term is preferred. But we, in common with many other theory-oriented scholars, are probably viewed as peripheral to the community that defines itself as being jurisprudential *stricto sensu*. We believe that jurisprudence offers valuable insights into law and legal thought and should be central to legal studies generally. However, we feel that unfortunately jurisprudence has become remote from legal practice and most legal scholars, and it is no longer a broad church. We have for a number of years attempted to connect jurisprudence with practice — to see it as the study of a legal process in action — and have utilised a primarily socially oriented view of the nature of law to do this. Such attempts may well have been useful, and may even have been noticed in the legal community generally, but have hardly fitted the intellectual *milieu* of jurisprudence.

[2] See further, A Bradney, *Conversations, Choices and Chances: The Liberal Law School in the Twenty First Century* (Oxford, Hart Publishing, 2003).

In an early project we criticised Herbert Hart in the *Jurisprudence of Orthodoxy*[3] from the perspective of a (slightly tongue in cheek) 'Belfast school'.[4] The critique was undertaken primarily because Hart claimed to be investigating a process (as a sociological investigation)[5] when he — to our minds as members of a socially aware law school — was doing no such thing. Some 15 years later, we believe that the critical essays still hold true, and that they offered a wide-ranging challenge to those who still asserted the usefulness of the Hartian model. Having produced the critique it seemed sensible to move on and to develop ideas on how legal philosophy might interact with practice and legal process, and we thus carried out various studies of law in action, with a mind to contribute to the understanding of law as based in the multiple interactions of actors. We thus argue for a social, neo-Wittgenstinian perspective of law.[6]

We hold that jurisprudence should emulate science. It should be based on empirical study and theoretical critique of the results of that empiricism. It should try to understand science as a post-Newtonian activity where the observer is part of the experiment. We suggest that the most interesting question at the moment for jurisprudes is just how this notion of a legal science might be put into action, not that of how to find mind-independent objective entities. The methodology we propose is thus social, but what of the topics which the methodology should be applied to? We suggest that jurisprudence is a concern with certain theoretical constructs:

— Nature of legal rules/principles;
— Morality and law;
— Power and authority;
— Legitimacy.

[3] P Leith and P Ingram (eds), *The Jurisprudence of Orthodoxy: Queen's University Essays on HLA Hart* (London, Routledge, 1988)

[4] Thus the 'Queen's University Essays' countered the *festchrift* for 'Oxford Jurisprudence': see AWB Simpson (ed), *Oxford Essays in Jurisprudence, Second Series* (Oxford, Oxford University Press, 1973).

[5] According to its preface, *The Concept of Law* was offered as an 'essay in descriptive sociology' (above n 1, vii).

[6] The argument that Hart was Wittgenstinian is not, in our view, supportable. The school of linguistic philosophy certainly took elements of a Wittgenstinian approach, but rather than viewing language as the boundary of knowledge, the linguistic philosophers transformed this into a situation where 'common usage' became the core of knowledge. Wittgenstein remains an influential figure in philosophy, but linguistic philosophy, withered many years ago. Our theoretical position is best laid out in our *The Barrister's World and the Nature of Law* (London, Open University Press, 1992). Wittgenstein does remain problematical as a philosopher — his work, based in mathematics, requires significant development in order to act as a full-blown descriptor of the world and social power. However, the argument that mathematics is a fully social phenomenon must surely support the view that legal knowledge, too, is a fully social phenomenon.

These are indeed the traditional concerns of jurisprudence, so we are not arguing for a radical reappraisal of the conceptual foundations of the subject, only the manner in which those conceptual foundations are examined. The way in which we see these best illuminated is through the analysis of the legal system as a social system. Such a perspective is hardly novel in these times, but is certainly little appreciated in jurisprudence which remains firmly attached to analytical methods. Generally, analytical philosophical approaches are coming under attack from a variety of empirical methods. As with all science, measurement is the key to advance: we suggest that sociological techniques are sufficiently robust to provide measurement (of a sort) to provide advance in jurisprudence.

We will briefly discuss our work in studying barristers,[7] government, governance and governmentality,[8] and judging in intellectual property matters[9] to demonstrate our strategy.

JURISPRUDENCE AND SOCIAL THEORY IN THE 1960S — WHERE IT ALL WENT WRONG

Our argument is intimately connected with the role of Herbert Hart in the reconstruction of jurisprudence in the 1960s, a figure we see to have been a *locus* around which a new way of seeing legal theory was built. It is not difficult to see that Hart occupies a prestigious position — almost a symbolic location — in legal theory: Oxford's jurisprudes still list him on their web site[10] as though he was still with them in spirit. It is a position which some appear to feel should protect him from critical onslaught. For example, Lacey, in her critique of our *Jurisprudence of Orthodoxy*, suggested that 'attacks on orthodoxy which focus on one author are invidious', and that social theory will not be much advanced 'if its focus is confined to

[7] J Morison and P Leith (above n 6).

[8] See especially J Morison, 'The Government — Voluntary Sector Compacts: Governance, Governmentality and Civil Society' (2000) 27 *Journal of Law and Society* 98; 'Democracy, Governance and Governmentality: Civic Public Space and Constitutional Renewal in Northern Ireland' (2001) 21 *Oxford Journal of Legal Studies* 287; and 'Modernising Government and the e-government Revolution: Technologies of Government and Technologies of Democracy' in P Leyland and N Bamforth (eds), *The Multi-Layered Constitution* (Oxford, Hart Publishing, 2003), 131–62. See also chs 1 and 8 of D O'Mahony, R Geary, K McEvoy and J Morison, *Crime, Community and Locale: The Northern Ireland Communities Crime Survey* (Aldershot, Ashgate, 2000).

[9] P Leith, 'Judicial and Administrative Roles: the Patent Appellate System in a European Context' (2001) 1 *Intellectual Property Quarterly* 50.

[10] 'Welcome to the public web site of the jurisprudence community at the University of Oxford! Oxford has had unparalleled strength in the philosophy of law ever since HLA Hart became Professor of Jurisprudence in 1952. Fifty years on, according to the Philosophical Gourmet Report 2002, "Oxford University continues to be the world leader in legal philosophy, and by a wide margin: no school anywhere else in the English-speaking world has either Oxford's depth or breadth."' Oxford Jurisprudence Web Site: <http:// www.law.ox.ac.uk /jurisprudence> (website accessed 24/09/04).

selective attacks on critical author's constructions of one example of "Oxford Jurisprudence".'[11] Such a defence is difficult to give credence to — it is clear that Hart was a central figure in both Oxford jurisprudence and the wider jurisprudential world. As the Oxford website still insists, Hart continues to be the most widely read figure in legal philosophy in the world. (Lacey, of course, may not demur to a defence of an orthodoxy which focused on one figure so long as it contained 'interesting memories'.)[12]

Hart was of course central to the orthodoxy, and attacking his position is not invidious but essential to critical understanding of the demise of jurisprudence. Moreover, attacking the central text of Hart, *The Concept of Law*, should surely not be invidious given its role in Hart's position in legal theory. Harari, too, suggested that it was not unfair:

> I think it is not unfair to judge Hart's contribution to legal philosophy by concentrating on his most influential, most ambitious, and most widely advertised work, The Concept of Law (1961). Were it not for —
>
> (1) the sorry state of legal philosophy in Britain and in the other English-speaking countries,
> (2) Hart's elevated and prominent position as Professor of Jurisprudence in the University of Oxford, and consequently,
> (3) the number of 'livings' (some of them very good ones) which he had in his gift,
> (4) the fact that his book was published by the Oxford University Press, and
> (5) the unusually large number of advertisements of it which were placed in various legal periodicals,
>
> I doubt very much whether it would have received anything remotely like the attention which it actually received. And this, not because it is a systematic, methodical, and thus, for English lawyers, a difficult book, but simply because it is a bad book.[13]

Campbell too, in his essay on the 'career' of *The Concept*, noted the critical assessment at the time of publishing from most commentators — critical assessments which had never really been answered — but also noted the loyalty of those around Hart:

[11] N Lacey, 'Review of *The Jurisprudence of Orthodoxy*' (1989) 6 *Journal of Applied Philosophy*.
[12] 'HLA Hart, who was professor of jurisprudence at the University of Oxford, 1952–68, and visiting professor of legal philosophy at HLS, 1956–1957, is the subject of a biography by Nicola Lacey, Professor of Criminal Law at the London School of Economics and Political Science. She would like to hear from anyone with information about, interesting memories of, or correspondence from Hart.' *Harvard Law Bulletin*, Spring 2001. See the resulting (and strangely readable) *A Life of HLA Hart: The Nightmare and the Noble Dream* (Oxford, Oxford University Press, 2004).
[13] A Harari, 'Open Letter' (1972, Unpublished). The 'Open Letter' was disseminated amongst legal philosophers prior to Harari's death. Somewhat intemperate — Harari himself, p 20, noted that many of the critical assessments by others were made in 'immoderate terms' — it remains a substantial critical assessment of Hart's *The Concept of Law*.

> There is little doubt that the influence of Hart has been significant. My argument, of course, is that that influence has been exaggerated and magnified by the adoption of his approach as something of an orthodoxy by the self-styled Oxford School of Jurisprudence. The prolific writings of members of the School have supported and sustained the life of The Concept, rehearsing its concerns and reiterating its themes, even if some revisions have been introduced. Jurisprudence in Britain in large part has operated within a particular paradigm, one inspired by Hart's work. Many prominent writers in jurisprudence were friends, pupils or colleagues of Hart (no harm in that) and their loyalty is clear.[14]

Harari's critique remains the most aggressive and detailed, but there is a mountain of criticism of *The Concept* which has rarely been seriously considered by those who continued through the 1980s and 1990s to advocate this as incisive work.[15] This is not the place to detail those criticisms in full, but as a simple example of the magnitude of confusion in *The Concept*, just consider the *central theoretical foundation* of his system of rule-based philosophy. Hart wrote of the core conjunction of primary and secondary rules:

> The main theme of this book is that so many of the distinctive operations of the law and so many of the ideas which constitute the framework of legal thought, require for their elucidation reference to one or both of these two types of rule, that their union may be justly regarded as the 'essence' of law, though they may not always be found together wherever the word 'law' is correctly used.[16]

Just what is being said here to be the central theme? Is there an 'essence' of law — the conjunction of primary or secondary rules — or not? If law is found where there is no conjunction, then is there still an 'essence of law'? The idea:

'Essence' of Law = Union (Primary Rules, Secondary Rules)[17]

[14] CM Campbell, 'The Career of the Concept', in P Leith and P Ingram (above n 3), 21.

[15] One distinguished later criticism is Moles's attempt to locate what John Austin actually did say from the misinterpretation of Hart: see RN Moles, *Definition and Rule in Legal Theory: A Reassessment of HLA Hart and the Positivist Tradition* (Oxford, Basil Blackwell, 1987). It is a sad fact that most jurisprudes today have never read the later lectures of Austin, where he outlines the more socially relevant perspectives on the legal system and thus demonstrates that the earlier lectures (taken by some as his only relevant contribution to the discipline) are an outline descriptor rather than a full legal theory.

[16] HLA Hart (above n 1), 151.

[17] We use a 'logical' technique to demonstrate the illogicality of Hart's thesis. It is interesting to note that many researchers saw a more logical than sociological aspect to Hart's work. See, for example, how the logicality of Post's 'production system' became the basis for a way of implementing Hartian justified software applications in law — see P Leith, *Formalism in AI and Computer Science* (London, Ellis Horwood, 1990).

seems clear and simple, but does this mean — when the union elements are 'not always to be found together' — that the essential qualities of law are still met:

'Essence' of Law = Union (Primary Rules, (NOT Secondary Rules))

'Essence' of Law = Union ((NOT Primary Rules), Secondary Rules)

Therefore:

'Essence' of Law = OR (Primary Rules, Secondary Rules)?

It is, of course, intellectual sleight of hand, where we are never quite sure what is being claimed and where each claim is anyway protected from fuller analysis by *escape clauses*.[18] The overall effect is that it looks reasonable (so long as it is not read critically) and almost common sensible. It is, of course, not reasonable, sensible nor understandable. An intemperate — invidious even — critic might suggest it to be 'rubbish'.

Our major criticism of Hart is that his 'theoretical' view was that of the anti-theoretical practising lawyer, claiming that we simply need to look at the everyday usage of language to determine the meaning of law. There is, in the Hartian perspective, no need for deep analysis, little need for social investigation, no requirement for empiricism — in total, an anti-theoretical smugness which was too often found in the writings of the linguistic philosophers.[19] Little wonder that a legal philosophy which became so dominant in the 1960s and 1970s had such a disarming effect upon the development of jurisprudence. Such an approach, advocating the investigation of 'everyday usage' of legal grammar and legal speech, undermined the empirical project. Why bother with fieldwork or consideration of methodology, when we simply need to use our 'commonsense' approaches to the world around us? Hart's view seems designed to appeal to a notional, thoughtful barrister who might, after a long day at the bar, wish to sit in his study, club or common room and reflect.

Connected to this criticism is the charge of conservatism — an anti-theoretical perspective which attempts to describe the legal world 'commonsensibly' is hardly likely to call for critical assessment of that legal world. As Skillen suggested of Hart:

> Hart's legalism, his 'apolitical' absorption in officialdom and its forms vitiates his account of what law is and what place it has in social life, turning what

[18] For example, 'In this and the next two chapters we shall state and criticise a position which is, in substance, the same as Austin's doctrine but *probably* diverges from it at certain points.' HLA Hart (above n 1), 18. Our emphasis.

[19] See Bertrand Russell's critique in *Portraits From Memory: And Other Essays* (London, George Allen & Unwin, 1956).

> sets out as a humanistic critique of positivism into an idealist apology for the *status quo*. Moreover, by erecting his faith in officials and experts into a full-blown social philosophy, Hart rules out of consideration the possibility that society might be organised along radically different lines.[20]

It also of course follows from this essential conservatism that Hart's account of how the law works may well fail to resonate very strongly with those versions of feminism, critical race theory, queer theory, etc which focus on very different life experiences in the law.

Hart gave us a 'fresh start', but one which also offered a golden age of law: simple, regulated, based on the caring professional lawyer. Little wonder that in countries where social and political change are the order of the day — in South America, the old Soviet bloc — Hart's ideas still hold sway with legal philosophers who want to hide away from this upheaval, wrapped in a cloak of legalism. Hartian philosophy was thus the orthodoxy which those who entered the discipline of jurisprudence followed, and it defined the limits of the field. Those who came after (Dworkin, for example) could never return to a pre-Hartian philosophy and had to set their own positions out primarily in regard to that of Hart. Who, for example, ever bothers to read John Austin since Hart effectively side-lined him? And where, as another example, do we see the traditional legal philosopher attempting even to acknowledge the empirical evidence which has multiplied since the 1960s with the rise of socio-legal studies?

OTHER JURISPRUDENTIAL APPROACHES

There are other ways than the Hartian (or those moulded in Hart's framework) to investigate jurisprudential issues. We have said above that it was the unhappiness with Hart and related perspectives which made us think more deeply about what was going on in the legal world. We found that much of what we were concerned about was — in the context of jurisprudential theory — under-researched and practically ignored, and thus of great interest to us. What we found when we began to look at these kinds of questions, though, was that our findings were of limited interest to jurisprudes, and thus our conscious membership of the field began to decline. At a lower level than consciousness though, we have continued to be interested in exactly the same questions which grabbed the attention of our younger selves: the nature of legal rules/principles; morality and law; power and authority; legitimacy.

Our approach remains directed towards a sociologically inspired jurisprudence, surely just one of the valid approaches which lie outwith the analytical framework. In the following sections we give an outline of how

20 A Skillen, *Ruling Illusions: Philosophy and the Social Order* (London, Harvester, 1977).

we feel this social input — forged through a belief in empirical evidence — can be useful in jurisprudence.

1 The Nature of Legal Rules in the Barrister's World

In *The Barrister's World and the Nature of Law* we looked at the use of law by practitioners. Drawing upon a series of interviews with barristers and some other figures in the legal systems of England and Wales, Scotland, Northern Ireland and the Republic of Ireland, we sought to examine what it is that barristers actually do and how this differs from what legal theorists believe that practitioners do. What we found was that the legal world is an essentially social one, where relationships with solicitors, clerks, other barristers and judges condition fundamentally what it is that amounts to law in action.

We had been struck by early research on a sample of solicitors which suggested that on average they would spend only about one hour each week on legal research with the rest of their working time being taken up with client management, negotiation, routine procedures and so on.[21] Who is doing the law in legal practice? Could it be that while solicitors are generalists, perhaps akin to family doctors in the medical world, barristers, like hospital consultants, are the specialists with detailed knowledge?

In fact our research revealed that most often barristers deal not with law in the law school sense of rules that can be applied to facts, but with a wider idea which we characterised as 'legal knowledge'. This commodity, which includes law in the strict sense but is much wider than simple rules, is located and used within a strongly social setting. Here the various personalities within the legal *milieu* exercise a determining influence on how the barrister operates. Thus the barrister must be seen in a world where he or she is attempting to build or maintain a career and must negotiate the hazards and opportunities offered by solicitors, clerks, other barristers and, perhaps most importantly of all, judges.

Thus, for example, we learned that the barrister–solicitor relationship is central in the barrister's world. He or she regards the solicitor as the client who is the party that must be satisfied rather than the lay client. This may involve providing a service for the solicitor which facilitates the solicitor's practice by providing efficient turnaround of paperwork and cases; unburdens the solicitor of difficult, indecisive or unrealistic clients; or enhances the solicitor in the eyes of the client who may provide repeat business. Similarly the personalities in a given case may exercise an important influence. Barristers told us that they were always very aware of the standard of

[21] C Campbell 'Lawyers and their Public' in DN MacCormick (ed), *Lawyers in Their Social Setting* (Edinburgh, W Green, 1976), 195–214.

the brief supplied by the solicitor, the quality and record of the opposition barrister, the credibility of any witnesses and, most of all, the personality and preferences of the presiding judge. This last factor in particular is especially important, with judges who like to intervene, or dislike too many precedents being cited or are sympathetic to the prosecution being accommodated as far as possible. Even beyond this, there were elements such as the degree of 'busy-ness' of an opponent, or the time in the financial year and thus the levels of funds left in the compensation funds of insurance companies, that might effect how hard a personal injuries claim is pressed.

This is not to say that law is not involved. However, it is less central than might be supposed from looking at the view of law in the law school or in the imagination of some jurisprudes, who still insist upon a sharp distinction between rules and facts. We developed an idea of *legal information* as a mix of strictly legal material and more rhetorical and socially rich information which strongly conditions how the barrister acts. Law is not a system which can be accurately modelled by a division into law and fact as though these were clear and distinct categories which are of central importance. Our argument is that law is richer than this. Law is a social process where information is constructed, passed on, mediated and developed through myriad ways. It exists with a highly social world where clients fight for freedom, money or revenge, and barristers struggle to develop and maintain careers in a busy and hostile world inhabited by clerks, solicitors, clients, other barristers and judges, who may or may not behave as the barrister would like.

To the jurisprude of a certain persuasion this context (which we found to be central and determining) is ignored. The view of rules that is deployed within some versions of legal philosophy is stripped of all context and reality. There, 'vehicles' are forbidden from entering the park, reasonable men can expect not to find themselves guilty of stealing their own umbrella and syllogisms, along with the finer reasoning of upper court judgements, provide the context of rules. Such a view is unreal and anti-sociological. It neglects the pressures on barristers to find work, the time limits, peer-group pressures and exigencies of running a case in court alongside maintaining and developing a career within a largely hostile *milieu* which preclude academic research of the sort envisaged by some academic lawyers. It ignores the way in which barristers, in common with the other actors in the world of practice, act within a social world that constrains and conditions what it is that they do. That is not to say that what barristers are doing is less than ideal, or that they fail in practice to deliver what it is that they are supposed to do. Rather it is to argue that the world of legal practice is richer and more social than is imagined by those who see only rules being applied to facts.

Legal knowledge is essentially practical: it is about problem-solving, and negotiation and settlement are central in both civil and criminal practice. (Indeed, the practical, end-oriented nature of legal practice perhaps explains why many barristers see procedure as equally important as, or more important than, law.) Persuasion is at the heart of the legal process, and the barrister's job is to ensure that solicitors and clients, witnesses and opponents, as well as judges and juries, are persuaded to see the world in the way that the barrister urges. Rules are not platonic/atomic structures with a core and a penumbra: they exist to be used in a rhetorical context where particular views can be urged and specific solutions to real problems achieved.

Of course law, in the sense of rules, is part of this, but law alone does not exhaust the material with which the barrister works. To see legal practice as being about mainly rules, or even rules as applied to 'facts', is to miss out on the richness of what is occurring. It ignores the contestable nature of facts and misrepresents the nature of law in action. For someone like Hart to take this view, and then further to represent it as a sociology of law, represents in our view a very considerable mistake.

Of course not all jurisprudence takes this view. Indeed, in *The Barrister's World* we took up a neo-realist view and sought to develop the work of Jerome Frank in developing a sociology on legal knowledge. But here again we see the influence of the formalist, Hartian perspective which misrepresented this realist account [22] and urged instead an impoverished, formalist view of law.

2 Government, Governance and Governmentality

There is another area, within public law scholarship, which illustrates how the formalist view no longer provides an adequate framework for understanding some of the major issues within legal inquiry. Mainstream legal scholars in general and public lawyers in particular now are increasingly coming to terms with ideas that the whole project of *government* is becoming reduced, or at least changed, as there is a loss of decision-making power and accountability to bodies beyond the traditional state.[23] It seems that their whole subject of study has altered and that now the site of government has shifted. Government does not now take place only within a single, unified national territory, or by means of a unified, single system. The effects of globalisation mean that territory, like economy and culture, are increasingly multiple and plural rather than unified and national. In this context government acts not so much by simply issuing commands or making law, but by developing strategies, techniques and procedures which operate across the countless, often competing value systems and concentrations of power that exist across state and non-state institutions and centres of power and expertise.

[22] See S Livingstone, 'Of the Core and the Penumbra: HLA Hart and American Realism' in P Leith and P Ingram (eds) (above n 3), 147–72.

[23] See further, J Morison and S Livingstone, *Reshaping Public Power: Northern Ireland and the British Constitutional Crisis* (London, Sweet & Maxwell, 1996) and 'The Case Against Constitutional Reform?' (1998) 25 *Journal of Law and Society* 510.

Ideas of multi-level government have evolved from a simple recognition that there are layers beyond the national state to more sophisticated ideas of how power is dispersed into a multiplicity of sites, constituting nodes in a heterarchical network rather than layers in a hierarchical pyramid, which operate in a relationship of mutual influence rather than control.[24] There are also ideas emerging that the activities of government are complex and *multi-format* too. There are now many more agencies and bodies from civil society, the private sector, as well as from government and quasi-government, and these operate at every level from the local, regional, national and European to deliver both the policy and services of government. As well as formal institutions, networks, partnerships and project groups, and individuals themselves are involved in the business of government.

Some of this change is captured well in ideas of governance and is well-developed in the literature of politics and the social sciences. Of course here there are, inevitably, disputes about what the term governance means. Rhodes, for example, talks of it having at least six distinct meanings clustered around the idea of 'governing without government'.[25] Kooiman, on the other hand, emphasises that modern governance is defined by being less about the direct intervention of government and more about the ways in which the environment of action for private actors can be shaped by the state.[26] Others, such as Skelcher, put the emphasis on notions of the 'congested state' where there is a complex of networked relationships between public, private, voluntary and community actors which has produced a dense, multi-layered and largely impenetrable structure of public action.[27]

The influence of these ideas largely has translated now from political science to law. Most constitutional theorists now accept in general terms that there has been a movement from government to governance, and that the role of the state has changed from being a guarantor and provider of security, wealth and law towards being more of a partner or facilitator for a variety of other bodies and agencies at various levels as they concern themselves with such issues. The additional value that lawyers may add to this

[24] See, for example, N Bernard, *Multilevel Governance in the European Union* (New York, Kluwer, 2002), or M Keating's account of the 'reterritorialisation of politics' as involving 'a dual process of sub-state mobilisation and supra-state integration' and a 'search for new levels of political action' in 'Europe's Changing Political Landscape' in P Beaumont, C Lyons and N Walker (eds), *Convergence and Divergence in European Public Law* (Oxford, Hart Publishing, 2002), 7.

[25] See further, R Rhodes, *Understanding Governance: Policy Networks, Governance, Reflexivity and Accountability* (Milton Keynes, Open University Press, 1997). See especially ch 1. For recent work from this perspective see M Bevir and RAW Rhodes, *Interpreting British Governance* (London, Routledge, 2003) and the Special Issue of 81 (2003) *Public Administration*.

[26] J Kooiman, *Modern Governance: New Government Society Interactions* (London, Sage, 1993).

[27] C Skelcher, 'Changing Images of the State: Overloaded, Hollowed Out, Congested' (2000) 15 *Public Policy and Administration* 3.

debate is in developing and articulating further notions of 'good governance' as promoting values of transparency, democracy and human rights, and in providing something of a normative framework to begin to evaluate new forms of governance.[28]

Jurisprudential scholars working within the shadow of Hart's account of law do not, however, appear to have noticed this fundamental practical change, or worked through the consequences for their subject matter. For them the nature of law continues to be about norms, primary and secondary rules, the state and most of all sovereignty. This focus on a 1950s version of a legal reality denies the opportunity to jurisprudes to contribute to the challenge to legal scholarship that such developments involve. It was this reason that this writer, along with many others who might equally describe themselves as jurisprudential in orientation, left behind the limited framework offered by this jurisprudence of orthodoxy and moved instead to richer sources of understanding. In particular, there is the governmentality approach associated with the later writing of Michel Foucault and some significant, subsequent critical work.[29]

Foucault's earlier account of discipline, with its emphasis on 'docile bodies' as surfaces for the inscription of power, has been supplemented by later work which stresses the importance of the active subject as the entity through which and by means of which power is actually exercised. The governmentality approach suggests that power exists beyond the state and that the centres and levels of governmental power, like its objectives and its techniques, are multiple and differentiated. Power is less about rules or imposing sovereign will and more about engaging with the many networks and alliances that make up a chain or network which translates power from one locale to another. Individuals relate to power not as simple coerced objects, but as autonomous subjects whose objectivity is shaped by their active engagement with the powers that govern them and by which they 'govern themselves'.

[28] Thus, for example, the Commission of the European Communities offers five principles — openness, participation, accountability, effectiveness and coherence — which it maintains underpin good governance. See further Commission of the European Communities, *European Governance A White Paper*: COM (2001) 428 final: (27 July 2001) 10.

[29] See especially M Foucault, 'Governmentality' in JD Faubion (ed), *Michel Foucault, Power: The Essential Works Volume 3* (London, Allen Lane Penguin Press, 2000); L Martin, H Gutman and P Hutton (eds), *Technologies of the Self: A Seminar with Michel Foucault* (London, Tavistock, 1998) and P Rabinow (ed), *Michel Foucault: Ethics* (London, Penguin, 1997). There are also a number of important writers who have taken up this approach and developed it further. In particular, see N Rose, *Powers of Freedom: Reframing Political Thought* (Cambridge, Cambridge University Press, 1999) and M Dean, *Governmentality: Power and Rules in Modern Society* (London, Sage, 1999). There have been some efforts to apply governmentality to law generally, most notably A Hunt and G Wickham, *Foucault and Law: Towards a Sociology of Law and Governance* (London, Pluto Press, 1994); V Tadros, 'Between Governance and Discipline: The Law and Michel Foucault' (1998) 18 *OJLS* 75; R van Krieken, 'Legal Informalism, Power and Liberal Governance' (2001) 10(1) *Social and Legal Studies* 5.

Government is a domain of strategies, techniques and procedures through which different forces and groups attempt to render their programme operable. Instead of thinking about one, overarching, single web of the public or the constitutional, with law as its sole or main expression, we should be considering the countless, often competing, value systems and their various methods of promulgation that exist across state and non-state institutions and centres of power and expertise.[30] The role of law here is different too. Just as the spaces of government can be seen to extend beyond the traditional boundaries of the constitutional, so too the techniques or technologies of government can be seen to encompass much more than just law in the sense of command. Law is now part of the framework that may establish and go towards defining a space of government. Law provides much of the context, and it underpins and gives effect to many of the ways in which various technologies of government are expressed. Law is thus an important element, but its role is as part of the multiform tactics of government.

This seems to provide a fuller framework for understanding how government now operates than more traditional Hartian ideas. It allows us to consider the problem of government outside the juridical framework of sovereignty and the state. As Rose puts it, governmentality

> rejects the view that one must account for the political assemblages of rule *in terms of* the philosophical and constitutional language of the nineteenth century, or that one must underpin this misleading account with a theoretical infrastructure derived from nineteenth-century social and political theory which accords 'the state' a quite illusory necessity, functionality and territorialisation.[31]

Governmentality allows us to look at the complex of governmental strategies, technologies and powers that exist across many different centres of power, and that are framed or expressed in law (as well as in other ways) but are not exhausted by reference to the state and law. Governmentality allows us to look at what Foucault termed the 'governmentalisation of the state'[32] which emerged in the nineteenth century and developed in the course of the last century. Foucault is here referring to the way in which the state has diffused within a whole range of other political centres and linked up with a whole range of micro centres of power in order to develop a mode of governing that will allow it to survive within contemporary power relations and escape from the irrelevancy of older modes of government based on discipline, sovereignty and territory.

[30] For a fuller account see J Morison 'Modernising Government and the e-government Revolution: Technologies of Government and Technologies of Democracy' in P Leyland and N Bamforth (above n 8).
[31] Rose (above n 29), 17–18.
[32] See 'Governmentality' in *Michel Foucault: Power, The Essential Works* (above n 29), 220–1.

In this way governmentality is directing us to a whole series of heterogeneous fields of government activity where various bodies, authorities and forces have sought to govern 'populations' and their conduct through a whole range of strategies and techniques. Governmentality is thus widening the scope of study far beyond formal statutes and case law, and even the more informal practices and understandings of the major officials who provide the internal aspect. It is directing study to a space that encompasses the traditional political and legal institutions but extends far beyond them to include a whole range of other discourses and vocabularies, mechanisms and strategies, rationalities and technologies. The consequences of this for more general legal theory are of course huge. As Cotterrell argues,

> The strength of Foucault's work for legal scholarship has been to emphasize the ubiquity of power and its necessity in structuring social relations. As Foucault revolutionized views of power, socio-legal scholarship should revolutionize views of law: from an image of exceptionality and pathology to one of normality and pervasiveness. Law, like power should be seen as a resource operating routinely in innumerable social sites and settings. Work on law as constitutive of social institutions, practices, ideas and identities, on law's ideological significance and rootedness in culture, on legal consciousness and on images of law in everyday life all point in this direction.[33]

Foucault complained that when he first studied power relations there were no tools of study: 'we had recourse only to ways of thinking about power based on legal models, that is: what legitimates power? Or we had recourse to ways of thinking about power based on institutional models, that is: what is the state?'[34] This approach still dominates jurisprudential thinking of the Hartian stamp. However, the governmentality approach can provide us with a valuable way of understanding how power is exercised at a distance and indirectly.

3 Legitimacy: 'Judging' and the European Patent Office

Legitimacy is central to jurisprudential thinking — whether of the legal system as a whole (eg, 'sovereignty'), the argumentation used in that system (validity of legal reasoning), or in the more particular details of legitimacy of the actors involved in the system (judicial and legislative competence).

For those interested in the theoretical construction of legitimacy — particularly related to these questions in an ever-tightening European legal

[33] R Cotterrell, 'Subverting Orthodoxy, Making Law Central: A View of Sociolegal Studies' (2002) 29 *Journal of Law and Society* 632 at 639.
[34] M Foucault, 'The Subject and Power' in *Michel Foucault: Power, The Essential Works* (above n 29), 327.

framework — the European patent system is a fascinating example of attempts to formalise structures as 'legitimate'. We have a cohesive trans-European body of advocates — 'the European Patent Attorney' — which connects with a powerful European organisation — the European Patent Office (EPO). The EPO, standing apart from the other European bodies, demonstrates independence from the EU and European Parliament but also a considerable influence over national bodies and courts. Its success (in terms of numbers of patents granted and influence upon patentability) is more than could have been expected in its life of some 25 or so years. Despite this, there is indeed a legitimacy problem with the EPO.

In the judicial sphere, litigation is still based on national jurisdiction and we lack, because of the interminable gestation of the 'Community Patent', an effective appellate system to ensure harmonisation of interpretation and procedure in European patent law. The judicial system in European patenting is thus complex and confused. Judicial decisions on validity can be made in national contexts and appealed only in that context too, since the European Patent is, as often noted, 'a bundle of national patents'. But decisions are also made outside litigation: the Boards of Appeal of the EPO consider many more cases of validity, breadth of claim, etc, than do individual national courts, and these 'administrative decisions' have considerable influence over the thinking of national courts. Though the courts in national countries look for guidance[35] to the decisions of the EPO, delays cause problems — for example the 'Soya' patent[36] had only completed its opposition period in 2003, some 10 years after it was first granted and some 15 years after application date. It may yet be on its way to the Boards of Appeal. The sound in the appellate system is thus considerable, but there is a lack of order and cohesion which leaves us with the music of Cage rather than Mozart.

How should the European patent appellate system be developed? What are the strengths of the current system which might form the basis of a unified patenting system in Europe? And how does this all fit in with the single market and the goals of the European ideal? And, is there, as Clifford Lees suggests some believe, a 'devilish plot to transfer the "ownership" — and certainly the administration — of the EPO to the Commission'?[37] There is a distinct lack of clarity over where the authority over patent law actually lies — and yet the system appears to work with reasonable effectiveness. How can such a system be *legitimate*?

[35] 'These decisions are not strictly binding upon courts in the United Kingdom but they are of great persuasive authority; first, because they are decisions of expert courts (the Boards of Appeal and Enlarged Board of Appeal of the EPO) involved daily in the administration of the EPC.' Lord Hoffman in *Merrell Dow Pharmaceuticals Inc v HN Norton & Co Ltd* [1996] Reports of Patent, Design and Trade Mark Cases 76.

[36] EP 301749. This relates to Monsanto's genetic engineering of plants and is of considerable economic import. Patents are granted for 20 years from date of application in most instances.

[37] C Lees, 'EPO — The Question of Power', *CIPA Journal*, August 1999.

Set up as part of an administrative system, the Boards of Appeal have become more 'judicial' as the EPO has developed, and the proposed parallel Community Patent (with its judicial system) has failed to appear. Indeed, the Boards of Appeal took great heart from a judgment of one of their critics, when he suggested that they were 'Judges' in everything but name.[38] From that point in time, the members of the Boards of Appeal have tried to turn this suggestion of their judicial role into a 'fact'. Such a development has not been easy — most of the Board members (and usually the most influential ones) have not had a legal background, rather being promoted through the EPO system for being 'good examiners' with a technical background.

In a study which one of us undertook it appeared that those with a 'legal' role were frequently not as influential in decision making as those with a technical role. The study appeared to be relatively uncontroversial — relating the results of interviews within the organisation, and developing from a previous study of the lower levels of the EPO. However, that perception quickly left, as the study was attacked from within the Boards of Appeal and the policy sections of the EPO and substantial effort was made to stop it being published. To those outside the EPO it was not a particularly controversial study (nor was it to ex-members of the EPO, who saw it as a reasonably accurate description of their ex-colleagues), but to groups attempting to locate themselves and manoeuvre a position in a developing European patent system, any criticism was to be attacked: academic study was too 'political' in the atmosphere of the late 1990s and following period when the European Commission was considering how to integrate the patent system. Members of the Boards of Appeal, it appeared, wanted to be judges in the true sense of the word, and an article which suggested their legal ability to partake of a role to be less than the role they desired to play, was a damaging document. This, of course, was an argument about *legitimacy* in its most explicit expression — an administrative organisation bent on projecting a positive image (though one which few outside the organisation accepted).

To the more traditional jurisprude, of course, legitimacy is not a practical, day-to-day issue. To the traditionalist it is about the more rarefied issues of thinking of the political system as a coherent, logical framework which can be inspected, rather as we might look at the workings of a clock. Which cog, in this view, is 'sovereign'? If that is found then it is from there that legitimacy derives.

In our view day-to-day matters are crucial and legitimacy is not something which is necessarily structured in a formal system. It is argued over, positions are attacked and defended, and the system is organic rather than

[38] 'They are judges in all but name — and it is rather a pity that they were not so-called by the Convention.' Jacob J in *Lenzing AG's European Patent (UK)* [1997] Reports of Patent, Design and Trade Mark Cases 245.

logical. In this perspective, the empirical method becomes the only way in which we can determine where legitimacy arises, the constraints under which it operates, and what its component aspects are in that particular context and time.

4 Morality and Law: Privacy and Obligations of Confidentiality

The reader should be now be getting the flavour of our approach: to look at what is happening on the ground (empiricism) and then try to make sense of that in a more theoretical manner (jurisprudentially). It seems to us that almost all legal problems can be investigated in this manner, and we can point to an area where one of us is now working — how social mores and feelings impact upon development of case law. This is of course 'morality and law' in the traditional sense. The work is underdeveloped and not yet published, but we can point to the approach being taken.[39] The introduction of UK Human Rights legislation, with its derivations of Arts 8 and 10, ECHR, is the focus of the problem in rights to privacy. In formal terms, these two articles provide a tension, and there is no formalistic way of resolving any particular dispute over rights:

> Art 8(1): Everyone has the right to respect for his private and family life, his home and his correspondence.
> Art 10(1): Everyone has the right to freedom of expression. This right shall include freedom to hold opinions and to receive and impart information and ideas without interference by public authority and regardless of frontiers ...

There is no way of resolving any particular problem relating to privacy in a logical or analytical manner, for if *you* claim rights to privacy you are denying *me* my freedom of expression to talk about you. The two rights must be read in conjunction with each other and thus — it appears to us — the only location of any rationale for decision must be on a *moral basis.* That is, that the judge is faced with the difficult position of having to construct an argument on particular facts, with concern for particular results, but also aware that that result will have general and perhaps wide-ranging effect. On reading the developing case law we see the difficulty of each judge and often how badly they perform in these situations. The difficulties

[39] Of course, like any empiricist project the problem is really only time and funding. Funding has always been difficult in the legal sciences — more so than in any other 'science', we feel — yet if we are to develop a scientific approach then we need scientific levels of funding in order to carry out the project. Funding which simply supports library effort is of more limited use, since the world which the law tries to interact with does not lie within the library walls. Further, there is a considerable problem with lawyers in assessing proper methodological approaches — too often they simply wish to follow the Popperian positivistic approach and deny any validity in approaches which may produce better and more insightful results. Our position is that results and methodology must be read together for interpretation — there can be no socio-legal methodology which produces results which stand separated from the method used.

are so profound that the real issues of judging on privacy/freedom of expression have to a very large extent been cast aside and replaced by something which is more 'technical' — breach of confidence. No doubt, the feeling of the judiciary is that such a technical resolution to their problem is more manageable, but it has to be suggested that this step, which we see as an attempt to extricate themselves from the moral choices open to them, can never really do this.

Breach of confidence law, as is being applied to privacy cases, is now far removed from the original commercial sense of obligations in trade secrets: there is no requirement now for a relationship between the parties in order for there to be a relationship. Little wonder that reading the judgments, one is reminded of the suggestion that where a judge uses the word 'clearly' to indicate logical steps in his argument, clarity is often most lacking.[40]

So far this is just traditional legal thinking — looking at case law and far from an incisive form of jurisprudence. How might it be expanded in the empiricist tradition? There are several ways — looking at the evidence presented in court and re-assessing that in the critical context of the judge's judgment, interviews with the individuals involved, and so forth. When we read a case report on privacy it strikes us as enormously strange — why should an individual who wants privacy to be central to his life go all the way to the European Court of Justice for a minute financial reward and lose all that privacy forever?[41] Why should a radio DJ who used sexual innuendo in her morning broadcasts (heard by a nation of young schoolchildren and their parents on the school run) be so annoyed that her nudity on an open (though we are told 'private' – ie, paid for) beach is photographed and reported?[42] What is this claim to privacy really about? And why are so many of these privacy claims not related to information, but to images? We

[40] For example, 'In my judgment the information giving details of her regular attendance at Narcotics Anonymous meetings for therapy must have been imparted in circumstances importing an obligation of confidence. The undisclosed source whether a fellow sufferer of drug addiction attending Narcotics Anonymous meetings or a member of Miss Naomi Campbell's staff or entourage owed her an obligation of confidence in relation to the information; whether or not that information was supplemented by a Mirror reporter attending a Narcotics Anonymous meeting or by covert photography. The information *clearly* bore the badge of confidentiality and when received by the defendants they, Mr Morgan and the Mirror journalists were clothed in conscience with the duty of confidentiality.' Morland J in *Campbell v Mirror* [2002] EWHC 499(QB). Our emphasis.

[41] See *Peck v UK* (44647/98) (2003) 36 EHRR 41, where the applicant's life was saved by CCTV during an attempt to cut his wrists *in a public place*. The applicant's complaint was that the use of the images was a breach of his right to a private life. The Court agreed: 'As such, the disclosure constituted a disproportionate and therefore unjustified interference with his private life and a violation of Article 8 of the Convention.' The award was €11,800 in respect of non-pecuniary damage.

[42] Sarah Cox accepted £50,000 in out of court settlement from the *Sunday People*, June 2003. She has been said to represent 'ladette' culture — variously blamed by diverse studies for the rise in binge drinking amongst women, transmission of sexual disease (STD, HIV+, etc), lung, throat and mouth cancers (due to smoking), breast cancer (linked to alcohol consumption), increasing levels of violence by women against other women, etc.

can go along with the rhetoric presented in the courtroom, but really we know very little of the social and legal context and impetus of this growing 'right'. Yet judges are taking the claims on a level — a moral level — which the sceptic would suggest is worthy of further study.

Morality and law is difficult enough for judges in practical terms, as it is for the rest of us. Little wonder that they try to find technical legal techniques to resolve these problems without concern for closer investigation for the moral basis of the claims. Such techniques are often at the very heart of legal developments, and the analysis of their use and elucidation appears to us to be at the heart of jurisprudence too.

CONCLUSION: WHAT ABOUT 'SCIENCE'?

Our title talks of 'science' but we have not discussed the nature of science. We can think of the problems of considering 'jurisprudence as a science' as being many, but at the most basic level we are talking about jurisprudence being the central discipline which tries to make sense of 'law' and, in that attempt, tries to utilise empirical evidence in ways which help that task. Moreover, jurisprudence should help us develop ways of *talking* about the legal world: we can have a multitude of methods and ways of thinking about those methods, but the aim is understanding and to develop grammars and vocabularies to describe that world. Unless we extend our language it does not seem to us we are moving forward in a scientific manner. Returning to Hart — it is not doing science when one simply describes the way that concepts are being used in 'common usage', rather it is hiding from the scientific method and wider knowledge of reason (and thus no wonder that Russell was so contemptuous of the linguistic philosophers).

There are many models of science available — from the rigidly 'empirical' project of Popper to what we would see as more enlightened realisations that the 'logical, detached perspective' of classical science has never really been valid. We see 'social science' as being problematic but also closer to the model we believe relevant for jurisprudence, but are not ideologically committed to a rigid version of this — in particular we look with some horror at the US sociologists of law and their obsession with methodological questions. Our position is more that empiricism and critical reason are at the heart of science, and that social science is one of the most difficult sciences to do well: we agree with the many scientists who realise they are no longer Newtonians (looking on, detached) but are now part of the experiment and their views impact upon the experiment itself — just like lawyers and law.

We feel rather like Robert Dick, the early geologist, who did so much to progress the discipline into a science. Samuel Smiles, the Victorian commentator on science and scientists (as well as 'self help' and 'character'), gave us Dick's view of those who interpreted 'evidence' which was not based on empirical findings and who worked from pre-conceived theory:

> His writing is very good, but his premises are incorrect. He cannot have seen the rocks, except from a gig, when he passed along the road; and now he drags them in to elucidate his theory. When I want to know what a rock is, I go to it. I hammer it; I dissect it. I then know what it really is. I object to this eternal theorising. My idea is that we know very little of geology, yet these men have got it dignified by the name of a science. The science of geology! Why, don't they see that there are only a very few exposed rocks which we can study. It is only a small bit of the crust of the earth that we can inspect. What are the rocks that we can see, compared with the immense mass lying underground, or forming the ocean bed which we can never see? No, no; we must just work patiently on, *collecting facts*, and in course of time geology may develop into a science.[43]

Dick's criticism could so easily have been applied to Hart and his project: theorising without evidence and showing little eagerness to get down to the hard work of collecting the facts. The lesson surely to be learned is that it is the empirical enterprise that will make jurisprudence a science in the future.

[43] S Smiles, *Robert Dick, Baker of Thurso, Geologist and Botanist* (London, John Murray, 1878), 130.

Index